BEYOND THE MARKET

Beyond the Market: the European Union and National Social Policy examines the impact of the European Union on the formation and content of national social policy. The contributors explore the key issues, focusing on the four larger member states:

- France
- Germany
- Italy
- the UK

The contributors use theory and empirical evidence to highlight the factors that influence the formation and content of social policy and why some states have been able to resist EU policy initiatives and maintain their autonomy.

David Hine is Official Student (i.e. Tutorial Fellow) at Christ Church, University of Oxford. **Hussein Kassim** is Lecturer in Politics at Birkbeck College, University of London.

THE STATE AND THE EUROPEAN UNION
Edited by Anand Menon,
Oxford University, Centre for European Politics,
Economics and Society,
Hussein Kassim,
Birkbeck College, London
and David Hine,
Christ Church, Oxford

This new series presents books based on an ERSC-funded interdisciplinary seminar series on the theme of state autonomy in the European Union. The series considers the impact of the EU's institutions, policy processes and laws on the policies of member states. The series will consider the impact of the EU on the autonomy of the member states. The primary focus is on France, Germany, Italy and the United Kingdom.

THE EUROPEAN UNION AND NATIONAL INDUSTRIAL POLICY
Edited by Hussein Kassim and Anand Menon

THE EUROPEAN UNION AND NATIONAL DEFENCE POLICY
Edited by Jolyon Howorth and Anand Menon

THE EUROPEAN UNION AND NATIONAL MACROECONOMIC POLICY
Edited by Anand Menon and James Forder

BEYOND THE MARKET

The EU and national social policy

*Edited by David Hine and
Hussein Kassim*

London and New York

First published 1998
by Routledge
11 New Fetter Lane, London EC4P 4EE

Transferred to Digital Printing 2004

Simultaneously published in the USA and Canada
by Routledge
29 West 35th Street, New York, NY 10001

Typeset in Baskerville by Routledge

British Library Cataloguing in Publication Data
A catalogue record for this book is available from the British Library

Library of Congress Cataloguing in Publication Data
A catalogue record for this book has been requested

ISBN 0–415–15238–0 (hbk)
ISBN 0–415–15239–9 (pbk)

CONTENTS

CONTENTS

CONTRIBUTORS

Jens Bastian is DAAD Lecturer in German Political Economy at the European Institute, London School of Economics and Political Science.

David Freestone is Legal Advisor, Environment and International Law, Washington DC and Professor of International Law, Law School and Institute of European Public Law, University of Hull.

Michael Gold is Lecturer in European Business and Employee Relations, School of Management, Royal Holloway, University of London.

David Goodhart is the Editor of *Prospect*.

David Hine is an Official Student (i.e. Tutorial Fellow) in Politics at Christ Church, Oxford.

Richard Jackman is in the Department of Economics, London School of Economics and Political Science.

Hussein Kassim is Lecturer in Politics, Department of Politics and Sociology, Birkbeck College, University of London.

Giandomenico Majone is External Professor of Political Science, Department of Political and Social Sciences, European University Institute, Florence.

Sonia Mazey is Tutor and Director of Studies in Social and Political Sciences, Churchill College, Cambridge.

Aaron McLoughlin is Ph. D. candidate, Law School, University of Hull and sometime political assistant to MEPs on the environment and formerly the Research, Energy and Technology Committee, Office of Dr Gordon Adam, MEP.

Susan Milner is Senior Lecturer in European Studies, School of Modern Languages and International Studies, University of Bath.

Martin Rhodes is Senior Research Fellow, Robert Schuman Centre, European University Institute, Florence.

PREFACE

This volume is based on a series of ESRC-funded research seminars entitled 'State Autonomy in the European Community', held in Oxford in the academic year 1993–4. The seminars examined the impact of EC action on the content of national policy and on the relationship between policy actors at the national level, with the aim of assessing both the implications of EC policy for the member states and the extent to which their autonomy has been circumscribed, or indeed enhanced. The seminars, which were interdisciplinary, addressed developments in the following areas: industrial, financial and service sectors; social policy, environmental protection and consumer policy; macroeconomic policy; and defence policy. The impact of EU membership on national administrative systems was also the topic of a seminar.

Neither the Research Seminar Series nor this book would have been possible without the support of ESRC Award No. A 451 264 400 248.

ACKNOWLEDGEMENTS

We are grateful to the Governing Body of Christ Church, Oxford, which kindly supported the seminar on which this volume is based at the college in January 1994.

We should like to thank all participants of the seminar on social, environmental protection and consumer policy for making it such a stimulating event. We should also like to express our appreciation to Anand Menon for helping to organize the seminar and for his important role in turning the results into an edited volume.

Our greatest debt of gratitude is owed to the contributors for their efforts and patience in producing this volume.

1

INTRODUCTION

The European Union, state autonomy and national social policy

David Hine

The scope of this book

This book, like others in the series,[1] examines the impact of the European Union on the autonomy of its member states.[2] Its focus is social policy – broadly understood as the principles by which a government seeks to affect the distribution of income, working conditions, and other social circumstances, according to a politically defined criterion of need and desert, through tax and benefits arrangements, labour-market regulation, health and safety regulation, and special opportunities for vulnerable or underprivileged groups. Social policy can be conceived broadly or narrowly. It could at EU level be said to cover a wide range of activities, including regional aid policies, social intervention to assist restructuring in sectors like steel or shipbuilding, or the Common Agricultural Policy's extensive intervention in agricultural markets, one essential purpose of which is income support. Since the focus of the series as a whole is more on the impact of EU action on the autonomy of the state, than on the content of policy itself, the editors have opted here for a narrower definition concentrating on the core areas of social policy, traditionally conceived, and focusing on labour market policy, training, equal opportunities, and social partnership. The one exception to this is the chapter on EU environmental policy. This has been included not only because it involves intervention to mitigate market outcomes, in terms of the broad social benefits it brings, but also because the style of EU policy development in this sector offers interesting parallels with that in the traditional areas of social policy.

In examining the impact of European Union action on member states, the concept of state *autonomy* is in many respects preferable as an analytical tool to its older and more juridically rooted counterpart state *sovereignty* (see Kassim and Menon 1996). It captures the range of mechanisms by which member-state governments are constrained to pursue particular policies even when, in formal-legal terms, they are free to do otherwise. The distinction is certainly not a new one, and in the twentieth century it has shed light on the ways in which, for example, economic interdependence, transnational flows of information, and massive differences in military power, have affected the capacity of states to obtain objectives in pursuit of which, formally speaking, they retain *de jure* independence. As the introduction to the first book in this series put it, 'sovereignty identifies one attribute of the state, it does not capture all aspects of its power' (Kassim and Menon 1996: 3)

The concept of autonomy is especially apt because, as most contemporary commentators observe, policy making in the EU is pursued through multi-tiered institutions, and through complex and often obscure processes, many of which are informal. The actors involved often have multiple objectives and divided loyalties, and the networks in which they become involved cross national boundaries and operate in overlapping legal frameworks. Students of the modern state, and its autonomy in relation to domestic political and economic interests, have long recognised the significance of its inability unilaterally to determine its own destiny. The modern liberal state is not 'autonomous' and those who control the offices of government, albeit by democratic election, are not able to choose policy goals freely or to implement their policy preferences as they desire. They are constrained by the checks and balances of liberal institutions, and by the social pluralism that creates the powerful interest-group actors with which they must reckon. It would therefore have been surprising if the literature which has developed on European institutions and policy making over the last two decades had not developed a similar conventional wisdom about the impact of action and policy development by the EEC/EC/EU on the autonomy of member states.

Looking at the system from the top down, it is possible to see the Union as a political system with its own authority structure, an established identity and legitimacy, and procedural rules and conventions (see Andersen and Eliassen 1993; Wessels 1997). However, it is clearly not a federal state like any other, and even when a policy competence has been attributed to the Community by treaty, its influence on the member states, and its ability to make policy and ensure its implementation, depends not just, and indeed perhaps not primarily, on its legal authority. The same may be said from the reverse perspective. Member states retain formal control over policies in many areas, but in order to achieve objectives in other areas they are periodically constrained to yield to pressures to conform to centrally determined choices. Thus a member state may lose control of the policy process not only when it is outvoted in majoritarian decision procedures, but also, and more often, when it realises it must make compromises with other member states to achieve some of its objectives; or when the judgement of market forces constrains its government to adopt policies it would prefer not to adopt; or when contacts and linkages with the European policy-making environment change the attitudes and values of important interests, of significant sectors of domestic public opinion, or even of key elements of the administration of the member state itself.

EC social policy in the 1980s

The role of social policy at EC level has become a good deal better understood in the last two decades than in the earlier years of the Community's existence, and the arguments surrounding it have been placed in sharper focus. Partly this is because academic analysts have themselves developed a better grasp of the processes involved and of the motives and justifications of the actors, as we shall see below. Partly, it is because the passage of time has made clear how policies adopted for one set of purposes have consequences in other directions. This frequently generates new policy demands, and new policy initiatives. This process, known in technical jargon as 'spillover', occurs inside national political systems, as well as between them, and is present in any complex system of government where policies have significant and often unforeseen side effects. Its special significance with respect to the relationship between the EU and the member states is that it generates arguments about the degree to which it is a one-way process shifting the location of power from national capitals to Brussels. It is not clear that any such migration is inevitable, as demonstrated by the debates about subsidiarity in the 1990s; nor will policy leadership move inevitably into the hands of the Commission. In fact, it may be difficult to identify any clear central locus of power. But it does make it likely, for reasons described above, that the policy autonomy of member states will be under greater threat, and that they will, at the very least, face a new policy agenda and a new policy community.

The case of social policy provides a ready example of this. The European Community – by far the most important dimension of integration in Western Europe – was from its outset a market-driven process. It is true that its predecessor, the Coal and Steel Community, involved a high degree of regulatory intervention, and that a major political *quid pro quo* of the integration of industry and services through the removal of tariff and non-tariff barriers to trade was the interventionist Common Agricultural Policy. Nevertheless the creation of a single market was informed above all by the philosophy of the market, and the removal of barriers to free competition. In the 1980s, that process was accelerated with the internal market programme, and was further challenged by forces in the wider international economic order, notably the globalisation of capital markets, enhanced competitive pressures from newly industrialising economies, and major programmes of business restructuring which increased job insecurity and exacerbated income differentials. When these developments occurred, a policy reaction raising the issue of EC-led action to redress the balance away from a purely market-driven process of integration was always likely.

The counter-pressures of the 1980s, in the shape of demands for policy initiatives at the Community level, that would safeguard the benefits of traditional models of social protection, were therefore at least in part the result of an accelerated drive towards market building. This is not to argue that Western Europe had or has an homogenous and undifferentiated social model to defend. On the contrary, as Martin Rhodes discusses in chapter 3, there are several different models. However, in the face of a set of powerful, and largely unidirectional economic changes, perceptions of a common threat arose in most member states, and in this sense helped persuade at least some governments and many other social actors to think in terms of common solutions where previously they had been unwilling to do so.

The themes that emerged in this debate were complex, and not always internally coherent. A major preoccupation was that growing economic interdependence was exposing larger proportions of national labour forces to the impact of the locational preferences of businesses and employers. The extent to which this phenomenon – known pejoratively as 'social dumping' – was a real threat was much disputed (see Goodhart in chapter 5). Nevertheless it fitted into the new and more sophisticated thinking that was taking place about market building at least in so far as the mobility of capital seemed increasingly responsive to variables such as labour market regulation and practice, welfare costs, trade union strength, skill and productivity levels. What governments do to influence those factors, so the argument ran, had always contributed to, or detracted from, the level playing field on which European firms are supposed to compete, and this had not hitherto been sufficiently recognised. The impact of such policies on relative competitiveness was never going to be as immediate or visible as, for example, rapid changes in exchange rates, state aids, or non-tariff barriers, but, by the late 1980s, it was nevertheless an important and increasingly discussed complication to the integration process. If the long-term implication was that market building implied downward competitive pressures on social provision at member-state level, with national governments ultimately losing their freedom to define their own domestic social agenda, one solution was to regain control at Community level. The prospect of monetary union, and the pressures for budgetary convergence that accompanied it, further eroded member-state control of social agendas, and thus served only to strengthen this argument.

It was therefore difficult to exclude social issues from the EC agenda, particularly in view of the prominence attributed to the social dimension by the Commission President, Jacques Delors, and the French President, François Mitterrand. A series of initiatives in the mid-1980s, not all of which were successful, culminated in the 1989 Community Charter of the Fundamental Social Rights of Workers, which was later enshrined, albeit ambiguously, in the so-called 'social chapter' of the 1993 Treaty of European Union. At least at the level of public utterances, therefore, the 1980s and 1990s brought the issue of social policy much more squarely onto the EC policy agenda.

The antecedents: the struggle for citizenship

These initiatives were, of course, built on pre-existing foundations. Social policy was enshrined as a legitimate area of EEC action in the Treaty of Rome, with several articles touching on the issue, the most important of which are found between articles 117 and 128. DG V, today covering employment, industrial relations and social affairs, became the main vehicle within the Commission for promoting policy in the sector, and over the years a variety of working groups, networks and monitoring systems were set up alongside DG V to facilitate the

gathering and dissemination of information and to encourage mutual understanding across the great range of national agencies and interest groups involved
in social policy.

However, the remit of the Community in social policy was always ambiguous,
both in terms of its constitutional foundation, and in terms of the political will
behind it. Social policy failed to take off as an important portfolio within the
Commission, or as one in which the Commission played a major role in policy
leadership or in the formal process of policy harmonisation. Its role was limited
by many factors: the dominance of the member states in policies involving direct
redistribution of income and the unanimity requirement in the Council of
Ministers; political fears that taxpayers would resist large interstate transfers for
welfare purposes (admittedly this happened through the CAP, but here it was
concealed as market intervention); the limited budgetary resources and weak
institutions of the EC itself, which would have had to have been enormously
expanded to distribute resources efficiently and fairly; and the significant variations in the style and content of welfare support across the EC.

For these reasons, the particular conception given to social policy was essentially one in which policies were justified by virtue of their contribution to the
building of markets, and in which policies were applied above all to participants
in those markets, namely, workers and employers, rather than on the basis of
universal citizenship rights. Hence article 119 dealt with the principle of equal
pay, and article 121 dealt with common social security arrangements for migrant
workers, while articles 123–8 (the European Social Fund) provided minimum
funding to encourage training and job mobility. Much the same applied to the
philosophy behind programmes of regional development assistance that started in
the 1970s. Such programmes undoubtedly entailed some modest transfers of
income, but they were justified in terms of aid to less developed regions, to assist
the long-term capacity of the economies of such areas to compete in the wider
European market. And they were never more than minor adjuncts to the real
exercise in redistribution and social regulation, which remained anchored firmly
at the level of the member states.

During the 1960s and 1970s, relatively little occurred to change this picture.
The Commission continued to proselytise, and in 1974, following a Council
resolution, DG V launched a Community social action programme concerned
with a range of issues linked to employment, the encouragement of social
dialogue, and the enhancement of working conditions. In subsequent years this
programme spawned several new agencies and initiatives, such as the advisory
committee on safety, hygiene and health protection at work, an action programme
in the field of education, and another on equal opportunities for women.
However, the possibility of further action or the launching of more far-reaching
initiatives was limited by the unwillingness of the member states to commit themselves to any notion that social policy should be pursued at EC level in virtue
of the concept of Community-based universal citizenship rights. Only in the
1980s, with the long battle to transform an economic community into a political

union, pursued through three successive treaty revisions, was this question raised
explicitly.

Even when it was finally raised, however, the question proved difficult to resolve.
The discussion preceding the 1989 Community Charter on 'Fundamental Social
Rights' suggested that the drafters were now thinking in universal citizenship
terms, but in the event the final document not only included the suffix 'of
Workers' in the title, but subordinated almost all the rights it identified to employment status (Hantrais 1995: 197–9). The 1993 Treaty of European Union
eventually remedied this in the main body of its text, referring for the first time to
'citizenship' of the European Union, though the rights established were exclusively political. The Agreement on Social Policy – which was detached from the
main body of the treaty and appended to the TEU as a Protocol at the insistence
of the UK – was closely linked to concepts of social partnership, but still focused
almost exclusively on workers. And at a moment when the debate on the newly
fashionable concept of 'social exclusion' (Kennett 1994: 23–9) was identifying the
real needs of social policy as lying in the direction of the various categories of
non-worker (the unemployed, the old, casual workers, immigrants, and new
entrants to the job market), the Agreement itself offered these categories little
hope. Finally, in 1997, the most recent – and unratified at the time of writing –
round of constitutional revision again turned its attention to social policy, this
time against the background of even greater concern about the effects of unemployment as the labour-market costs of the long recession of the mid-1990s
mounted. Yet, notwithstanding the insertion in Section II, chapters 3–7 of the
draft Amsterdam Treaty of a long chapter on 'employment' and other chapters
on 'social policy', 'the environment', 'consumer protection' and 'public health' the
wording, absence of compulsion and restrictions on funding suggested to sceptics
that the length of the constitutional text was in inverse proportion to the real
underlying commitment and the probability of immediate action. As in 1991–2,
the preparatory work of the *Comité des sages*, which was charged by the IGC and
the Commission with reviewing the Social Charter in preparation for treaty
reform, produced an ambitious blueprint to incorporate a range of fundamental
social citizenship rights into the new Treaty, but these were set aside at the IGC
itself in favour of bland phrases and extensive qualifications about their meaning.

Neo-liberal economics and the constraints of the 1990s

The fundamental explanation of why the momentum built up in the 1980s
proved so difficult to translate into an effective EC-led social policy was, of course,
that that momentum arrived too late. By the time the universal citizenship issue
and the social exclusion problem were raised, other conditions had also changed.
The lack of resources to engage in widespread redistributive social programmes
at the European level had become starker than ever. Successive financial-
perspective planning exercises undertaken by the Community underlined that
its resources were to be capped at a level barely above one per cent of GDP

throughout the 1990s, and ever-tightening domestic budgetary pressures simply reinforced this. Meanwhile the concerns in the early 1990s at the growth of the ambitions of both the Commission and the Court of Justice (the latter, as we shall see, as important a player in EC social policy as the former) made several governments increasingly restive about the attribution of new policy competencies. Most important of all, however, was the changed climate in which economic issues were now being discussed. The drive towards the market may have been responsible for the explicit recognition that market-building policies implied a levelling-down of social-policy provision, but those implications were being read in very different ways: although on the one hand there were those who argued for a full-blown European social policy, there was an equally powerful school of thought which argued that it was the European system of social protection, in its various national manifestations, which would have to change in order to enable the EC as a whole to draw real benefit from its own economic integration. 'Market optimist' critics of an activist social policy at European level argued that harmonisation should be left to the market, which would determine the most appropriate form of national social policy stance, and which would gradually be adopted by other governments as they perceived its superior qualities. No less opposed to an EC-level social policy were 'market-pessimist' critics, who argued that harmonisation would have perverse consequences since the structure of labour markets across the EC was too diverse to make a uniform system of regulation appropriate.

The events of the 1990s, with which this book is primarily concerned, reflect the continuing tension between these two opposed philosophies. There is no doubt that the perspectives of all actors in the social policy community have altered during this period. The apparently inexorable rise of widespread unemployment has broadened the focus of possible remedies. Thus, the social chapter has brought new objectives (social protection, social dialogue and human resource development), while majority voting has gradually been extended to cover not just health and safety but also working conditions and equality questions. The Commission itself has come to accept that, with unemployment growing and the employment consequences of monetary union difficult to predict if labour mobility remains low, minimal norms, rather than detailed top-down harmonisation, are a more appropriate policy response, and are less likely to conflict with the goals of a more flexible labour market. The action programmes set by the Commission in 1994 and 1995 accordingly reflect a much scaled-down set of ambitions from that of the 1980s.

Erosion of state autonomy without centralisation: the influence of EU institutions

The chapters of this book do not, however, simply demonstrate that the EU's failure to implement an activist and universal system of social regulation, superseding national differences, has left member states with complete autonomy to determine their own social policy stances. This is so firstly, and most obviously, because, while social policy is traditionally associated with measures mitigating or modifying markets, state autonomy in the social policy field is affected not just by an activist social policy at the supranational level, but also, in so far as they have implications for social policy, by the economic liberalism of market-building measures. Secondly, there are a number of ways in which, through mechanisms other than the classic top-down EC directive, the autonomy of member states has been very significantly curtailed. These include the didactic activism of the Commission in its non-legislative and non-regulatory activities; business practices and market forces that are only indirectly related to legal and political aspects of the integration process; and the continuous, albeit often unpredictable, intervention of the Court of Justice.

The activism of the Commission is documented in a number of ways in the chapters of this book. In the field of social policy, it is a promoter and an impresario, as much as a legislative leader. As analysis of the domain underlines, the Commission has brought interests together, monitored developments, commissioned studies, established agencies and promoted dialogue. The Council of Ministers may remain the ultimate arbiter of legislation, but the Commission has been able to set agendas and establish terms for discussion. It has done so in the fields of unemployment, social partnership, vocational training, women's rights, the protection of children, assistance to the disabled, family policy, health and safety at work and several other areas. Bringing together representatives of national administrations, national interest groups, national monitoring agencies, and others involved in the delivery of social policy, it has created at the European level networks that have profoundly influenced the context in which social policy is delivered. In this way it has helped shape the intellectual framework in which even national governments think about social policy, gradually pushing out the boundaries of what is seen as a legitimate area of concern and involvement for the Community. None of this gives it authority, still less control, and every inch of the ground it seeks to occupy has to be fought over, but it finds potential allies in unusual quarters among governments, employers' organisations and major corporations, many of which, though unwilling to see a full-blooded transfer of regulatory and distributive powers to the centre, are concerned, in the face of impersonal market processes, that for many social issues there needs to be a central forum which, at the very least, is seen as the legitimate arena in which questions can be discussed. Most of these actors are unwilling for good reasons to leave that forum role to the European Parliament, anxious though that body is to play a major role in social policy. And they are aware that the Council of Ministers itself is not always the best place for such activities, since it can exacerbate national differences and tends to exclude the diversity of interests represented in any one member state. The range of monitoring and consultative agencies in the social field, assembled over the years by the Commission, has therefore become an important magnet for those interested in maintaining contact across national borders, co-ordinating responses, exchanging information and engaging, if not in outright 'social partnership' at the very least in a continuous social dialogue.

As far as the Court of Justice is concerned, its opportunity to influence social policy unwinds over many years after a piece of legislation comes into force, and, in so far as national social policy legislation can be annulled or constrained by Court judgements linked to EC treaty or legislative objectives that are themselves quite outside those in the social policy field, this can be a negative, even unintended restraint, rather than a positive one. Once a piece of EC legislation has been agreed, it cannot easily be removed, even long after the national governments which agreed it have given way to others. A British Conservative government found in 1994, for example, that an apparently modest directive the so-called Acquired Rights Directive concerning employee rights facing transfer of business ownership, agreed by a Labour government in 1977, and implemented without much controversy into national law by a Conservative government in 1981, could be interpreted by the ECJ in a completely unexpected manner that affected UK domestic policy in regard to the contracting out of public-sector services under rules requiring compulsory competitive tendering (Adnett 1996: 259). Even though, as with most such court-driven policy, the logic which guides it emanates less from an integrated view of policy needs, as from somewhat haphazard deductions about legal consistency, court-affected policy has, as Leibfried and Pierson have argued (1995: 51–65), and as several chapters in this book confirm, had a key influence on the parameters in which national social policy operates. The Court has delivered over 300 judgements affecting policy in connection with the mobility of labour, access to and portability of benefits, forms of discrimination against foreigners in areas such as professional qualifications, education and health-service provision, and numerous other areas.

The contents of the book

These issues are explored in detail in the chapters which follow. The chapter which follows this introduction, by Giandomenico Majone, examines the growth of regulatory powers and agencies at EC level, of which the area of social policy provides some striking examples. His explanation of this growth lies not only in the entrepreneurialism of the Commission's search for alternative mechanisms to expand its power when its budgetary resources are tightly limited, but also in the demand for regulation at the level of member states. The latter has expanded in a fairly indiscriminate way as a response to problems of the low credibility, in an integrated market, of a system of regulation based on pure intergovernmentalism; member states do not trust one another to regulate fairly and effectively, and can in any case through EC regulation delegate difficult but necessary decisions, and the blame for them, up to a supranational level. This growth in regulatory powers and agencies is then compounded by the dynamics of delegation and control, which tend to work against effective control by national governments, and which therefore facilitate the growth of policy networks which follow substantive rather than national lines.

In the following chapter, Martin Rhodes reviews the development of EC social policy over the last three decades, against the background of different models of national social policy, and the current crisis in welfare state provision. In what he identifies as 'realist' mode, he concludes that the EC neither can, nor should, put in place a federal welfare state to substitute for the growing difficulties at the national level, but that the EC can establish an important floor of standards, and can assist in implementing best-practice policies to aid processes of national social-policy adjustment.

Richard Jackman examines the causes of the long-term growth of EC unemployment in chapter 4, asking whether EC policies have themselves contributed to that growth, and what policy options are available to reverse the trend. He concludes that the explanation lies both in global economic changes and in the requirements of the internal market, that it is destined to worsen as the EC's economic ties with central and eastern Europe grow, that most EC member states have failed to update their labour-market institutions effectively to cope with these challenges, and have off-loaded a disproportionately large share of the burden of providing a social safety net on employers.

Moving from the effects of policy uniformity to those of policy differentiation, David Goodhart examines the vexed issue of 'social dumping' in chapter 5. Goodhart seeks to assess how widespread the phenomenon is, and how far the EC has attempted to act against it. He concludes that while social dumping undoubtedly does exist, labour cost differences inside the EC are less significant than they frequently seem, that the costs of moving production location are generally very high, that anecdotal evidence from business supports this view, and that even for the Commission the problem does not rank very highly compared with other social-policy issues. Reducing standards of social protection beyond a certain point, in fact, appears to produce sharply diminishing returns. In any case most companies in high-quality sectors of the economy are unaffected by minimum-standards legislation.

In chapter 6, Jens Bastian discusses how national governments and the EU have sought to address the challenges posed by unemployment in western Europe. He traces the way in which work-sharing emerged as a possible solution to growing joblessness at the national level with the support of governments, employers and some trade unions. He also considers the debates that have taken place in and between EU institutions, highlighting the willingness of the member states, with the notable exception of the United Kingdom, to develop a common approach to labour market issues. As in other fields, so in this area, Bastian finds that state autonomy has been constrained by action at the EU level. The emergence of Brussels as a decision-making centre has enabled subnational actors to fight, and often to win, domestic battles in supranational forums. Not only have trade unions, for example, been able to find allies in EU institutions and to build coalitions in order to advance positions that are at odds with the approaches preferred by their national governments, but interventions by the European Court of Justice have had important implications for national policy, compelling states to abandon or modify existing practices, to recognise new rights and obligations, and to introduce legislation that departs from traditional orientations.

In chapter 7, Michael Gold explores the implications for member states of the development of social partnership initiatives, particularly against the context of practices which have developed since 1985, and which were encapsulated formally in the so-called 'social chapter' of the Maastricht Treaty on European Union. Drawing on the lessons of developments at both industry-wide and sectoral levels, he concludes that to date constraints – especially concerning the representational status of the parties involved, enduring differences in the social and legal frameworks of industrial relations systems, and significant problems of implementation and enforcement – have held back its impact on the development of social and labour policies of the member states. However, the legal and institutional framework is still very new, and although there will be no 'big bang', there is now considerable potential for information disclosure, consultation and negotiation to evolve into a set of shared values and practices, led most notably by the multi nationals, and stimulated especially by the recent Works Council Directive.

In her chapter, Sonia Mazey provides evidence of the somewhat mixed results stemming from the efforts of EC institutions – the Commission and the Court of Justice in particular – to force issues onto national political agendas and progressively 'Europeanise' important, though in several member states much neglected, areas of social rights. Mazey examines the way in which the EC, as 'purposeful opportunist', was a catalyst in extending national sex equality laws in the workplace, and in providing women with a new means of legal redress in cases of sex discrimination. There remain many shortcomings in the resulting legislation, and implementation remains a problem, particularly when combined with the rise of a neo-liberal economic agenda in the 1990s. However, in this area, the development of formal institutional frameworks at both EU and national level, providing arenas for discussion, information exchange, action programmes, and monitoring, as well as implementation, have certainly influenced the context in which national governments operate, and have tentatively begun to extend the issue beyond the explicitly 'social affairs' arena, sensitising policy makers in other policy sectors. Nevertheless, Mazey also underlines the extensive margin for manoeuvre which national governments retain in this sector and the extent to which national traditions and styles have effected the way in which policy is implemented.

These limitations emerge even more clearly in chapter 9, by Susan Milner, which examines the efforts of the EC to steer training policy between the very divergent national styles which operate across the Community. Although there has for some years been a consensus on skill enhancement in general, it continues to mask radically different approaches between member states. These differences are difficult to bridge, and Milner argues that the EC's method of working, which involves extensive compromise, is not well adapted where there are sharp ideological differences at stake. Much of the convergence which has taken place is therefore driven by global economic pressures, though the EC has been able to act as a significant catalyst for change through its role as facilitator, forum provider and menu setter.

Chapter 10 by David Freestone and Aaron McLoughlin, examines, predominantly from a lawyer's perspective, the impact of EC environmental policy on members states, showing, as in the case of sex equality, a further example of 'Community opportunism.' Environmental policy has gradually been pushed up the EC policy agenda, from an almost non-existent starting point, to become a significant limitation on state competence. However, the locus of power cannot be defined with precision. Relationships are still evolving, and the strength of particular actors varies according to political context and the constellation of alliances, including, most notably, those between the Commission and particular member states. As in other sectors, moreover, as the nominal competence of the Community expands, problems of implementation and enforcement are thrown into ever sharper relief.

Notes

1 Kassim, H. and Menon, A. (eds) (1996) *The European Union and National Industrial Policy*, London: Routledge; Howorth, J. and Menon, A. (eds) (1997) *The European Union and National Defence Policy*, London: Routledge, and Menon, A. and Forder, J. (eds) (1998) *The European Union and National Macroeconomic Policy*, London: Routledge.
2 Using the terms 'European Union' and 'European Community' with consistency and accuracy, but without pedantic repetition, presents problems whenever the time period or events under analysis straddle the ratification of the Maastricht Treaty of European Union. By convention, the 'European Community' is coming to represent the economic and social pillar of the European Union, and where only that pillar is being referred to, or where the reference is to events completed before the ratification of the Treaty of European Union, it is appropriate to use that term. In other cases, particularly in a book concerned with social policy, it has been considered appropriate to use the term 'European Union'.

References

Adnett, N. (1996) *European Labour Markets*, London: Longman
Andersen, S.S. and Eliassen, K.A. (1993) *Making Policy in Europe. The Europeification of National Policy*, London: Sage
Hantrais, L. (1995) *Social Policy in the European Union*, London: Macmillan
Howorth, J. and Menon, A. (eds) (1997) *The European Union and National Defence Policy*, London: Routledge
Kassim, H. and Menon A. (1996) 'The European Union and state autonomy' in Kassim, H. and Menon A. (eds) *The European Union and National Industrial Policy*, London: Routledge, 1–10
Kennet, P. (1994) 'Exclusion, post-Fordism and the "new Europe"', in Brown, P. and Crompton, R. (eds) *Economic Restructuring and Social Exclusion*, London: UCL Press, 14–32
Leibfried, S. and Pierson, P. (1995) 'Semisovereign welfare states: social policy in a

multitiered Europe', in Leibfried, S. and Pierson, P. (eds) *European Social Policy: Between Fragmentation and Integration*, Washington DC: The Brookings Institution, 43–77

Menon, A. and Forder, J. (eds) (1998) *The European Union and National Macroeconomic Policy*, London: Routledge

Wessels, W. (1997) 'An ever closer fusion? A macropolitical view on integration processes', *Journal of Common Market Studies*, 35:2, June

2

UNDERSTANDING REGULATORY GROWTH IN THE EUROPEAN COMMUNITY[1]

Giandomenico Majone

1 Introduction

The prominent place given to the principle of subsidiarity in the Maastricht Treaty reveals widespread concerns about the accumulation of regulatory powers in Brussels, but also raises several theoretically interesting questions. First, how is over-regulation at the European level possible, given that national governments are strongly represented at every stage of the policy-making process? Again, member states strive to preserve the greatest possible degree of sovereignty and policy-making autonomy, as shown for example by their stubborn resistance to Community intervention in areas such as macroeconomic policy and indirect taxation. Why, then, have they accepted many regulatory measures not foreseen by the founding treaty and not strictly necessary for the proper functioning of the common market? Finally, concerning the quality rather than the quantity of Community regulations: how is innovation at all possible in a system where the formal rights of initiative of the Commission, as well as its executive functions, seem to be so tightly controlled?

There can be little doubt about the determination of the member states to limit the Commission's discretion at every stage of policy making. Political initiative comes from the heads of state or government (European Council); political mediation takes place in the framework of the Committee of Permanent Representatives of the member states (COREPER); formal adoption is the prerogative of the Council of Ministers; and implementation is in the hands of the national administrations. Before final adoption by the Council, a Commission proposal will typically have been discussed in a working group comprising for the most part national officials; submitted to an advisory committee which includes outside experts; transmitted to COREPER to be discussed in the working group of national officials it sets up; reviewed by COREPER once more, and finally placed before the Council for approval.

The Commission's discretion in the execution of Council directives has been tightly regulated by Council Decision 87/373/EEC of 13 July 1987 on the 'comitology' system. The system consists of a large number of committees associated with the Commission in the exercise of its executive functions. Over the years, the system has become increasingly complex, including both advisory and oversight (so called 'management' and 'regulatory') committees. Regulatory and to some extent also management committees can block a Commission measure and transmit the case to the Council which can overrule the Commission.

Not surprisingly, many students of European integration have concluded that policy innovation in the EC is only possible when national preferences converge toward some new approach. Intergovernmentalist writers, in particular, rely on a model of least-common-denominator bargaining, a sort of Ricardian theory of Community policy making. As in Ricardo's theory of economic rent, the price of a good is determined by the unit cost of the output produced by the marginal firm so, according to intergovernmentalists, the quality of policy decisions in the EC is determined by the preferences of the least forthcoming (or marginal) government. Hence, barring special circumstances, the outcome will converge toward a least-common-denominator position.

Also writers not belonging to the intergovernmentalist school have denied the possibility of genuine policy innovation. According to these writers, the Community can hope, at best, 'to generalize and diffuse solutions adopted in one or more member states by introducing them throughout the Community. The solutions of these member states normally set the framework for the Community solution' (Rehbinder and Stewart 1985: 213).

Not even neo-functionalists thought it necessary to offer a theory of policy innovation. Ernst Haas explained the growth of European competences in terms of the 'expansive logic of sectoral integration' (Haas 1958). He assumed a process of functional 'spillovers' in which the initial decision of governments to delegate policy-making powers in a certain sector to a supranational institution inevitably creates pressures to expand the authority of that institution into neighbouring policy areas. Economics and technology, rather than political demands or policy entrepreneurship, would drive the result. Recent versions of neo-functionalism show greater awareness of the growing importance of innovation in the EC policy making system. Thus, the notion of 'political spillover' (George 1993) emphasises the role of supranational institutions and subnational actors in the process of functional spillover. Such empirical observations are not developed, however, into an explanation grounded in general theories of institutional behaviour.

In attempting to provide theoretical, rather than *ad hoc*, explanations for the apparently unstoppable growth of European regulations, I have found it useful to distinguish different dimensions of policy growth: quantitative growth; technical complexity; task expansion; and policy innovation. The usefulness of this analytic distinction is due to the fact that rather different causal factors operate along the various dimensions.

The chapter is organised as follows. Section 2 presents some examples and selected empirical evidence concerning the quantitative and qualitative growth of

EC regulation in recent years. The crucial importance of regulation in EC policy making is explained in section 3 by means of a model which has among its main variables the limited size of the Community budget and the low credibility of purely intergovernmental agreements in the field of regulation. Section 4 discusses the dynamics of delegation and control, while section 5 reviews some recent theories of policy entrepreneurship. Section 6 derives a number of positive and normative implications from the analysis developed in the previous sections. The chapter concludes with some remarks on institutional reform.

2 Some examples

Each of the three questions raised at the beginning of the introduction rests on a body of empirical evidence which is too extensive to be reviewed here; only a few suggestive examples will be presented. Concerning the phenomenon of over-regulation, one can mention the almost exponential growth in the number of directives and regulations produced, on average, each year: 25 directives and 600 regulations by 1970; 50 directives and 1,000 regulations by 1975; 80 directives and 1,500 regulations per year since 1985.

To compare: in 1991 Brussels issued 1,564 directives and regulations as against 1,417 pieces of legislation (laws, ordinances, decrees) issued by Paris, so that by now the Community introduces into the corpus of French law more rules than the national authorities. Moreover, according to some estimates, today only 20 to 25 per cent of the legal texts applicable in France are produced by the parliament or the government in complete autonomy, that is, without any previous consultation in Brussels (Conseil d'Etat 1992). It seems that Jacques Delors' often-quoted prediction that by 1998, 80 per cent of economic and social legislation will be of Community origin, while perhaps politically imprudent, did not lack solid empirical support.

Reporting such statistics, the French Conseil d'Etat speaks of normative drift (*dérive normative*) and luxuriating legislation (*droit naturellement foisonnant*), doubting that any government could have foreseen, let alone wished, such a development. It also points out, however, that the same member states that deplore the *furie réglementaire* of the Brussels authorities, are among the major causes of over-regulation – a point we shall examine more closely below.

Concerning the continuously expanding agenda of the Community, a suggestive indicator is the number of specialised councils of ministers, which went from fourteen in 1984 to twenty-one in 1993. In addition to the traditional councils of the ministers of economics, finance, agriculture, trade and industry, we now have regular meetings of the ministers of the environment (since 1974), education (since 1974), research (since 1975), consumer affairs (since 1983), culture (since 1984), tourism (since 1988), civil protection (since 1988) and telecommunications (since 1988).

Of seven important areas of current policy development – regional policy, research and technological development, environment, consumer protection, education, cultural and audiovisual policy, and health and safety at work – only the latter was mentioned in the Treaty of Rome, and then only as an area where the Commission should promote close co-operation among the member states (article118, EEC). In the case of environmental protection, for example, three Action programmes were approved before the Single European Act (SEA) explicitly recognised the competence of the Community in this area. If the first Action Programme (1973–6) lacked definite proposals, concentrating instead on general principles, subsequent documents became increasingly specific. The second programme (1977–81) indicated four main areas of intervention, while the third (1982–6) stressed the importance of environmental impact assessments and of economic instruments for implementing the 'polluter pays' principle. Concrete actions followed. The number of environmental directives/decisions grew from ten in 1975, to thirteen in 1980, twenty in 1984, twenty-five in 1985, and seventeen in the six months immediately preceding the passage of the SEA.

Consider, finally, genuine policy innovation as distinct from mere quantitative growth or task expansion. As already mentioned, many (perhaps most) students of EC policy making hold that Community policies cannot move beyond least-common-denominator solutions, unless the interests of the most important member states favour some new approach. Thus, according to intergovernmentalist accounts of the internal market programme, the emphasis of the 1985 White Paper (COM(85)310, final) on mutual recognition reflects a change in the preferences of the member states in the direction of less interventionist economic policies and a corollary shift toward deregulatory programmes (Keohane and Hoffman 1990: 288). Starting from the same assumption that the decisions of supranational institutions mirror the policy preferences of the most powerful political and economic actors in Europe, other authors have argued that the *Cassis de Dijon* ruling, which gave prominence to the principle of mutual recognition, was based on the reading of the European Court of Justice (ECJ) of the interest of the most influential member states (Garrett 1992; Garrett and Weingast 1993).

A more careful analysis of the evidence reveals a rather different picture. First, there is no indication that in justifying the *Cassis* decision the ECJ was following anything but its own convictions. There is no mention of the idea of mutual recognition either in the argument of the plaintiffs' lawyers or in the observations of the Commission and the conclusions of the Advocate General (Dehousse 1994). Moreover, countries with a high level of health and safety standards, such as France and Germany, realised that mutual recognition of such standards would entail competition among national regulators. Regulatory competition, it was feared, creates the conditions for 'social dumping' as each country attempts to gain advantages for its own industry and to attract foreign investments by lowering the level of regulatory constraints which firms must meet. Hence countries with advanced systems of social regulation tended to support the traditional method of harmonising national standards rather than their mutual recognition (Alter and Meunier-Aitsahalia 1993).

In fact, the Commission, rather than the member states, had a strong reason for favouring reform of the traditional approach to harmonisation. By the early 1980s, if not earlier, it had become clear that the attempt to achieve an integrated market by harmonising thousands of laws and regulations of six, nine, and finally twelve countries at various levels of economic development and with vastly different legal, administrative and cultural traditions, was bound to fail. A new approach was clearly needed. Already in autumn 1979, the Internal Market Commissioner suggested before the European Parliament that the harmonisation policy should take a new direction, based on the *Cassis* judgement. In July 1980, the Commission sent an 'interpretative Communication' to the member states, the European Parliament and the Council, boldly stating that *Cassis* would serve as the foundation for a new approach to harmonisation. The member states reacted with concern to the broad policy implications drawn by the Commission, in particular to the prospect of direct competition among national regulators. The Legal Services of the Council delivered a counter-interpretation of the case, arguing that the Commission's generalisation of the Court's argument was excessive, and concluding that the *Cassis* ruling changed virtually nothing (Alter and Meunier-Aitsahalia 1993). In the event, the Commission's broad interpretation prevailed. At the Milan meeting in June 1985, the member states endorsed the White Paper and its mutual recognition strategy.

Even in the case of day-to-day policy making, the prevailing view seems to be that the Commission can at best diffuse throughout the Community solutions adopted in the most advanced member states. There are, it is admitted, some examples of genuine policy innovation. Thus, the Polychlorinated Biphenyl (PBC) Directive (76/769/EEC) 'had no parallel in existing Member State regulations', while the Directive on sulphur dioxide limit values (80/779/EEC) established, on a Community-wide basis, ambient quality standards, which most member states did not previously employ as a control strategy (Rehbinder and Stewart 1985: 214). However, lacking adequate theoretical explanations, such examples tend to be dismissed as special cases of no general significance.

Such a cavalier attitude can no longer be maintained. The SEA, by introducing qualified majority voting not only for internal-market legislation but also for important areas of social regulation, has created suitable conditions for the development of striking regulatory innovations. For example, the framework Directive 89/391 on Health and Safety at Work goes beyond the regulatory philosophy and practice even of a country like Germany (Feldhoff 1992). Among the notable features of the directive are its scope (it applies to all sectors of activity, both public and private, including service, educational, cultural and leisure activities), the general obligations imposed on employers, the requirements concerning worker information, and the emphasis on participation and training.

Equally innovative are the Machinery Directive (89/392/EEC) and, in a more limited sphere, Directive 90/270 on health and safety for work with display screen equipment. Both directives rely on the concept of 'working environment', which opens up the possibility of regulatory interventions in areas traditionally considered to be outside the field of occupational safety, and consider psychological factors like stress and fatigue as important factors to be considered in a modern regulatory approach. It is difficult to find equally advanced principles in the legislation of any major industrialised country, inside or outside the EU.

In order to explain such policy outputs we need new, more analytical theories of the policy process in the Community. Such theories should be capable of explaining the qualitative deepening of EC regulation as well as its apparently unstoppable growth.

3 A model of regulatory policy making

To understand policy making in the EC one must start from the basic fact that the budget of the EC is quite small, even after the significant increases of recent years. It represents less than 4 per cent of all the central government spending of the member states and less than 1.3 per cent of the gross domestic product (GDP) of the Union. By comparison, between 45 and 50 per cent of the wealth produced in the member states is spent by the national governments. The Community budget is not only small, but also rigid: almost 70 per cent of total appropriations consists of compulsory expenditures for programmes such as the Guarantee Section of the European Agricultural Guidance and Guarantee Fund (EAGGF).

Second, it is important to distinguish between regulatory policies and policies involving the direct expenditure of public funds. Examples of the latter type are redistributive policies, which transfer resources from one group of individuals, regions or countries to another group, and distributive policies, such as public works or financial support for research and technological development, which allocate public resources among different activities. Now, an important characteristic of regulatory policy making is the limited influence of budgetary limitations on the activities of regulators. The size of direct-expenditure programmes is constrained by budgetary appropriations and, ultimately, by the size of government tax revenues. In contrast, the real costs of most regulatory programmes are borne directly by the firms and individuals that have to comply with them. Compared with these costs, the resources needed to produce the regulations are trivial. It is difficult to overstate the significance of this structural difference between regulatory and direct-expenditure policies. The distinction is especially important for the analysis of Community policy making since not only the economic but also the political and administrative costs of implementing EC regulations and directives are borne, directly or indirectly, by the member states.

Third, I assume that the European Commission, like any other bureaucratic organisation, attempts to maximise its influence, subject to budgetary, political and legal constraints. The present discussion focuses on the budgetary constraints. As already noted, the financial resources of the Community go, for the most part, to the Common Agricultural Policy and to a handful of distributive and redistributive programmes. The remaining resources are insufficient to support large-scale initiatives in areas like industrial policy, energy, research or technological innovation. Hence, the only way for the Commission to increase its role is to expand the scope of regulatory activities, even beyond the functional require-ments of the common market.

As we saw in the preceding section, this strategy has been remarkably, some would say too, successful, but the reasons for the success cannot be found only in the preferences of the Commission. The EC policy-making system includes many actors: industrialists, trade unions, public-interest groups, national and subna-tional politicians and bureaucrats, independent experts, and so on. The Commission plays a key role in the *supply* of Community regulation; we must now consider the *demand* side. In order to simplify the exposition, I shall only consider the most important actors on the demand side, the national governments (for a more detailed analysis, see Majone 1992, 1994a).

It may seem illogical, if not plainly wrong, to discuss the role of the member states in the development of Community regulation under the heading of demand. After all, most legally binding acts have to be approved by the Council which represents the interests of the national governments and is supposed to be the real legislator in the EC system. Why not place the member states and the Commission on the same side of the demand-and-supply equation, as 'co-producers' of the regulatory outputs? Although this is the formally correct view, several factors suggest that from a policy making point of view it is more useful to consider that national governments demand, rather than supply, EC regulation.

To begin with, there is considerable evidence that many Commission proposals are introduced at the suggestion of member states (as well as of other actors such as the European Parliament, the Council of Ministers, the Economic and Social Committee, and private interests). For example, the German and Dutch govern-ments played a key role in the initiation and drafting of EC directives concerning vehicle emission control, while the British government exerted considerable pres-sure on the Commission to liberalise the market for life and non-life insurance where British insurers enjoy a comparative advantage over their competitors on the continent. According to the report of the French Conseil d'Etat cited above, of the last 500 proposals of regulations and directives presented by the Commission as of 1991, only 6 per cent appear to be 'spontaneous initiatives', so that the over-whelming majority of proposals would actually be produced on the demand of member states or other actors.

A second and theoretically more important factor has to do with the issue of policy credibility. As noted in the introduction, it is not *a priori* obvious why member states would be willing to delegate regulatory powers extending well beyond the level required by the founding treaty or by the logic of functional spillovers in an increasingly integrated market. As Ronald Coase (1960) has shown in a famous article, the presence of negative externalities does not in itself prevent effective co-ordination among independent actors.

A significant implication of Coase's theorem is that the rationale for suprana-tional regulation is *regulatory failure* rather than market failure. Market failures with international impacts, such as transboundary pollution, could be managed in a co-operative (intergovernmental) fashion without the necessity of delegating regulatory powers to a supranational body, *provided* that national regulators were willing and able to take into account the international repercussions of their choices; that they had sufficient knowledge of one another's intentions; that the (transaction) costs of organising and monitoring policy co-operation were not too high; and especially that they could trust each other to implement in good faith their joint decisions.

International regulatory failure occurs when one or more of these conditions are not satisfied. For example, it is usually difficult to observe whether intergovernmental regulatory agreements are kept or not. This is because much economic and social regulation is discretionary. Because regulators lack information that only regulated firms have, and because governments for political reasons are reluctant to impose excessive cost on industry, bargaining is an essential feature of the process of regulatory enforcement. Regardless of what the law says, the process of regulation is not simply one where the regulators command and the regulated obey. A 'market' is created over the precise obligations of the latter (Peacock 1984). Since bargaining is so pervasive, it may be impossible for an outside observer to determine whether or not an international regulation has been, in fact, violated.

When it is difficult to observe whether governments are making an honest effort to enforce a co-operative agreement, the agreement is not credible. One solution is to delegate regulatory tasks to a supranational authority with powers of monitoring and of imposing sanctions. Sometimes governments have problems of credibility not just in the eyes of each other, but in the eyes of third parties such as regulated firms. Thus, where pollution has international effects and fines impose significant competitive disadvantages on firms that compete internationally, firms are likely to believe that national regulators will be unwilling to prosecute them as rigorously if they determine the level of enforcement unilaterally rather than under supranational supervision. Hence the transfer of regulatory powers to a supranational authority like the European Commission, by making more stringent regulation credible, may improve the behaviour of regulated firms (Gatsios and Seabright 1989). Also, because the Commission is involved in the regulation of a large number of firms throughout the European Union, it has much more to gain by being tough in any individual case than a national regulator: weak enforcement would destroy its credibility in the eyes of more firms. Thus it may be more willing to enforce sanctions than a member state would be, even if its direct costs and benefits of doing so are no different (ibid.: 50). The fact that the Commission is involved in the regulation of a large number of firms throughout Europe also explains why it is less vulnerable to the risk of 'regulatory capture' than national regulators.

Perhaps the greatest advantage of EC membership in a period of far-reaching policy changes, is the possibility of delegating politically difficult decisions (such as the elimination of state aid to industry, the enforcement of competition rules, trade liberalisation and strict implementation of environmental regulations during economic recession) to supranational non-majoritarian institutions (Majone 1994b). By showing that their hands are tied by European rules, member states can increase the international credibility of their policy commitments and, at the same time, reduce the power of redistributive coalitions at home. In sum, the low credibility of purely intergovernmental agreements, together with the advantage of shifting politically difficult decisions to a non-majoritarian institution, explains the willingness of member states to delegate important regulatory powers to the Commission. In the next section, we explore the consequences of this delegation.

4 The dynamics of delegation and control

The delegation of extensive powers of adjudication and policy making to supranational institutions is what distinguishes the EC from more traditional international regimes. Its implications are still poorly understood, however. Neither neo-functionalists nor intergovernmentalists have seriously considered the dynamics of delegation and control; the former because of their faith in the automatism of functional spillovers, the latter because of their assumption that supranational institutions simply provide a smooth, faithful translation of national interests into policy. To analyse the consequences of the delegation of policy making powers, and the possibilities of political control one must turn to the literature on political–bureaucratic and principal–agent relations rather than to traditional theories of European integration.

The thrust of much recent research on political–bureaucratic relations is that bureaucracy has a substantial degree of autonomy, and that direct political control is rather weak (Wilson 1980; Moe 1987, 1990; Majone 1994c). Oversight for purposes of serious policy control is time consuming, costly, and difficult to do well under conditions of uncertainty and complexity. At any rate, legislators are concerned more with satisfying voters to increase the probability of re-election than with overseeing the bureaucracy. As a result, they do not typically invest their scarce resources in general policy control. Instead, they prefer to intervene quickly, inexpensively and in *ad hoc* ways to protect particular clients in particular matters (Mayhew 1974). Hence legislative oversight is un-coordinated and fragmented. Similarly, the literature on the budgetary process has cast doubts on the budget as an effective tool of control. As Wildavsky (1964) discovered, budgeting is decentralised and incremental, resulting in automatic increases that further insulate the bureaucracy from political control.

New theories based on the principal–agent model give a somewhat more positive assessment of the possibility of political control of the bureaucracy. According to agency theory, political control is possible because elected politicians create bureaucracies. They design administrative institutions with incentive structures to facilitate control, and they monitor bureaucratic activities to offset information asymmetries. Thus, agency theory, like recent versions of intergovernmentalism (Moravcsik 1993), posits well-informed central decision makers who systematically mould the preferences of bureaucratic agents and are capable of exercising rational political control (Wood and Waterman 1991: 803).

However, the process is considerably more complex than envisaged by these theories. In the delegation phase, political principals do have the freedom to select their agents and impose an incentive structure on their behaviour. Over time, however, bureaucrats accumulate job-specific expertise, and this 'asset specificity' (Williamson 1985) alters the original relationship. Now politicians must deal with agents they once selected, and in these dealings the bureaucrats have an advantage in technical and operational expertise. As a result, they are increasingly able to pursue their objective of greater autonomy. As Terry Moe (1990: 143) writes:

> Once an agency is created, the political world becomes a different place. Agency bureaucrats are now political actors in their own right: they have career and institutional interests that may not be entirely congruent with their formal missions, and they have powerful resources – expertise and delegated authority – that might be employed toward these 'selfish' ends. They are now players whose interests and resources alter the political game.

This recent research on political–bureaucratic relations throws considerable light on the dynamics of delegation and control in the EC context. Also, for the representatives of the member states in the Council of Ministers, oversight for purposes of serious policy control is costly, time-consuming, and difficult to do well. Hence their unwillingness to invest scarce resources in such activities. As was mentioned in section 2, the 'comitology' system is an attempt to control the Commission's discretion in the execution of Council directives. Regulatory and management committees created under this system can block a Commission measure and transmit the case to the Council, which can overrule the Commission. Even in the case of such committees, however, the Commission is not only in the chair, but has a strong presumption in its favour (Ludlow 1991: 107). According to the more detailed empirical study of the comitology system to date 'Commission officials generally do not think that their committee significantly reduced the Commission's freedom and even less that it has been set up to assure the Member State's control' (Institut für Europäische Politik 1989: 9). According to the same study, the Council acts only rarely on the complex technical matters dealt with by the comitology committees, but when it does, its decisions mostly support the Commission's original proposals (ibid.: 123). In fact the Commission has reported overwhelming (98 per cent) acceptance of its proposals by the various regulatory committees (Eichener 1992).

The case of policy initiation, the formal procedure according to which Commission proposals are discussed in a working group comprising national experts, submitted to an advisory committee, and reviewed by COREPER, also gives an impression of tight control that does not correspond with reality. What is known about the *modus operandi* of the advisory committees and working groups suggests that debates there follow substantive rather than national lines. A good deal of 'copinage technocratique' develops between Commission officials and national experts interested in discovering pragmatic solutions rather than defending political positions (Eichener 1992). By the time a Commission proposal reaches the Council of Ministers all the technical details have been worked out and modifications usually leave the essentials untouched.

In part, this is because although the Council with its working groups can monitor the activities of the Commission, it cannot complete with the expertise at the disposal of the Commission and its Directorates (Peters 1992: 119). The offices of the Commission responsible for a particular policy area form the central node of a vast 'issue network' that includes, in addition to the experts from the national administrations, independent experts, academics, environmental, consumer and other public-interest advocates, representatives of economic interests, professional organisations and subnational governments.

Commission officials engage in extensive discussions with all these actors but remain free to choose whose ideas and proposals to adopt. The variety of policy positions, which is typically much greater than at the national level, increases the freedom of choice of European officials. It may even happen that national experts find the Commission a more receptive forum for new ideas than their own admin-istration. The important Machinery Directive (89/392EEC) mentioned in section 2, offers a striking example of this. The crucially important technical annex of the directive was drafted by a British labour expert who originally had sought to reform the British approach to safety at the workplace. Having failed to persuade the policy makers of his own country, he brought his innovative ideas to Brussels, where they were welcomed by Commission officials and eventually became European law (Eichener 1992: 52).

5 Policy entrepreneurship

The existence of large margins of regulatory discretion is a necessary but not a sufficient condition for genuine policy innovation. We must also consider the capacity of Commission officials to play the role of policy entrepreneurs. Kingdon (1984) describes policy entrepreneurs as constantly on the look-out for windows of opportunity through which to push their preferred ideas. Policy windows open on those relatively infrequent occasions when three usually sepa-rate process streams – problems, politics and policy ideas – come together. Policy entrepreneurs concerned about a particular problem search for solutions in the stream of policy ideas to couple to their problem, then try to take advantage of political receptivity at certain points in time to push the package of problem and solution.

A successful policy entrepreneur possesses three basic qualities: first, he must be taken seriously either as an expert, as a leader of a powerful interest group, or as an authoritative decision maker; second, he must be known for his political connections or negotiating skills; third, and probably most important, successful entrepreneurs are persistent (Kingdon 1984: 189–90). Because of the way they are recruited, the structure of their career incentives, and the crucial role of the

Commission in policy initiation, Commission officials often display the qualities of a successful policy entrepreneur to a degree unmatched by national civil servants.

In particular, the Commission exhibits the virtue of persistence to an extraordinary degree. Most important policy innovations in the EC have been achieved after many years during which the Commission persisted in its attempts to 'soften up' the opposition of the member states, while waiting for a window of opportunity to open. A textbook example is the case of the Merger Control Regulation approved by the Council on 21 December 1989, after more than twenty years of political wrangling.

As far back as 1965, the Commission argued that the Treaty of Rome was seriously deficient without the power to control mergers. The following year it asked a group of experts to study the problem of concentrations in the common market. The majority of the group held that article 85 of the Rome Treaty could be applied to 'monopolising' mergers, but the Commission chose to follow the contrary opinion of the minority. It did, however, accept the majority view concerning the applicability of article 86 to mergers involving one company already in a dominant position in the common market. The European Court of Justice followed the Commission's interpretation in the *Continental Can* case (1973).

At the beginning of 1974 the European Parliament and the Economic and Social Committee approved by large majorities a proposal for a merger control regulation, but the member states were not yet prepared to grant the Commission the powers it requested. A long period of inaction followed. The process was again set in motion by the path-breaking *Philip Morris* Judgement of 17 November 1987 in which the Court of Justice held, against the then prevalent legal opinion, that article 85 does apply to the acquisition by one company of an equity interest in a competitor where the effect is to restrict or distort competition. The Commission warmly endorsed the Court's decision. It was clear that another important step, after *Continental Can*, had been taken on the road toward the control of merger activities with a 'Community dimension'. In the meanwhile, the 'Europe 1992' programme for the completion of the internal market had stimulated waves of mergers. This development opened the window of opportunity the Commission had been waiting for so long. Centralised merger control of Community-wide mergers could now be presented as essential for success in completing the internal market. Finally, the convergence of Kingdon's three streams of problems, politics, and policy ideas produced the 1989 Merger Control Regulation.

This episode in the history of EC policy making provides a clear illustration of the persistence and entrepreneurial skills of the Commission, but also supports a more general point, namely that an adequate explanation of policy development in the EC must be rooted in the dynamics of the entire system, and must pay serious attention to the relationships of mutual dependence among European institutions. Thus, in section 2 we mentioned the strategic significance of mutual recognition for the Commission, rather than for the member states. Only through this new approach to harmonisation could the objectives of the internal market programme be achieved in time. In turn, the new approach was made possible by the actions and decisions of both the Commission and the Court of Justice. The relationship of mutual dependence of these two institutions has been expressed very well by Alter and Meunier-Aitsahalia (1993: 19) 'The *Cassis* decision advanced the idea of mutual recognition, and the entrepreneurship of the Commission put the issue on the table and forced a debate. Both the decision itself and the Commission's response were necessary to produce the new harmonisation policy. The legal decision was needed to encourage the Commission to issue its bold Communication. . . . The Commission's Communication, however, was also necessary in order to bring the legal decision into the political arena.'

Combining concepts from public choice theory with historical case studies, William Riker (1986) provides additional insights into the strategies used by policy entrepreneurs to change existing political coalitions. He argues that through agenda setting, strategic behaviour, and especially through the introduction of new policy dimensions to political debate, the entrepreneur can break up existing equilibria in order to create new and more profitable political outcomes. The successful entrepreneur 'probes until he finds some new alternative, some new dimension that strikes a spark in the preferences of others' (ibid.: 64).

A good example of this strategy is the introduction by the Commission of the concept of working environment into the Europe-wide debate on health and safety at work. As was mentioned in section 2, this concept opens up the possibility of regulatory interventions in areas such as ergonomics traditionally considered to be outside the field of occupational safety. In view of the claims by intergovernmentalists that Community policy making is under the control of the most powerful member states, it should be pointed out that the important Machinery Directive and other equally innovative directives in the area of occupational safety (see section 2) were inspired by the regulatory philosophy of two small countries – the Netherlands and Denmark, which first introduced the concept of working environment into their legislation – and opposed by Germany in order to preserve the power and traditional approach of its own regulatory bodies (Feldhoff 1992; Eichener 1992).

6 Positive and normative implications

As was suggested in the introduction, in order to understand the development and growth of regulatory policies in the EC it is important to distinguish between different manifestations of the phenomenon: quantitative growth, regulatory complexity, task expansion and 'deepening', that is, genuine policy innovation. The theories discussed in the preceding pages suggest a number of observations concerning these various dimensions of development and growth.

The model of demand and supply of EC regulation sketched in section 3 seeks to explain regulatory origin rather than the ongoing regulatory process. Nevertheless, the model has significant implications for the issues raised in this chapter. It will be recalled that the main explanatory variables, in addition to the

Commission's desire to increase its influence, are the budget constraint and the low credibility of intergovernmental regulatory agreements.

Paradoxically, the attempt of the member states to limit the scope of supranational policies by imposing a tight and rigid budget constraint on the Commission, has favoured the development of a mode of policy making that is largely immune from budgetary discipline. As an American student and practitioner of regulation writes:

> Budget and revenue figures are good summaries of what is happening in welfare, defense, or tax policy, and can be used to communicate efficiently with the general public over the fray of program-by-program interest-group contention. In the world of regulation, however, where the government commands but nearly all the rest takes place in the private economy, we generally lack good aggregate numbers to describe what is being 'taxed' and 'spent' in pursuit of public policies. Instead we have lists – endless lists of projects the government would like others to undertake.
>
> (De Muth 1984:25)

Thus, continuous expansion is a structural feature of regulatory policy making, and not only or even primarily the result of functional spillovers and the 'expansive logic of sectoral integration' as neo-functionalists argued. Two additional factors contribute to the seemingly unstoppable growth of European regulation. First, it has already been mentioned that the great majority of recent EC regulations and directives are not the result of 'spontaneous initiatives' of the Commission, but rather of demands coming especially from individual member states and the Council, but also from the European Parliament, the Economic and Social Committee, regional governments, and various private and public interest groups. The possibility granted by the Maastricht Treaty to the European Parliament to ask the Commission to submit legislative proposals can only strengthen this trend.

While the responsiveness of the Commission to such requests may increase its political legitimacy, uncontrolled and un-coordinated demands can produce a number of negative consequences, of which legislative inflation is the most obvious one. These consequences are aggravated by institutional factors. Because the European Commission is a collegial body, central co-ordination of the regulatory programmes of the different Directorates-General (DGs) is quite difficult. Lack of central co-ordination leads to serious inconsistencies across and within regulatory programmes, lack of rational procedures for selecting policy priorities, and insufficient attention to the cost-effectiveness of individual rules.

One method of reducing over-regulation would be to create an institution with the power to oversee the entire regulatory process and to discipline the activity of the DGs by comparing the social benefits of proposed regulations with the costs imposed on the European economy by the regulatory requirements.

Such an institution or 'regulatory clearing house' should be established at the highest level of the Commission. DGs would be asked to submit draft regulatory programmes to it annually for review. When disagreements or serious inconsistencies arise, the President of the Commission or a 'Working Committee on regulation' would be asked to intervene. This review process would help the Commission to screen demands for EC regulations and to shape a consistent set of regulatory measures to submit to the Council and the European Parliament. The usefulness of the procedure could be enhanced by co-ordinating the regulatory review with the normal budgetary review, thus linking the level of budgetary appropriations to the cost-effectiveness of the different regulatory programmes (Majone 1992).

Let us now consider the issue of regulatory complexity. Many students of EC policy making have observed that EC directives exhibit a much greater level of technical detail than comparable national legislation. The widespread opinion that this level of complexity is due to the technical perfectionism of the Commission lacks plausibility: the Commission is very small relative to its tasks, has limited resources, and is largely composed of generalists, not of technical experts. Rather, it is distrust of the member states which is largely responsible for regulatory complexity. Doubting the commitment of other governments to honest implementation of European rules, and being generally unfamiliar with different national styles of administration, national representatives insist on spelling out mutual obligations in the greatest possible detail, including at times chemical, statistical or mathematical formulae.

Member states not only mistrust each other; they also mistrust the Commission. As noted in section 4, in order to limit the discretion of the Commission they have created a complex system of working groups and advisory committees largely staffed by national experts. For the reasons given above, the system is not very effective in reducing the freedom of choice of the Commission, but it introduces a strong technical bias into the regulatory process. This is because most national experts are narrow technical specialists more interested in process and technical details than in cost-effective and easy-to-implement solutions. This technical bias, combined with the reluctance of the Council to engage in serious policy control and the lack of central oversight at the Commission level, is probably another factor contributing to regulatory complexity.

This hypothesis is supported by more general theoretical considerations. Some economists have argued that an explanation of regulatory complexity does not need to rest on peculiar interests of the regulators but on economic interests of third parties, namely specialists in various aspects of regulation such as lawyers, accountants, engineers or safety experts. Unlike other interest groups, these experts care more about the process than the product of regulation. They have an interest in regulatory complexity because complexity increases the value of their expertise. Thus 'red tape' may not simply be evidence of bureaucratic inefficiency or ineptness. Rather, in part, 'red tape' is a private interest that arises because a complex regulatory environment allows for specialisation in rule making and ' rule intermediation' (Kearl 1983; Quandt 1983).

In 1985 the Commission introduced a new approach to technical regulation with the explicit objective of reducing regulatory complexity (COM(85)310, final). In essence, the new approach proposes a conceptual distinction between matters where harmonisation of national regulations is essential, and those that can be left to the sphere of voluntary technical norms (the principle of 'reference to standards'), or where it is sufficient that there be mutual recognition of the requirements laid down by national laws. In practice, the new approach replaces the multitude of *specification* standards (also called process or engineering standards) by a few *performance* standards which a product must satisfy in order to secure the right of free movement throughout the single European market.

The technical specifications formulated by European standardisation bodies (such as the European Standardisation Committee, CEN, and the European Standardisation Committee for Electrical Products, CENELEC) are not binding and retain their character of voluntary standards. However, governments are obliged to presume that products manufactured in accordance with European standards (or, temporarily, with national standards when no European ones are yet available) comply with the 'fundamental requirements' or performance standards stipulated in the directive (Pelkmans 1987). The system is completed by the mutual recognition of testing and certification procedures.

The new methodology is a highly innovative approach to supranational regulation in general, and to the problem of regulatory complexity in particular, but its success depends crucially on the level of mutual trust among the member states. In the absence of mutual trust, national regulators may upset the delicate balance between different and potentially conflicting objectives – satisfying essential requirements of health and safety and preventing the creation of non-tariff barriers through regulation – on which mutual recognition rests. The experience with the mutual recognition of approvals of new medical drugs provides a graphic illustration of this point.

For more than two decades the Commission has attempted to harmonise national regulations for new medical drugs by means of a set of harmonised criteria for testing new products, and the mutual recognition of toxicological and clinical trials conducted according to EC rules. Under the 'multi-state drug application procedure' (MSAP) introduced in 1975, a company that has received a marketing authorisation from the regulatory agency of a member state may ask for the mutual recognition of that approval by at least five other countries. The agencies of the countries nominated by the company must approve or raise objections within 120 days. In the case of objections, the Committee for Proprietary Medicinal Products (CPMP) – which includes national experts and Commission representatives – has to be notified. The CPMP must express its opinion within sixty days; within another thirty days it may be overruled by the national agency that has raised objections.

Unfortunately, the procedure has not worked well: national regulators did not appear to be bound either by decisions of other regulatory bodies, or by the opinions of the CPMP. Even a new, simplified procedure introduced in 1983 did not succeed in streamlining the approval of process, since national regulators continued to raise objections against each other almost routinely (Kaufer 1990). These difficulties finally convinced the Commission to propose the establishment of a European Agency for the Evaluation of Medicinal Products and the creation of a new centralised Community procedure – compulsory for biotechnology products and certain types of veterinary medicines, and available on an optional basis for other products – leading to a Community authorisation (Commission of the European Communities 1990).

As this example shows, a good deal of decentralisation would be possible if only national regulators would trust each other more. Often mistrust reflects insufficient appreciation of different regulatory philosophies and national styles of policy making. However, in some cases regulators have low international credibility because they lack, or are perceived as lacking, the scientific and technical expertise, financial resources and policy infrastructure needed to deal effectively with complex regulatory issues. In such cases, Community assistance may be needed to ensure that all member states achieve a level of competence sufficient to support mutual trust and make mutual recognition possible.

The gist of the argument presented so far is that national governments and regulatory authorities bear a considerable share of the responsibility for the volume and complexity of EC regulation. Hence, remedies should first be sought at the level of the member states, although more centralised control of regulatory programmes within the Commission would be helpful too. Where the policy entrepreneurship of the Commission becomes important is in explaining the progressive 'deepening' of EC regulations.

In sections 4 and 5 I have discussed in general terms the conditions which make policy entrepreneurship possible, and the most important strategies followed by successful entrepreneurs. Here I consider a particular, but significant, aspect of 'deepening': the fact that some of the most striking examples of policy innovation in the EC are in the area of social regulation (see section 2). There is, of course, a straightforward explanation for this. Clearly, there is limited scope for innovation when policies are either prescribed by treaty – the case of competition, agriculture or trade policies – or represent a necessary response to the functional needs of an increasingly integrated market – rules concerning the free movement of goods, services, capital and people. At least since the Single European Act, social regulation does not have to be justified in functional terms, and thus offers greater scope for entrepreneurship and innovation than traditional EC policies.

However, a more interesting explanation is suggested by James Q. Wilson's well-known taxonomy of regulatory policies according to the pattern of distribution of benefits and costs (Wilson 1980: 366–72). In this taxonomy, entrepreneurial policies correspond to policies that confer general (though perhaps small) benefits at a cost to be borne by a small segment of society. Most social regulation falls into this category. The costs of cleaner air and water, safer products and better working conditions are borne, at least initially, by particular segments of industry. Since the incentive is strong for the opponents of the policy but weak for beneficiaries, social regulatory measures can be passed only if there is a policy entrepreneur who can mobilise public sentiment, put the opponents of the measures on the defensive, and associate the proposed regulation with widely shared values.

According to Wilson, the entrepreneur is vicarious representative of groups not directly part of the legislative process. The observation helps us understand the growing importance of social regulation, and hence of entrepreneurial politics, in the EC. Historically, diffuse interests have been poorly represented in Europe because traditional forms of state intervention tended to favour producers – capitalists and unionised workers – at the expense of consumer interests. Also, political systems characterised by strong party control of both the executive and the legislature, and highly centralised public bureaucracies, impeded the emergence of independent political entrepreneurs.

On the other hand, the insulation of the Commission, a non-majoritarian institution, from partisan politics, the activism of the European Court of Justice, and the efforts of the European Parliament to define its own distinctive role, are all factors that explain why diffuse interests are often more effectively protected at the European than at the national level. Critics of regulatory growth in the EC should not forget than in most member states consumer-protection legislation and even environmental policies were poorly developed, when not entirely lacking, before national governments were forced to implement European directives in these areas.

7 Conclusion: toward institutional reform

There is a general agreement that a Community of sixteen, twenty or more members could not function under present rules: institutional reform is urgently needed. Although this chapter is not specifically concerned with this vast topic, some of its findings may be relevant to the broader issue.

A first point of methodological interest is that one should not overemphasise the *sui generis* nature of the Community, but rather attempt to distinguish between idiosyncratic problems and those that can be more generally ascribed to a mode of policy making or method of governance. Thus, over-regulation is a general problem, though it may be aggravated by the particular institutional arrangements and peculiar politics of the Community. It follows that reform proposals should not be devised on an *ad hoc* basis, but should be inspired by general principles.

This applies also to fundamental political issues like the 'democratic deficit' of Community institutions, in particular the Commission. As I have argued elsewhere, a problem of democratic accountability arises whenever policy-making powers are delegated to non-majoritarian institutions such as politically independent central banks and regulatory commissions. To discuss the problem exclusively in the context of EC institutions is to run the risk of neglecting relevant experiences in favour of *ad hoc* and possibly flawed solutions.

Second, our discussions of over-regulation and regulatory complexity suggest that it is unhelpful, as well as unfair, to blame the Commission for all the dysfunctions of policy making at the European level. If it is true that the member states have their share of responsibility then institutional reform should begin at home. One of the central themes of this chapter is the overwhelming importance of trust among the member states. We saw that mutual recognition cannot succeed when national regulators do not trust each other. But similar problems will arise in the practical applications of the principle of subsidiarity. This is because national and subnational governments may be more attuned to individual tastes, but they are unlikely to make a clean separation between providing public goods for their citizens and engaging in policies designed to advantage the country or region at the expense of its neighbours. For example, local authorities have sometimes controlled air pollution by requiring extremely tall smokestacks on industrial facilities. With tall stacks, by the time the emissions descend to ground level they are usually in the next city, region or country, and so of no concern to the jurisdiction where they were emitted. Until regulators can trust each other to avoid such selfish strategies, centralisation of regulatory authority is the only practical way of correcting transboundary externalities, or preventing the local regulation of a local market failure from becoming a trade barrier.

One final point about decision-making procedures. As already mentioned, the regulatory activities of the Commission are supported by a dense network of consultative, regulatory, and management committees. Moreover, at the end of October 1993, decisions were taken by the member states concerning the establishment of ten new administrative bodies. These include, in addition to the forerunner of the European Central Bank, the European Monetary Institute located in Frankfurt, the European Environmental Agency, the Office of Veterinary and Phytosanitary Inspection and Control; the European Centre for the Control of Drugs and Drug Addiction; the European Agency for the Evaluation of Medicinal Products, and the Agency for Health and Safety at Work.

The proliferation of technical committees and specialised agencies further aggravates one of the most serious defects of the Community institutions: the lack of transparency of their decision-making process. Because of the opacity of the procedures, it is difficult for the citizens of the Union to identify the body which is responsible for decisions that apply to them, and the legal remedies that are available to them.

A similar situation arose in the United States at the time of the New Deal, which saw a dramatic growth in government intervention. The establishment of new specialised agencies, the functions of which were extremely complex and varied, created a need for rules to ensure that they did not act arbitrarily or unlawfully. In the absence of a true administrative law tradition, the rules governing the federal administration had developed in a piecemeal fashion and they have been worked out in response to *ad hoc* needs. However, such an approach was deemed insufficient to cope with the changes under way. The Administrative Procedures Act (APA), adopted by Congress in 1946, aimed to legitimise the growth of federal bureaucracy by providing a single set of rules explaining the procedures to be followed by federal agencies and providing for judicial review of many of their decisions.

I submit that the Community could usefully draw on such a precedent. The enactment of an EC Administrative Procedures Act would provide the Community with a unique opportunity to decide what kind of rules are more likely to rationalise decision making, to what extent interest groups should be given access to regulatory process, or when judicial review is necessary. Even if it were to limit itself to the writing of existing practices into the law, as the APA largely did, the adoption of a single set of administrative rules would at least provide for a hard core of provisions applicable to the developing regulatory process. Such a move would bear witness to the willingness of the EC and its member states to allow an unregulated growth of the Community's administrative functions.

Note

1   Following the terminology of the Maastricht Treaty, I use the expression European Community (EC) to denote the economic and social 'pillar' of the European Union. This chapter does not deal with the other two pillars – the common foreign and security policy, and co-operation in the fields of justice and home affairs. 'European Union' is used here only to refer to the collectivity of the member states.

References

Alter, Karen J. and Sophie Meunier-Aitsahalia (1993) 'Judicial Politics in the European Community: European Integration and the Pathbreaking *Cassis de Dijon* Decision', Paper presented at the European Community Studies Association Conference, Washington DC, May 27–29, 1993.

Coase, Ronald (1960) 'The Problem of Social Cost', *The Journal of Law and Economics*, 3, 1–44.

Commission of the European Communities (1985) *Completing the Internal Market*, COM(85)310, final. Luxembourg: Office for Official Publications of the European Communities.

—— (1990) *Future System for the Free Movement of Medicinal Drugs in the European Community*, COM(90)283, final, Luxembourg: Office for Official Publications of the European Communities.

Conseil d'Etat (1992) *Rapport Public 1992*, Paris: La Documentation Française, Etudes et Documents No. 44.

Dehousse, Renaud (1994) *La Cour de Justice des Communautés Européennes*, Paris: Montchrétien.

De Muth, Christopher C. (1984) 'A Strategy for Regulatory Reform', *Regulation*, 4, 25–30.

Eichener, Volkner (1992) *Social Dumping or Innovative Regulation?*, Florence: European University Institute, Working Paper SPS No. 92/28.

Feldhoff, Kerstein (1992) 'Grundzüge des Europäischen Arbeitsumweltrechts', mimeo., Bochum: Ruhr Universität.

Garrett, Geoffrey (1992) 'International Cooperation and Institutional Choice: The European Community's Internal Market', *International Organization*, 46, 533–560.

33

Garrett, Geoffrey and Barry Weingast (1993) 'Ideas, Interests and Institutions: Constructing the European Community's Internal Market', in J. Goldstein and R. Keohane (eds) *Ideas and Foreign Policy*, Ithaca, NY: Cornell University Press.

Gatsios, Kristos and Paul Seabright (1989) 'Regulation in the European Community', *Oxford Review of Economic Policy*, 5, no. 2, 37–60.

George, Stephen (1993) 'Supranational Actors and Domestic Politics: Integration Theory Reconsidered in the Light of the Single European Act and Maastricht', Sheffield: mimeo.

Haas, Ernst (1958) *The Uniting of Europe: Political, Social and Economic Forces, 1950–1957*, Stanford, CA: Stanford University Press.

Institut für Europäsche Politik (1989) *'Comitology': Characteristics, Performance and Options*, Bonn: Preliminary Final Report.

Kaufer, Erich (1990) 'The Regulation of New Product Development in the Drug Industry', in G. Majone (ed.) *Deregulation or Re-Regulation?*, London: Pinter Publishers, 223–51.

Kearl, John R. (1983) 'Rules, Rule Intermediaries and the Complexity and Stability of Regulation', *Journal of Public Economics*, 22, 215–26.

Keohane, Robert and Stanley Hoffman (1990) 'Community Policy and Institutional Change' in W. Wallace (ed.) *The Dynamics of European Integration*, London: Pinter Publishers.

Kingdon, John W. (1984) *Agendas, Alternatives and Public Policy*, Boston: Little, Brown.

Ludlow, Paul (1991) 'The European Commission', in R. Keohane and S. Hoffman (eds) *The New European Community: Decisionmaking and Institutional Change*, Boulder, CO: Westview Press, 85–132.

Majone, Giandomenico (1992) 'Market Integration and Regulation: Europe after 1992', *Metroeconomica*, 43, 1–2, 131–56.

—— (1994a) 'The Rise of the Regulatory State in Europe', *West European Politics*, 17, 3, 78–102.

—— (1994b) 'Independence vs. Accountability? Non-Majoritarian Institutions and Democratic Government in Europe', in J.J. Hesse (ed.) *The European Yearbook on Comparative Government and Public Administration 1994*, Oxford: Oxford University Press.

—— (1994c) 'Controlling Regulatory Bureaucracies: Lessons from the American Experience', in H.U. Derlien, U. Gerhardt, F.W. Scharpf (eds) *Systemrationalität und Partialinteresse*, Baden-Baden: Nomos, 291–314.

Mayhew, David R. (1974) *Congress: The Electoral Connection*, New Haven, CT: Yale University Press.

Moe, Terry M. (1987) 'Interests, Institutions and Positive Theory: The Politics of the NLRB', *Studies in American Political Development*, 2, 236–99.

—— (1990) 'The Politics of Structural Choice: Toward a Theory of Public Bureaucracy', in O.E. Williamson (ed.) *Organisation Theory from Chester Barnard to the Present*, Oxford: Oxford University Press, 116–53.

Moravcsik, Andrew (1993) 'Preferences and Power in the European Community: A Liberal Intergovernmentalist Approach', *Journal of Common Market Studies*, 31, 4, 473–524.

Peacock, Alan (1984) *The Regulation Game*, Oxford: Basil Blackwell.

Pelkmans, Jacques (1987) 'The New Approach to Technical Harmonization and Standardization', *Journal of Common Market Studies*, 25, 3, 249–69.

Peters, Guy, B. (1992) 'Bureaucratic Politics and the Institutions of the European Community', in Alberta M. Sbragia (ed.), *Europolitics*, Washington DC: The Brookings Institution.

Quandt, Richard E. (1983) 'Complexity in Regulation', *Journal of Public Economics*, 22,199–214.

Rehbinder, Eckhardt and Richard Stewart (1985) *Environmental Protection Policy*, Berlin: de Gruyter.

Riker, William (1986) *The Art of Political Manipulation*, New Haven, CT: Yale University Press.

Wildavsky, Aaron (1964) *The Budgetary Process*, Boston: Little, Brown.

Williamson, Oliver E. (1985) *The Economic Institutions of Capitalism*, New York: The Free Press.

Wilson, James Q. (1980) *The Politics of Regulation*, New York: Basic Books.

Wood, Dan B. and R. W. Waterman (1991) 'The Dynamics of Political Control in the Bureaucracy', *American Political Science Review*, 85, 801–28.

3

DEFENDING THE SOCIAL CONTRACT

The EU between global constraints and domestic imperatives

Martin Rhodes

Introduction

In the space of a decade, the mood concerning the nature of Europe's welfare states and the role to be played by European integration in shaping and protecting them has gone from cautiously optimistic to bleak. Europe's 'social contracts' – the complex webs of relations linking governments with citizens and citizens with each other in the EU's member states – are unlikely to be defended against global or domestic forces for change by a federal or even quasi-federal system. Some would argue that this reflects a transition from unfounded idealism to a more realistic assessment of the essentially limited contribution that pan-European harmonization or convergence can make. Others lament the fact that the 'great European project' has become primarily market driven, with social policy consigned to the margins and notions of a federal welfare state abandoned. As proof of their views, both would point to the shift in priorities from social protection and standard raising to 'competitiveness' and 'flexibility'.

Much has been written on the sclerotic development of the 'European Social Dimension'. Again, this literature is divided between the 'cautious optimists' and the Euro-pessimists (Trubeck 1996). The optimists point to the autonomy and purpose of key institutions in Europe's 'multilevel' polity and the capacity of the latter and the member states to create a regulatory order that bolsters Europe's national social contracts. Meanwhile, the pessimists argue that integration has contributed to the 'globalization' of the European economy in breaking down the borders of economic competition while contributing little to new institution – building or preventing 'social dumping' and regime competition from eroding social standards.

This chapter aims to explore these arguments by considering recent developments in European welfare states and labour markets. It presents an image of the EU as increasingly caught between global pressures and domestic imperatives for change, a supranational actor with little capacity or, it should be stressed, legitimacy for creating either a federal social policy system or direct intervention in the 'semi-sovereign' affairs of its member states. And yet, the net effect of achievements to date should not be discounted: the accretion of past pan-European policy initiatives has created a sphere of labour law and social legislation that is 'European' in character and not simply the amalgam of member states traditions; sovereignty in a number of important areas has been surrendered, often unwittingly, to supranational institutions; and the decision-making process no longer conforms entirely to the precepts of intergovernmentalism: although interstate bargains have underpinned the development of the 'social dimension', they have not been solely responsible for shaping or advancing it.

Nevertheless, it is also clear that European policy making and intervention cannot compensate for the loss of nation state steering capacity in an era of globalization. As argued below, somewhat paradoxically, pan-European policy initiatives were better suited in many respects to an era which is now rapidly passing – one in which nations could still control their national boundaries and when Fordism and all its attributes (traditional forms of economic organization, the standard male breadwinner-based family and the conventional life–work cycle) were still intact. Unfortunately, the window of opportunity for a European social policy created by a coalition of certain member states and supranational non-state actors from around 1987 to 1993 came at precisely the point when Europe was entering a period of low growth and far reaching changes in patterns of production, wealth creation and employment. These developments threaten to undermine the priority given in the recent past to higher levels of European social protection. In the late 1990s, both the future of European welfare states and the role of the European Union are uncertain. What *is* clear is that while the former are going through a period of change and even experimentation, this renewed focus on *national* priorities makes EU intervention increasingly problematic.

In analyzing these developments and their implications, the following takes neither the 'Euro-optimist' nor the 'Euro-pessimist' position. Unlike the 'Euro-optimist' viewpoint, described by Wolfgang Streeck as a tendency 'to minimize the significance of the disappearance of the supranational state perspective' and 'rather than dwell on what is not happening . . . prefers to deal with what is', the argument below seeks to understand why a federal European social order has failed to emerge and to consider the consequences of economic integration in the absence of a parallel state-building process (Streeck 1997). But unlike Streeck's own 'Euro-pessimist' position, it does not attribute Europe's present and emerging welfare and citizenship problems to the failure to replace the weakening national state with a supranational substitute (involving a tacit assumption that it was ever feasible to do so). Nor does it claim that all is lost for national policy in an economically integrated Europe without federal structures. Instead it seeks to show that while significant advances have been made in European social policy, there have always been and still are clear limits to the role it can play: in the contemporary period of new domestic and international challenges to welfare states, social policy

37

adjustments must proceed through a combination of national and European initiatives in which the former remain pre-eminent.

The EU and national social systems: what has been achieved?

Why no federal welfare state?

As George Ross has commented, judging Community accomplishments against aspirations for a federal European welfare state is quite unrealistic, 'given that the EC was constitutionally barred from most welfare-state areas, and it was not a nation state, let alone an instrument for the social democratic rebalancing of the international economy' (Ross 1995: 358). It is therefore inaccurate to assume or argue that the absence of a strong, redistributive European welfare-state project is the result of the victory of Margaret Thatcher's conception of Europe as a 'US-aligned free-trade zone' over Jacques Delors' 'supranational welfare-state building project' (Streeck 1996: 301–2). The fact of the matter is that the foundations for a federal welfare state were never put in place, nor, if they had been, is it easy to see how they could have been built upon.

Laying the foundations for a federal welfare state would have required a consensus on this matter from the early years of integration. But romantic attachment to the notion aside, in the real world of European policy making, the surrender of social policy sovereignty to supranational institutions has never been deemed desirable – even by the strongest supporters of European social policy such as the French. Although the latter came close to seeking the inclusion of full upward harmonization clauses and extensive regulatory powers in the Rome Treaty, this was due to self-interest rather than a commitment to European federalism. In any case, its principle partner in the integration project, Germany, was totally opposed. Indeed, the EEC Treaty reflects this basic Franco-German conflict. The French wanted unambiguous decision-making powers in the Treaty of Rome, believing that without some form of social security harmonization their high social charges would create competitive disadvantage. In addition, gender equality provisions in the French constitution would have to be transferred to the Treaty. But the Germans – defending their distinctive post-war 'ordo-liberal' position – were opposed to any legal competence for the EEC in this area (Rhodes 1998b). The result was an awkward Treaty compromise, providing a section on social policy with no clear guidelines on the scope of its provisions or the means for their implementation. The institutional prerequisites for supranational welfare-state building have therefore never existed, and until the *relance* of the 'social dimension' in the 1980s under the Mitterrand–Delors axis, there was little or no enthusiasm for it. Even then, the most ardent advocates of 'social Europe' (including Jacques Delors) sought an extension of Europe's regulatory role via standard intergovernmental procedures – albeit bolstered by greater majority voting – rather than 'progress from inter-governmentalism to supranationalism' (cf. Streeck 1996: 302).

Thus, the legal basis for a Community role in social and labour market policy (set out in articles 117 to 123 of the Treaty of Rome) remained ambiguous, even after the revisions of the Single European Act, which brought health and safety legislation under qualified majority voting (QMV) with article 118A. This ambiguity has forced the Commission – which has always adopted a broad interpretation of its powers – to forge alliances with member state governments and, where possible, interest groups, to fill the gap between formal competence and actual influence (Holloway 1981: 11–39). The Commission has also had to make a creative use of Treaty articles in order to push forward legislation, given that the original article 118 gave the Commission the task of promoting close co-operation between the member states in training, employment, working conditions, social security and collective bargaining, but without specifying how. Only article 119, which met the demands of the French in defining the equal pay principle, article 121 on social security measures for migrant workers and articles 123–8 on the European Social Fund were more explicit, explaining, in part, the advances more readily made in these areas, especially gender equality where article 119 made the Commission and the ECJ important actors (Holloway 1981; Hantrais 1995).

But even had there been a consensus on the construction of a federal welfare state, the task would have been a daunting one, encountering numerous structural impediments, including the historical link between nationhood and welfare-state building (and its absence in the European Community), the lack of societal prerequisites, the national embeddedness of welfare states and the diversity of social policy regimes.

Nationhood and welfare-state building   Although many factors have been important in building European welfare states – the fear of revolution and of the *classes dangereuses* was certainly instrumental in many countries, beginning with Bismarck's Germany – the origins of the welfare state also reveal a strong patriotic dimension and were linked to the consolidation and defence of nationhood. Wars were often instrumental in developing a sense of trade-off between the suffering that people had to endure during the conflict and their potential entitlements in times of peace and renewed growth. Because international conflicts imply a total dedication of the people to the objectives of the national government, unity and solidarity became the catch words and the key values. In the name of the defence of the nation, taxes were raised, women put to work and men were sent to the front. After the war, it was felt both by citizens and politicians that those who contributed to this collective effort had to be compensated. Skocpol (1992) shows how decisive in the construction of a nascent social policy was the financial contribution provided to the widows or the pensions paid to the soldiers of the American war of secession. Beveridge based his ambitious reforms in Britain on the fundamental opposition between the warfare states of the fascist and Nazi dictatorships and the welfare states of the democratic regimes. The same is true of the history of the French welfare state at the end of both the first and the second world wars. The claims were more nationalistic in tone after 1918 and more class based in 1945–6 (Rhodes and Mény 1998). But on both occasions, the idea of national solidarity was a key element in the rhetoric and the principles guiding reform and promoting the 'Priority of Compatriots' – the fact that 'the political borders of the state . . . delineate a sphere of individuals whose interests ground special, though not exclusive claims on their shared institutions' (Frøllesdal 1997: 145). The EU clearly lacks the historical moments and myths that merged nationhood with solidarity.

The national embeddedness of welfare states This is unsurprising given these origins. For the diversity of European national welfare regimes is reflected not only in large differences in social expenditure (although these are converging) but, more importantly, in embedded and historically shaped principles of *national* organization. Policy space, as well as administrative/organizational and fiscal space, is occupied by nation states, among which integration in the core areas of welfare-state regimes – education, health care and retirement security, not to mention forms of labour market organization – is consequently highly unlikely. This 'pre-emption of policy space' is a major obstacle to Europeanization beyond a loosely organized system of multi-tiered policy development with limited supranational authority. At the same time, the strong links between social policy development and political legitimacy, and the fact that governments have already surrendered national autonomy across a wide range of other policy areas, means that member states will resist a significant transfer of decision making and fiscal capacity and remain protective of their social policy authority (Pierson and Leibfried 1995; Majone 1996). Control of labour markets and social costs is, after all, one of the few areas in which member states can determine competitiveness in an integrated economy with a single currency, although a deregulatory spiral is unlikely. Moreover, if it is difficult to create solidarity between citizens with a common identity, the development of citizenship rights at the European level is even more so. Given the 'Priority of Compatriots' it may be quite utopian to imagine significant financial redistribution across national boundaries – especially in the light of German unification where the strains of such a policy have been severe. Hence, in part, the failure of proposals from the poorer southern states for a form of fiscal redistribution based on the German *Finanzausgleich* system.

The absence of societal prerequisites In most member states, the political coalitions that built on the early welfare foundations have been dependent on the incumbency of left-wing or social-market oriented Christian democracy, high union membership density, and union as well as employer centralization. At the European level, however, political movements are fragmented, union and employer representation is weak and the EU's 'quasi-state'-like structures provide none of the usual links between parliamentary representation and executive power. Furthermore, the creation of a redistributive welfare state is not only dependent on a political coalition supportive of such a project, but on a redistributive capacity which the EU lacks. Of course, there is the Common Agricultural

Policy, but this provides a perverse and distorted form of distribution rather than income support, while regional policy is a highly inefficient form of redistribution: its main effect, by transferring funds to regions rather than people, is to benefit rich people in poor regions the most (Majone 1996). Finally, the establishment of any form of European welfare state would require political structures whereby such major institutional innovations could be translated into policy. However, under even the most optimistic projections of 'sovereign-state' European structures, the EU's political institutions will continue to fragment power and decision making.

Social policy regime diversity   One of the objectives of European social policy has been to overcome traditional rivalries among the various philosophies of social protection, especially between the Bismarckian and Beveridgean schools, and promote a 'European model' based on three fundamental aims of social protection: a guarantee of a living standard consistent with human dignity and access to health care; social and economic integration; and the maintenance of a reasonable standard of living for those no longer able to work. But the institutional diversity of Europe's welfare regimes – the social democratic Scandinavian, the liberal Anglo-Saxon (the UK and Ireland), the continental corporatist (Germany and Benelux) and southern European types (Esping-Andersen 1990; Ferrera 1996) – has been preserved throughout the postwar period and a long period of economic growth. Their peculiar mixes of funding arrangements (taxation or employment-linked social charges), entitlements and benefits (employment-insurance-based or universal) and corresponding industrial relations systems (with different combinations of law and collective bargaining) have been far from conducive to spontaneous integration. Moreover, as discussed below, they continue to generate quite different 'solidarity dilemmas' and demands for reform. Convergence was actually greater in the EFTA countries than in the EC of nine (1973–1981), because of the similar constellations of political power in the former compared to the latter's political diversity (Montanari 1995). Enlargement has not simplified matters. While the accession of Greece, then Spain and Portugal, added a group whose institutional landscapes superficially resembled the continental corporatist model, their levels of social spending and social protection were initially well below the EU average and have only slowly crept towards it. And although Austrian membership expands the earnings-based corporatist group, Sweden and Finland tip the balance towards the tax-based Anglo-Saxon/Nordic group.

Policy making among 'semi-sovereign' welfare states

Even within the limited scope set by these parameters for a European 'social contract', the regulatory politics have been highly problematic. If alliances with interest groups and member states and the creative use of the Treaty have occasionally allowed the Commission to make policy advances with 'social action programmes' (the most ambitious after 1987), it has also heavily constrained it and fuelled battles over the appropriate type, level and voting basis of Community legislation (Rhodes 1995). Thus, from the very beginning, any attempt by the European Commission to set an agenda for the harmonization or approximation of rules and regulations, or promote supranational decision making, has provoked a two-way conceptual clash:

- between the competing philosophies of strongly and more moderately regulated labour markets and welfare states;
- and between 'solidarity' and 'subsidiarity' in the framing of European policies.

Neither of these clashes boils down to the pursuit of pure national interest: they are shaped by national political traditions, patterns of economic organization and the ideology of parties in power. It is important to appreciate the variety of positions to which this two-way clash can give rise, for the struggle at the heart of Europe has never been clearly between 'a free trade and a supranational welfare-state building project' (cf. Streeck 1996: 301ff), nor even today between clear-cut 'neo-liberal' or 'social/Christian democratic' strategies (cf. Hooghe 1997). While the pure 'free trade/neo-liberal' project has had relatively few adherents (even among European employers) (Rhodes and van Apeldoorn 1997), a large-scale, redistributive welfare project, with enforceable European rights and obligations, has never been firmly placed on the Community agenda, even if in certain periods, and in certain policies, there have been moves in that direction. From the late 1970s, it is true, there appeared to be a clear division between continental countries supportive of, and a British government opposed to, the promotion of a European system of citizenship rights, employment rules and industrial relations. But in reality, as illustrated by early Franco-German differences, and subsequent strains in that relationship (Rhodes 1998b), intergovernmental coalitions and disputes have been much more complex. At the same time, there has also been a clear clash of interests – *and* ideology – between Europe's employers and trade unions over forms and levels of regulation as well as the architecture of European policy making.

This two-way clash – which became particularly acute after the 1987 Single European Act (SEA) – has underpinned an ongoing debate and conflict of interests within a heterogeneous and fragmented policy community. It has been complicated still further by the diversity of Europe's national labour market regimes, among which there has been little hard evidence of convergence (Rhodes 1992; 1995). The result has been a sporadic although increasingly important process of European institution building and legislation, following two broad paths:

- rule making and the establishment of minimum standards across a range of areas, from health and safety standards, through equal opportunities, entitlements in the workplace and, most recently, the establishment of rights to consultation in transnational companies;
- the creation of a process of bargaining at the European level through the

social dialogue, initially as a process of forging agreement on general issues between still weakly organized European employers' organisations and trades unions.

Together, these twin pillars of the 'social dimension' provide neither a functional equivalent to a European welfare state, nor the basis for a social-democratic reconfiguration of Europe's political economy. But their significance should not be underestimated.

Despite the fragility of the alliance behind an expansion of the European social dimension, the interaction of France, Germany and other member states has created a European sphere of labour law and social legislation that is 'European' in character and not simply the amalgam of member-state traditions. A loosely structured regime has been put in place with important substantive elements (in the form of Community legislation and ECJ case law), procedural rules and innovations (especially with the expansion of QMV and the social partnership provisions of the Maastricht Social Protocol and Agreement) and methods of enforcement (strengthened by Maastricht's empowerment of the ECJ to fine dilatory member states) (Rhodes 1995). The result has been the creation of a multi-tiered policy system and a transition from sovereign to *semi*-sovereign welfare states (Leibfried and Pierson 1995). The resistance of nation states to the transfer of greater authority to the European Union is evidence of what Streeck (1995) has called the 'nation-state paradox' – i.e., the fact that, while nation states have progressively lost control of their economies, they have retained 'external' sovereignty in international relations. To date, European states have surrendered much more sovereignty to the market than they have to supranational institutions (Tsoukalis and Rhodes 1997). But the extent to which sovereignty has been 'pooled' in social policy should not be underestimated.

EU social policy making among semi-sovereign states displays the following features:

Joint decision making driven by a complex combination of national interest, ideology and practicability In contrast to the realist or intergovernmental interpretation of these developments, they are not simply the sum of compromises between the member states in pursuit of their own material interests (the defence of domestic organized interests or of the short-term electoral fortunes of government rather than ideological positions)(cf. Lange 1992; Moravscik 1993). Rich states do not always (or even often) seek to sustain their competitive status by imposing their social standards on others: the Germans, for example, have never attempted to 'export' their social costs to the rest of Europe but have rather sought a more *communautaire* development of minimum and flexible standards, often reining in the maximalist ambitions of the Commission and the French (Rhodes 1998b). Nor do poorer states simply engage in 'cheap talk' in backing higher social standards or accept them only because of side-payments through the Structural Funds (Lange 1992; 1993): such interpretations misunderstand the extent of high regulation already in place in these countries and their genuine ideological commitment to stronger welfare states (Threlfall 1997).

The creation of a policy network above and beyond the nation state Also in contrast to the liberal intergovernmental view (e.g. Moravcsik 1993), domestic interests do not only lobby governments which then forge bargains at the supranational level. They also strike alliances with supranational actors, successfully bypassing the national sphere, and when these relationships are institutionalized – as in the social dialogue provisions of the Maastricht Social Agreement – introduce important elements of multi-level governance. The EU has had an important impact on interest mobilization and representation in the member states over the years, with the ETUC (the European Trade Union Confederation), backed up by the powerful German labour movement, helping to bolster union capacities at the EU level, overcome fragmentation (in spreading support for integration among often hostile national unions) and institutionalize a 'social dialogue' with a reluctant European employers' organization (UNICE). Linked to the influence of other national union movements, such as the French CFDT, this activity creates a network of interests and influence on legislation and other policy developments that defies simple intergovernmental interpretations.

The creation of a social policy regime no longer fully controlled by its member states Not only are there sunk-costs and institutional lock-in effects once original concessions have been made (see Pierson 1996); but the complexity of decision making, the accommodation of diverse positions and attempts to resolve Treaty anomalies create enormous potential for unintended consequences and strengthen non-state actors, especially the Commission and the Court of Justice. In addition to its important agenda setting and process management roles (see Pierson and Leibfried 1995), the actual and potential influence of the Commission in the legislative process was amply demonstrated in the late 1980s and early 1990s when, in attempting to evade the British veto facilitated by unanimous voting, it tried – sometimes successfully – to shift the Treaty base of a number of directives to QMV (Rhodes 1995). The Court of Justice has played an extensive role in interpreting EC law and, like the Commission, has been innovative in expanding its own room for manoeuvre, although its role in building *positive* social policy, including social citizenship rights, remains constrained. (Leibfried and Pierson 1995; Ball 1996).

A reduction of the social policy autonomy of the member states through pan-European regulations Despite a noticeable shift to what Streeck (1995) calls 'neo-voluntarist regulation' (e.g., the use of non-binding recommendations instead of binding directives), a gamut of binding legislation (regulations and directives) is now in place as a result of the 'activist' policy making of the Commission and the Council of Ministers. These rules have set a floor under, and have sometimes upgraded, national regulations in the richer member states, while shaping the upward adaptation of social protection systems in the poorer ones. Although its implementation and enforcement remain problematic, European health and safety legislation has proliferated, especially since the adoption of QMV for health and safety under article 118A of the Single European Act, including the 1989 framework directive and the June 1991 directive on health and safety for atypical work, requiring important changes to the regulatory systems of member states (James 1993; Majone 1996). Equal treatment and opportunity directives, and ECJ case law deriving from them, has extended a binding set of rights across member states, forcing even 'paragons of European integration' like Germany to upgrade national legislation (Cox 1993; Ostner and Lewis 1995: 186ff). Binding directives and ECJ decisions in employment protection have governed collective redundancies, the transfer of businesses and the rights of employees of insolvent employers since the mid-1970s, while under the 1989 social action programme, directives have been passed enforcing health and safety rights for atypical workers, special treatment of pregnant women in the workplace, protection for young workers, 'core' terms and conditions for posted workers, proof of employment contracts, working time and rights to workers' consultation in multinationals.

A reduction of member state social policy autonomy via market compatibility requirements The market compatibility requirements (largely relating to freedom of movement) of the Treaty of Rome have resulted in an ECJ-led process of regulatory innovation which has begun to break down the borders of welfare-state development. The implications of this process, as set out by Leibfried and Pierson (1995) are that member states may no longer limit social benefits to their own citizens; they may no longer insist that their benefits are only consumed on their own territories (except in the case of unemployment benefits which are exportable for only three months); and, in a limited number of instances, they are losing control of how people living within their borders should be protected (e.g. controlling entitlement to disability and invalidity benefits established by an authority in another member state).

In sum, member states are now subject to a web of enforceable regulations resulting from EU legislation, and this will help shape if not determine their approaches to welfare-state reform. For even if these systems remain nationally specific and under the control of national authorities, critical areas of policy now fall outside the domain of unilateral member-state action. Although, as discussed below, the principal site for welfare-state adjustment and adaptation remains the nation state, the scope, scale and nature of reform is increasingly constrained or influenced by supranational regulation.

Much, on the other hand, has not been achieved and, as already indicated, even those areas of innovation in European social policy have failed to meet the expectations of many. Although many pieces of health and safety and equal opportunities legislation have ratcheted up standards across member states, especially those of the 1988–93 health and safety action programme – with the help of QMV under article 118A of the Single European Act – in other areas, intergovernmental bargaining has diluted major directives, notably the European Works Council Directive which, far from spreading the German co-determination system to the rest of Europe (the intention of its unsuccessful predecessor, the 1970s Vredeling Directive), has put in place minimal requirements for the consultation of workers in transnational companies (see Streeck 1997). Moreover, EU social citizenship rights remain underdeveloped, for much of the emphasis of 'positive EU social policy' has been on *industrial* citizenship rights, linked to employment and freedom of movement. As Closa (1998) argues, a richer contract in terms of social rights at the EU level is made difficult because it would need to embrace a degree of communitarianism incompatible with the EU's current direction.

One should also recognise the sea change in thinking, in both the Commission and the member states, since around 1993, when, having put in place at Maastricht the prerequisite mechanisms for freeing blocked legislation, several major developments began to transform the policy agenda: the demise of the Mitterrand/Delors axis and its replacement with a more centrist Commission President and a right-wing (although paternalist) French president; a growing resistance to a further transfer of authority to the EU, reflected more generally in the importance given to 'subsidiarity' in the Maastricht Treaty; and a recognition that high and rising rates of unemployment in Europe might require a rather different approach to labour markets and social policy than in the past. The result has been a shift in focus from employment protection towards employment promotion (if necessary, through a more flexible re-regulation of labour market rules), a questioning of cohesion policy priorities and plans to link the Structural Funds more closely to employment imperatives (Hooghe 1997). There have also been some new alignments in EU policy making and a sentiment in the Commission – where the departure of Delors has diminished the influence of DG V – that the social policy positions of Paris and Bonn have moved closer to British Euro-scepticism.

But beyond ideological shifts, the fact remains that the creation of a European economy has failed to elevate the level of logical social policy responses from the nation state to Europe, beyond pressures to facilitate the freedom of movement of workers and citizens and the creation of a minimum floor of rights and entitlements for workers. For not only do welfare states and labour market systems remain nationally embedded, but economic integration is helping make the *national* level an increasingly important site of conflict, innovation and regulatory reform. Whereas once the challenge for Europe was to produce an upward approximation of social protection and entitlements as and when convergence permitted – installing elements of a European social contract – there is a pressing need now to reform *national* social contracts, albeit within a framework which can and should be constructed at the European level.

Challenges to EU welfare states and labour markets

These recent developments, coupled with the acknowledgement that much EC/EU social policy has been linked to a market rather than state-building project, apparently confirms the fears of the Euro-pessimists. The above discussion has pointed out that, within the constitutional and intergovernmental constraints on European policy making, a substantial process of innovation has occurred in creating both the substantive and procedural dimensions of a European policy regime. Nevertheless, a combination of political opposition, legitimacy constraints and the sheer complexity of the regulatory task in Europe has placed evident limits on this project.

National social contracts and solidarity dilemmas

This last point is an important one, for despite the fact that the welfare-state systems of continental Europe were rooted in a similar ideological and political background, the policy variations among them have been great. Even leaving aside the British 'liberal' system, this makes it difficult to talk of a 'European Social Model' as such, beyond certain common general characteristics such as trade union rights to collective bargaining, extensive systems of workforce protection and redistributive policies. As Ferrera (1998) points out, although at a high level of abstraction there is a strong affinity among European systems, seen from below the 'European Social Model' 'shatters into a kaleidoscope of historical sediment and national specificity'. Welfare states emerged with quite different institutional structures and modes of operation (Esping-Andersen 1990): the Scandinavian model achieved a high degree of 'decommodification' (distancing the citizen from market dictates) and a cross-class commitment to high levels of welfare spending and taxation; the 'Germanic' continental model had a lower level of decommodification and a more status or occupational basis for welfare provision, but, nevertheless, a strong consensus behind a comprehensive system; meanwhile, the Anglo-Saxon model has always been less generous, providing flat-rate benefits based on taxation and a general social insurance system, and was built on a much narrower class coalition. A distinctive, and unevenly institutionalised variant of the continental 'social contract' emerged in southern Europe after the 1960s, dependent on a combination of state programmes and traditional (charity and family-based) welfare (Ferrera 1996; Rhodes 1997).

Given the diversity of the 'social contract' among – and within – Europe's 'welfare families', it is unsurprising that they now face rather different challenges. This applies as much to their labour markets as their benefit and social security systems, given the various combinations of rules that underpin them, the different balance between regulation based on law or on collective bargaining, and the way that employment systems are linked to welfare states via funding arrangements, either taxation, social charges or a mixture of the two. These systems remain distinctive, despite pressures for convergence. Just as these welfare families confront quite diverse solidarity dilemmas and political and institutional constraints on reform, they also have quite different understandings of the nature of social problems and traditions of responding to them. Thus, while poverty in

France is interpreted as a failure of society, producing a debate on how best to increase solidarity via social spending, in Britain – where a jump in inequality since the late 1970s has put more adults and children below the poverty line than in any other European country – poverty has revived the nineteenth-century discourse about the negative consequences of helping the poor (Paugam 1998). In Britain, the policy legacy of selectivity (rather than 'universalistic maintenance'), handed down from the time of the Poor Laws, has facilitated an erosion of 'solidarity' via the spread of targeted, means-tested services – an innovation much harder to introduce in continental Europe, given its greater institutional and symbolic commitment to 'contract-based' solidarities (Ferrera 1998).

Thus, at one level these systems all face common problems, including demographic change (the shift in the ratio of active citizens to passive welfare recipients); the rising cost of health care (due to 'demand-side' factors such as ageing, higher disposable incomes and greater insurance coverage, but also to technological improvements and rising real prices); low economic growth and high unemployment; and the changing nature of the labour market. The growing proportion of non-standard forms of work and the increasing workforce participation of women both challenge traditional arrangements – the first because such workers may be denied access to entitlements devised for permanent, full-time employees; the second because social protection is generally geared to male breadwinners and tends to penalise female careers. Yet responding to these common problems requires a quite different policy mix depending on the country, making a uniform European approach impossible. Thus, while some of these developments have attracted the active – and legitimate – intervention of the EU in setting a minimum floor below which entitlements cannot fall, other areas of intervention require a flexible national approach, especially if they encroach on the *droits acquis* of different professional groups or social categories. Moreover, not only do the different solidarity dilemmas generated by these systems need to be tackled within national settings (although European framework rules have their place), but they also indicate that the past emphasis of EU policy – on helping defend or raise the level of acquired rights and entitlements – may no longer be appropriate. A complex process of *re*regulation, involving a loosening of some regulations, shifting others from legal bases to collective bargaining or abolishing existing rules while compensating for them through social security or tax innovations will be needed to tackle unemployment and other social problems. In this context, the role of the Commission as a 'clearing house for ideas and a catalyst for action' (Commissioner Padraig Flynn cited in Hantrais 1995: 207), and the source of 'soft' forms of regulation (e.g., recommendations, flexible framework laws and agreements) may be more appropriate and feasible than blanket interventionism (cf. Streeck 1995).

The issue of unemployment shows how different national systems have to face the sometimes adverse consequences of existing social contracts and swallow the bitter pill of reform. Thus, in the Scandinavian countries, the distributional costs of generous social contracts were met by those in employment who have paid high taxes for an overdeveloped public sector to soak up the potentially unemployed. In continental Europe, governments, employers and labour unions have more or less agreed that the price of adjustment should be shouldered by the unemployed, comprised largely of younger, female and older workers (Esping-Andersen 1996). In southern Europe, an acute 'inside-outsider' problem has developed as a result of the fragmentation and disparities in the income support system for those without work, with large differences in the level of protection given to core and marginal workers (Rhodes 1997). But everywhere there is an emerging consensus that if labour market 'outsiders' are to become 'insiders', then changes to the regulations that cover both employment and the funding of welfare will have to be made. If income inequalities are not also to increase, such changes must be accompanied by other innovations such as work-sharing and reforms to taxation, e.g. the introduction of a negative income tax, alongside a *re*regulation of the sheltered sectors of continental economies, to price people with low or non-existent skills into work (Scharpf 1997a).

But there are big difficulties in moving forward with such an agenda, in part because European states have lost some of their margin for manoeuvre. First, there is the issue of domestic political opposition. The general feeling is that any change is a zero sum game which therefore encounters the fierce resistance of the political losers. While the welfare status quo is itself beginning to undermine the legitimacy of the social contract (from the viewpoint of young people, the unemployed or women for example), its evolution and adaptation are presented as an unacceptable attack on the entitlements and *droits acquis* of its present beneficiaries (Rhodes and Mény 1998). Second, there is the question of globalisation. Although the problems currently facing European labour markets and welfare states have been caused neither by an absence of a European welfare state nor by regime competition or 'social dumping', globalisation has become important in obliging certain reactions and restricting policy options.

The impact of globalisation

But what, precisely, is the impact of globalisation? This is a complex and controversial subject and can only be touched upon here (for a survey of arguments, see Rhodes 1996). The 'old' social contract – and its diverse institutionalisation in these welfare states – was very much part of the 'golden age' of western economic development, during which the preservation of national sovereignty, uninterrupted growth and the Keynesian welfare state all went hand in hand. National autonomy was preserved in the era of 'embedded liberalism' with the help of exchange and trade controls, even if economies became increasingly open after the 1950s (Ruggie 1982). This 'relative autonomy' allowed the construction of rather different types of welfare state and 'social contract', each with its own approach to the provision of public goods and the institutionalisation of 'solidarity'. But in the post-1970s era of 'disembedded liberalism', the ability of governments to fulfil their side of the welfare compact is wearing thin, due to the loss of government control in a global economy over employment and other broad economic policy objectives as the flow of goods and capital has been liberalised (Ruggie 1994; Rhodes 1996). Meanwhile, competitive pressures have allegedly created a decentralising dynamic in many European countries, as the most appropriate site for the organisation of production and innovation becomes the region and the most productive level for post-Fordist labour relations becomes the company or plant (Cooke *et al.* 1997). An increasingly popular metaphor to capture this phenomenon is the 'hollowing out of the state' as decision-making powers and steering capacity is surrendered to both higher and lower levels of authority. The increasingly central role for the firm in this context, and its demands for greater autonomy from 'inflexible' national systems of employment regulation also has evident implications for the role of the EU and supranational regulation.

However, as already argued, nation state decision making in social policy has not been fully surrendered to higher levels. EU member states remain 'semi-sovereign'. National governments may have lost their power to expand social spending at will, due largely to their inability to sustain growing public deficits, but they remain the architects of welfare states and employment systems. As for the decentralisation arguments, there are actually contradictory – although quite logical – tendencies at work. On the one hand, decentralisation in formerly centralised industrial relations systems has been induced by a combination of factors: the new international division of labour within large transnational firms and the introduction by multinationals of 'alien' elements into national bargaining arenas; cross-class 'flexibility' alliances between employers and workers have undermined 'social corporatist' systems, inducing a shift to a more sectorally-based form of bargaining (e.g. some Scandinavian countries) while employers in all systems are searching for greater company- and plant-level flexibility in three areas: internal (or functional) flexibility in the workplace; external (or numerical) flexibility *vis-à-vis* the wider labour market; and greater pay flexibility at local levels. Meanwhile, the creation of the single market and movement towards EMU are also placing pressures on wage-cost competition given the new constraints on competitive devaluation. This again focuses efforts on firm-level adjustment costs.

But at the same time, there are also pressures in favour of centralisation as well as both national and European employment protection regulations. For in response to competitive pressures, and the diffusion of new forms of 'best practice' management and work organisation, manufacturers – as well as certain service-sector companies – are embracing the principles and techniques of flexible specialisation, lean production and total quality management. This implies the creation or maintenance of *co-operative labour relations* and a *high-trust internal firm environment*. Well-designed systems of labour market rules remain essential in this context. The optimal world of internal flexibility in this environment is therefore built not by unilateral management action but on team work and low levels of hierarchy within firms. It also depends not just on high levels of skills but also on high capacities for skills acquisition and national education systems. At the same time, building and sustaining high levels of trust within the company/plant demands not a high degree, but a moderate degree of external flexibility, i.e. the capacity of entrepreneurs to hire and fire and adjust their levels of employment. Too high a level of external flexibility – i.e., the absence of regulatory constraints on firms – destroys trust and undermines internal flexibility. This trade-off – producing a productive form of 'regulated co-operation' – is a critical one for sustaining both competitiveness *and* consensus in European labour markets. Furthermore, both cost competitiveness and stability require more than simply a deregulatory strategy at the level of the firms: they also require a means of preventing wage drift and inflationary pressures in the labour market. This has focused the attention of governments in countries where trade unions are still significant actors on revitalising incomes policies, to keep inflation in line with Maastricht convergence criteria and prevent rising wage costs from damaging competitiveness and creating more unemployment (see Rhodes 1998a).

Thus, globalisation not only involves the state as an agent in the process of opening borders, liberalising markets and promoting the flow of finance and trade, but also, of necessity, in channelling, constraining and legitimising market power. The spread of market ideology (neo-liberalism) hits its functional limits when the dependence of the market on national institutions is revealed. Quite apart from ideological resistance, at that point a pure neo-liberal strategy becomes dysfunctional, for the effective functioning of market mechanisms still requires purposive state intervention, not just in deregulation but in reregulating the domains of welfare, taxation, innovation, employment and education. Although new rules have to be defined at the international level, as Boyer (1996: 110–11) argues, the next century 'will still be the era of nation-states in charge of disciplining and taming the markets (even if) the contours of this involvement are still largely unknown'.

Recasting national employment and welfare systems: what role for domestic and EU policy making?

As Boyer points out, the rules of the game are still being written. But there are already indications as to the direction of state involvement and the role for international regulation. As discussed above, recent institutional developments at the EU level suggest not only that social policy decisions will continue to be made largely by national government but that, contrary to a major theme in 'Euro-pessimism' and in much of the globalisation literature, nation states retain considerable capacity for a positive recasting of domestic social contracts. Moreover, the failure to constitute a pan-European corporatism does not detract from this capacity: indeed, there was always the danger, as recognised by the German unions, that transferring authority to Europe would *weaken* it. At present, many European countries are engaged in an agonising reappraisal of their welfare-state arrangements, and many governments are beginning to negotiate new social contracts. The outcome is as yet unclear; but the models competing for attention in Europe still offer multiple rather than single-path, future trajectories.

One of the futures that may prove appropriate for many European countries is that of 'competitive corporatist' social pacts which seek a consensual and, in so far as is possible, an equitable adjustment of European welfare systems and labour markets. The EU is seeking to play a role in this process by encouraging a European employment pact and promoting further advances in the European social dialogue. Although such pacts can be criticised as 'nationalist productivity coalitions', in which the power of capital is inevitably strengthened, they are certainly more desirable than unilateral neo-liberalism. For not only can they avoid a damaging breakdown in consensus on socio-economic priorities; they may even build a consensus and institutional supports in countries where the prerequisites for corporatism have always been weak or non-existent. Above all, they are a method of bolstering state steering capacity in the area of welfare reform at a time when it is being diminished by domestic resistance, the declining legitimacy of redistributive politics and global constraints.

There has been a growing number of such examples in Europe in recent years, including Belgium, Austria, Ireland, the Netherlands, Portugal, Italy and Spain.

- In *Ireland*, a rather comprehensive social pact negotiated in 1987, 1990, 1993 and again in 1996 has addressed tax, education, health and social welfare issues in addition to incomes. The emphasis has been on inflation-proof benefits, job creation and the reform of labour legislation in the areas of part-time work, employment equality and unfair dismissal. Pay rises have been subject to floor and ceiling levels. In return, trade unions have delivered industrial relations harmony.
- In *Italy*, negotiations in the early 1990s that initially focused on reforming Italy's automatic wage-indexation system were extended to include the rationalisation of bargaining structures, the reform of union representation in the workplace, improvements to the training system, the legalisation of temporary work agencies, assistance for the unemployed to enter the labour market and, the most significant step, the May 1995 agreement between the unions and the government on pension reform.
- In *Portugal*, there have been five tripartite pacts since 1987 focusing on incomes and social and labour market measures, including pay-rise ceilings and loosening rules on the organisation of work, the termination of employment and the regulation of working hours. The 1996 agreement also covers social security issues, including a minimum wage, a reduction of income tax for low income groups, and a more favourable tax treatment of health and education benefits and old age pensions.
- In *The Netherlands*, a flexible form of corporatism, involving a considerable degree of decentralisation in wage bargaining, has provided the basis for industrial relations peace, wage moderation and an ongoing process of labour market reregulation while preventing an increase in inequality and combatting unemployment (now one of the lowest in the OECD). There have also been agreements on social security contributions, work sharing and industrial

policy, training, job enrichment, the development of 'entry-level' wages and, in 1995, rights for temporary workers were strengthened in return for a loosening of dismissal protection for core workers (Rhodes 1998a).

Where these social pacts have been formed around general macroeconomic objectives and/or specific labour market objectives, it is much more likely that concertation over more general welfare issues can also successfully occur, especially where the 'emergency' character of such pacts has given way to a more embedded, institutionalised set of relationships. As mentioned above, these pacts have been criticised as 'post-social-democratic coalition-building' which embody an 'alliance between nationalism and neo-liberalism' (Streeck 1996: 305–13). Admittedly, the shift towards 'competitive corporatism' does represent 'the construction of national level coalitions to "modernise" the national economy', but it does not necessarily mean that 'all other political objectives (are) subordinate to that of increasing national competitiveness' (Streeck 1996: 311). First, while there may be elements of nationalism in the way European countries (and regions) still compete for inward investment, this is not the driving force behind these pacts and their policy innovations, nor is a more general process of regulatory arbitrage between competing welfare and labour market regimes. For 'social dumping' and 'regime shopping' by firms in tightly regulated labour markets with high social expenses is mitigated by the importance of a whole range of factors including unit labour costs, production organisation, skills and education provision, quality, marketing, market proximity and after-sales service as well as the 'constructive flexibility' that derives from productive forms of labour market regulation and industrial relations arrangements. More important are the more general competitive pressures that are driving changes in the form of production and nature of work in all European economies that all governments have to respond to. Moreover, while competitiveness may be a key concern, these pacts contain important trade-offs between equity and efficiency of the kind that have always characterised welfare states, even during their 'golden age'. Indeed, the new trade-offs are often responses to the solidarity dilemmas and contradictions generated by those earlier bargains and may actually improve on them if older equity gaps are filled and new forms of disentitlement prevented. Under such circumstances, far from the pursuit of an outright neo-liberal strategy, some elements of 'thirdpath','progressivecompetitiveness'or'incentivecompatible-egalitarianism' can be put in place (Bowles and Gintis 1995). These might include the generalisation of the following forms of innovation (Rhodes 1998a):

- a shift away from legislated or rule-governed labour market regulation to negotiated labour market regulation, e.g. in minimum wages, as in the Irish and Portuguese social pacts;
- the relaxation of high levels of security for full-time core workers, in return for greater protection for temporary and part-time workers, as in the Dutch 1996 agreement on 'Flexibility and Security';

- a reform of employment regulations to price the low-skilled and unskilled into work while providing compensation for income losses through other innovations, such as a negative income tax;
- a redesign of social security systems to prevent implicit or explicit disentitlements, in relation to two groups in particular: women workers (who are often discriminated against by male-breadwinner-oriented social security systems); and those not in permanent, full-time employment;
- and a parallel redesign of social security systems to allow a guarantee of access to skill acquisition and social services at any point during the life cycle, especially through education and training (Esping-Andersen 1994).

All of these adjustments attempt to respond to the dilemmas facing European welfare states in maintaining legitimacy by adjusting political expectations and maintaining or rebuilding supportive domestic coalitions. For while coping with pressures from the international economy (including the deflationary, cost-cutting impact of moves towards EMU), they must also maintain a balance between the three basic components of the traditional social contract – insurance against risk, the welfare safety net and the principle of solidarity (Sigg *et al.* 1996). Prioritising the insurance component (by basing a greater proportion of entitlements on employment-linked social contributions) risks penalising the poorer and inactive members of society. But prioritising social assistance and income redistribution threatens the support given to welfare programmes by the electorally and resource-important middle classes which are increasingly predisposed towards individualist solutions in social security, health and pensions. A loss of support from this quarter also threatens to undercut social solidarity. Welfare-state reform must of necessity negotiate a middle course between these two options if the European 'social contract', in all its national varieties, is to be defended.

But what role can the EU play in this era of national welfare innovation and change? As is clear from the above, the role – both actual and potential – for national governments is still much more than a vector for globalisation or 'the spearhead of structural transformation to market norms both at home and abroad' (Cerny 1997). For the nation state, while frequently an agent of 'commodification', remains the central focus for consensus, loyalty and social discipline. Moreover, while the institutional innovations achieved in recent years, especially with the Maastricht Social Protocol and Agreement, have begun to tackle the problems of the 'joint decision trap' (the clash between irreconcilable member state interests) (Scharpf 1988) and the 'corporatist decision gap' (the absence of effective bargaining between the European social partners), the member states have yet to fully escape them (cf. Falkner 1997). Indeed, it may be the case that the closer the EU comes to resolving such problems in the decision-making machinery, the more reluctant will the member states be to employ it, as suggested by the post-Maastricht concern with subsidiarity. Moreover, the EU has yet to acquire the legitimacy and capacity for intervention beyond certain boundaries, and these have been restricted, rather than extended, since Maastricht, especially with German opposition to new EU social exclusion and poverty programmes, again on the basis of subsidiarity. This is not necessarily a tragedy. For while it is important that common European labour standards prevent a 'race to the bottom' and 'regime shopping' by transnational companies, within these parameters, the recasting of European welfare states must be tackled by the member states. They remain the primary level for the achievement, adjustment and defence of trade-offs between equity and efficiency and for the complex bargains underpinning them.

Beyond more general policies with a positive impact on Europe's social system – such as a co-ordinated reflation of the European economy – a number of propositions can be advanced for a future EU role. Of course, a new consensus may emerge on advances in specific areas of social policy, with new legislation developed either by the Commission and the Council of Ministers or between the latter and the social partners, as allowed for under the Maastricht Social Protocol and Agreement. The latter's procedures will be strengthened by Britain's membership under the Blair government. There may yet also be agreement on the inclusion of a series of social rights in the Treaty, although recent divisions on this issue suggest it will be difficult to manage. More fruitful, and more important in relation to member-state efforts to recast their own welfare states, would be a new EU co-ordination role. Scharpf (1997a) has argued that this could be achieved in two ways. The first would be to allow differential levels of social protection, linked to varying levels of labour costs and social spending, preventing the poorer member states from vetoing upward harmonisation among the more prosperous. All European welfare states could be underpinned by an explicit agreement on a threshold below which welfare expenditure would not fall. Second, this floor could be supplemented by sub-European co-ordination among groups of countries (i.e. 'welfare families') which have similar institutions and policy mixes such as the wealthy 'corporatist' group of Sweden, Denmark, Germany and Austria. 'Coordinated reform strategies among countries that share critical institutional preconditions are more promising, in principle', argues Scharpf, 'than unilateral coping strategies' (1997b: 29).

However, such a role faces two predictable obstacles. The first is that the poorer member states may resist the creation of a two-tier Europe in social policy, especially if this accompanies a two-tier transition to full monetary union. Pro-welfare elites in those countries may fear that such a differentiation will consign them permanently to a second-class club and reduce pressures for an implementation of EU legislation already on the statute books. In fact, the EU needs to play a role in ensuring that an equitable balance in labour market reregulation and social policy reform is achieved in these countries as much as in their wealthier counterparts. For it is wrong to imagine that the poorer countries (especially those in southern Europe) are simply 'low regulation' countries. Indeed, one of the main features of these countries is the peaks of generosity in social transfers employment protection which exist alongside significant gaps in provision; and one aim of their social policy reforms should be to eliminate these shortfalls in equity. As already suggested, the innovative nature of these pacts makes them much more than 'coping strategies'. Second, the confinement of the southern and other member states to a lower level of regulation would not necessarily make social policy innovation any easier among the wealthy. As mentioned above, while the inclusion of two Nordic countries and Austria in the EU bolsters membership of the high-regulation country club, their domestic arrangements remain quite distinct. Moreover, Germany is now one of the principal opponents of further supranational regulation in this area. Once again, the complex nature of national trade-offs and social bargains, as well as their legitimacy, is at stake.

On the other hand, the idea of an agreed welfare floor is a good one and much more in keeping with EU tradition and practice than the creation of differentiated 'clubs'. This could be bolstered by the supranational reinforcement and encouragement of national bargains which tackle existing inequities in welfare cover and extend the natural constituency of the labour movement, as well as introduce new forms of flexible work and social security and tax reform. One specific area where an EU role is required is in helping to ensure that both labour and capital remain linked in national social pacts, given the low exit-costs in many countries without a corporatist tradition. As for capital, action by the Commission and member states at the EU level could ensure that the new European Works Councils play a role in locking large firms, especially multinationals, into national bargaining processes, and counter their tendency to break away, as in the Irish case. As for the problem of trade union exit, additional incentives for continued participation must be provided. At the national level this could be achieved by scheduling productivity-linked wage increases and employment creation in line with a return to non-inflationary growth. At the European level, the Commission and member states should also attempt to forge a link between national pacts and the European social dialogue: the conclusion of a European employment pact stressing the importance of education and training, as well as setting out the conditions for a co-ordinated strategy of European reflation, would make an important contribution.

Conclusions

In contrast to both the 'optimist' and 'pessimistic' positions, this chapter – which could be called a 'realistic' interpretation – has argued the following:

- that given the weak foundations for, and widespread antipathy to pan-European social policy initiatives, significant advances have been made in putting in place a loosely linked regime comprising substantive rules, procedural mechanisms and enforcement procedures that constrain and underpin member-state policies in this domain;
- that although one should not minimise the importance of European-level social policy developments, in either institutional or policy output terms, as traditionally conceived, European policy initiatives are inadequate for dealing with many of the pressing issues currently facing European social and labour market systems;

- that this inadequacy does not derive from the failure to put in place a federal welfare state – something that was neither politically possible nor economically feasible – but from a combination of challenges from within member-state systems and from beyond their borders;
- that a putative federal system would not necessarily assist in this process, given that the nature of these challenges requires a recasting of *national* welfare states and labour markets that must be dealt with primarily within domestic policy structures, either at the national or still lower levels of political organisation, allegiance and legitimacy;
- and that the appropriate and feasible role of the EU in this context is to establish a floor of standards, at a level acceptable to the majority of member states; ensure that inequalities that cannot be resolved by redistributive policies within member states are met with pan-European transfers; and help implement a set of 'best practice' policies to facilitate a process of consensual *national* adjustment.

References

Ball, C. A. (1996) 'The Making of a Transnational Capitalist Society: The Court of Justice, Social Policy and Individual Rights Under the European Community's Legal Order', *Harvard International Law Journal*, 37, 2, pp. 307–88.

Bowles, S. and H. Gintis (1995) 'Productivity-Enhancing Egalitarian Strategies', *International Labour Review*, 134, 4–5, pp. 559–85.

Boyer, R. (1996) 'State and Market: A New Engagement for the Twenty-First Century', in R. Boyer and D. Drache (eds) *States Against Markets: The Limits of Globalization*, London: Routledge, pp. 84–114.

Cerny, P. (1997) 'Paradoxes of the Competition State: The Dynamics of Political Globalization', *Government and Opposition*, 32, 2, pp. 251–74.

Closa, C. (1998) 'Some Sceptical Reflections on EU Citizenship as the Basis of a New Social Contract', in M. Rhodes and Y. Mény (eds) *The Future of European Welfare: a New Social Contract?*, London: Macmillan 1998.

Cooke, P., T. Christiansen and G. Schienstock (1997) 'Regional Economic Policy and a Europe of the Regions', in M. Rhodes, P. Heywood and V. Wright (eds) *Developments in West European Politics*, London: Macmillan, pp. 190–206.

Cox, S. (1993) 'Equal Opportunities', in M. Gold (ed.) *The Social Dimension: Employment Policy in the European Community*, London: Macmillan, pp. 41–63.

Esping-Andersen, G. (1990) *The Three Worlds of Welfare Capitalism*, Cambridge: Polity Press.

—— (1994) 'Equality and Work in the Post-Industrial Life Cycle', in D. Miliband (ed.) *Reinventing the Left*, Cambridge: Polity Press.

—— (1996) 'Welfare States without Work: the Impasse of Labour Shedding and Familialism in Continental European Social Policy', in G. Esping-Andersen, *Welfare States in Transition: National Adaptations in Global Economies*, London: Sage, pp. 66–87.

Falkner, G. (1997) 'Social Policy and the Various Decision Traps of Regional Integration', Paper for the Joint Sessions of the ECPR, Bern, 27 February–2 March.

Ferrera, M. (1996) 'The 'Southern Model' of Welfare in Social Europe', *Journal of European Social Policy*, 6, 1, pp. 17–37.

—— (1998) 'The Four "Social Europes": Between Universalism and Selectivity', in M. Rhodes and Y. Mény (eds) *The Future of European Welfare: a New Social Contract?*, London: Macmillan.

Frøllesdal, A. (1997) 'Do Welfare Obligations End at the Boundaries of the Nation-state?', in P. Koslowski and A. Frøllesdal (eds) *Restructuring the Welfare State: Theory and Reform of Social Policy*, Studies in Economics, Ethics and Philosophy, Vol. 12, Berlin: Springer, pp. 145–163.

Gold, M. (1993) *The Social Dimension: Employment Policy in the European Community*, London: Macmillan.

Hantrais, L. (1995) *Social Policy in the European Union*, London: Macmillan.

Holloway, J. (1981) *Social Policy Harmonization in the European Community*, Farnborough: Gower.

Hooghe, L. (1997) 'The Structural Funds and Competing Models of European Capitalism', paper presented at the conference on 'Territorial Politics in Europe: A Zero-Sum Game?', European University Institute, Robert Schuman Centre, Florence, April 21–22.

James, P. (1993) 'Occupational Health and Safety', in M. Gold (ed.) *The Social Dimension: Employment Policy in the European Community*, London: Macmillan, pp. 135–52.

Lange, P. (1992) 'The Politics of the Social Dimension', in A. M. Sbragia (ed.) *Euro-Politics: Institutions and Policy making in the 'New' European Community*, Washington DC: The Brookings Institution, pp. 225–56.

—— (1993) 'Maastricht and the Social Protocol: Why Did They Do It?', *Politics and Society*, 21, 1, pp. 5–36.

Leibfried, S. and P. Pierson (1995) 'Semisovereign Welfare States: Social Policy in a Multi-tiered Europe', in S. Leibfried and P. Pierson (eds) *European Social Policy: Between Fragmentation and Integration*, Washington DC: The Brookings Institution, pp. 43–77.

Majone, G. (1996) 'Which Social Policy for Europe', in Y. Mény, P. Muller and J.-L. Quermonne (eds) *Adjusting to Europe: The Impact of the European Union on National Institutions and Policies*, London: Routledge, pp. 123–36.

Montanari, B. (1995) 'Harmonization of Social Policies and Social Regulation in the European Community', *European Journal of Political Research*, 27, 1, pp. 21–45.

Moravcsik, A. (1993) 'Preferences and Power in the European Community: A Liberal Inter-governmentalist Approach', *Journal of Common Market Studies*, 31, 4, pp. 473–524.

Ostner, I. and J. Lewis (1995) 'Gender and the Evolution of European Social Policies', in S. Leibfried and P. Pierson (eds) *European Social Policy: Between Fragmentation and Integration*, Washington DC: The Brookings Institution, pp. 159–93.

Paugam, S. (1998) 'Poverty and Social Exclusion: A Sociological View', in M. Rhodes and Y. Mény (eds) *The Future of European Welfare: a New Social Contract?*, London: Macmillan.

Pierson, P. (1996) 'The Path to European Integration: A Historical Institutionalist Analysis', *Comparative Political Studies*, 29, 2, pp. 123–63.

Pierson, P. and S. Leibfried (1995) 'The Dynamics of Social Policy Integration', in S. Leibfried and P. Pierson (eds) *European Social Policy: Between Fragmentation and Integration*, Washington DC: The Brookings Institution, pp. 432–65.

Rhodes, M. (1992) 'The Future of the Social Dimension: Labour Market Regulation in Post-1992 Europe', *Journal of Common Market Studies*, 30, 1, pp. 23–51.

—— (1995) 'A Regulatory Conundrum: Industrial Relations and the Social Dimension', in S. Leibfried and P. Pierson (eds) *European Social Policy: Between Fragmentation and Integration*, Washington DC: The Brookings Institution, pp. 78–122.

—— (1996) 'Globalization and West European Welfare States: A Critical Review of Recent Debates', *Journal of European Social Policy*, 6, 4, pp. 305–27.

—— (1997) 'Southern European Welfare States: Identity, Problems and Prospects for

Reform', in M. Rhodes (ed.) *Southern European Welfare States: Between Crisis and Reform*, London: Frank Cass, pp. 1–22.

—— (1998a) 'Globalization, Labour Markets and Welfare States: A Future of "Competitive Corporatism"?', in M. Rhodes and Y. Mény (eds) *The Future of European Welfare: a New Social Contract?*, London: Macmillan.

—— (1998b) 'An Awkward Alliance: France, Germany and Social Policy', in D. Webber (ed.) *The Franco-German Relationship in the European Union: The Hard, the Rotting or the Hollow Core*, London: Routledge.

Rhodes, M. and B. van Apeldoorn (1997) 'Capitalism versus Capitalism in Western Europe', in M. Rhodes, P. Heywood and V. Wright (eds) *Developments in West European Politics*, London: Macmillan, pp. 171–89.

Rhodes, M. and Y. Mény (1998) 'Europe's Social Contract under Stress', in M. Rhodes and Y. Mény (eds) *The Future of European Welfare: a New Social Contract?*, London: Macmillan.

Ross, G. (1995) 'Assessing the Delors Era and Social Policy', in S. Leibfried and P. Pierson (eds) *European Social Policy: Between Fragmentation and Integration*, Washington DC: The Brookings Institution, pp. 357–88.

Ruggie, J. G. (1982) 'International Regimes, Transactions and Change: Embedded Liberalism in the Postwar Economic Order', *International Organization*, 36, 2, pp. 379–415.

—— (1994) 'Trade, Protectionism and the Future of Welfare Capitalism', *Journal of International Affairs*, 48, 1, pp. 1–11.

Scharpf, F. W. (1988) 'The Joint Decision Trap: Lessons from German Federalism and European Integration', *Public Administration*, 66, pp. 239–78.

—— (1997a) 'Employment and the Welfare State: A Continental Dilemma', Max-Planck-Institut für Gesellschaftsforschung Working Paper, No. 7, July.

—— (1997b) 'The Problem Solving Capacity of Multi-level Governance', Max-Planck-Institut für Gesellschaftsforschung, mimeo.

Sigg, R., I. Zeitzer, X. Scheil-Adlung, C. Kuptsch and M. Tracy (1996) 'Developments and Trends in Social Security, 1993–1995', *International Social Security Review*, 49, 2, pp. 5–126.

Skocpol, T. (1992) *Protecting Soldiers and Mothers: the Political Origins of Social Policy in the United States*, Cambridge: Harvard University Press.

Streeck, W. (1995) 'From Market-Making to State-Building? Some Reflections on the Political Economy of European Social Policy', in S. Leibfried and P. Pierson (eds) *Fragmented Social Policy: The European Union's Social Dimension in Comparative Perspective*, Washington DC: The Brookings Institution, pp. 389–431.

—— (1996) 'Public Power Beyond the Nation-State: The Case of the European Community', in R. Boyer and D. Drache (eds) *States Against Markets: The Limits of Globalization*, London: Routledge, pp. 299–315.

—— (1997) 'Citizenship Under Regime Competition: The Case of the 'European Works Councils'', Max-Planck-Institut für Gesellschaftsforschung Working Paper, No. 3, March.

Threlfall, M. (1997) 'Spain in Social Europe: A Laggard or Compliant Member-State', *South European Society & Politics*, 2, 2, pp. 1–33.

Trubeck, D. (1996) 'Social Justice after Globalization: the Case of Social Europe', paper presented to the seminar 'Globalization and the Law', European University Institute, Florence, Department of Law, November.

Tsoukalis, L. and M. Rhodes (1997) 'Economic Integration and the Nation-State', in M. Rhodes, P. Heywood and V. Wright (eds) *Developments in West European Politics*, London: Macmillan, pp. 19–36.

4

THE IMPACT OF THE EUROPEAN UNION ON UNEMPLOYMENT AND UNEMPLOYMENT POLICY

Richard Jackman

The rapid growth in unemployment during the 1970s and early 1980s, and the sustained high levels of unemployment since that time, in much of western Europe, must be counted one of the most conspicuous failures of the European Union. In the 1950s and 1960s, the nations of western Europe had achieved a remarkably successful record of full employment. Not only that but, and perhaps more worryingly, the recent experience of the EU countries has been very much worse than that of the major industrial nations outside the EU, in particular the United States and Japan (see figure 4.1). The working age population in the States has been growing at twice the rate of the EU countries, yet the peak US unemployment rate (in 1992) of 7.2 per cent was lower than the lowest rate achieved by the EU during the past decade. Closer to home, the low unemployment rates achieved by many of the smaller non-EU western European economies such as in Scandinavia, Austria or Switzerland (figure 4.2) during the 1980s can be contrasted with the sharp rise in unemployment in Finland and Sweden which has coincided with their accession to the EU.

It is clearly reasonable to ask how the major economies of western Europe have achieved so abysmal a record. Has the formation of the EU itself contributed to the growth of unemployment in the member states, and if so how? Have EU policies made matters worse, and if so in what ways? What can be done now, either by the EU itself or by the governments of member states?

The EU itself accepts that it has a responsibility for the unemployment rates of its member states. In this light, the White Paper, 'Growth, Competitiveness, Employment' (CEC 1993) proposed the objective of halving European unemployment, then standing at 10 per cent, by the year 2000. The White Paper focused on the perceived 'competitive weaknesses' of the EU economies and proposed policies of increased investment and labour market deregulation to improve competitiveness. This work formed the basis for a meeting of the European Council at Essen in December 1994, which urged EU countries to take

60

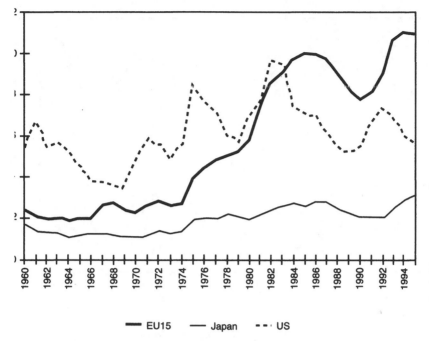

Figure 4.1 Unemployment rate EU 15, US, Japan
Source: European Economy (1995), no. 60, table 3.

action in five areas ('the Essen Conclusions'). These were:

i   investment in vocational education
ii   increasing the employment intensity of growth
iii reducing non-wage labour costs
iv   improving the effectiveness of labour market policy and
v   more help for groups particularly hard hit by unemployment.

These conclusions are clearly phrased in a manner to allow different member states to interpret them in accordance with their own perceptions. For example the UK government has instanced the growth of part-time employment as a contribution to 'increasing the employment intensity of growth'. It may be noted that the obligations are imposed on the governments of the member states rather than on the EU, but are at the same time phrased in such general terms as to impose no specific requirement on any member state. Not surprisingly, therefore, nothing has come of this initiative and, three years after the publication of the White Paper the EU employment rate still stood at 10.8 per cent.

Overshadowing these developments have of course been the moves towards Economic and Monetary Union (EMU). Monetary union requires not only the creation of supranational monetary institutions and the adoption of common monetary policies for participant countries, but also, as a result of the convergence criteria laid down in the Maastricht Treaty, the adoption of restrictive fiscal policies

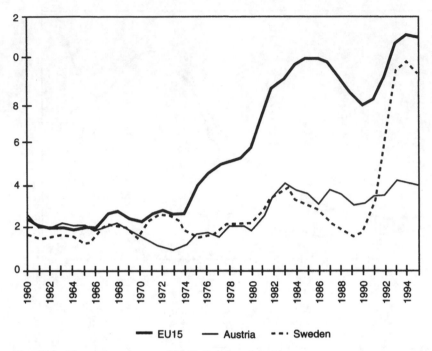

Figure 4.2 Unemployment rate EU 15, Sweden, Austria
Source: European Economy (1995), no. 60, table 3.

on the part of prospective EMU members. Arguably, the macroeconomic requirements of the Maastricht timetable have had a much greater influence on the evolution of unemployment in Europe in the last five years than any labour market measures.

In this chapter, I first set out the broad dimensions of the unemployment problem, contrasting recent experience in the EU with that of other OECD countries. The chapter then examines recent policy developments, and their impact on unemployment, in three main areas: macroeconomic management; trade unions, wage bargaining and employment legislation; and unemployment benefits and income support. The main conclusion of this chapter is that the adjustment to economic change in the labour markets of the EU countries is likely to entail a wide range of changes, and this argues for a deregulatory approach to wage and employment legislation, including legislation protecting trade union rights. Such an approach will harm the interests in particular of organised labour in the wealthier EU countries, in whose interests many EU initiatives in the labour market have been designed. With the move towards the single market and a single currency in the EU matched by even more far-reaching trade liberalisation in the world economy, not to mention the prospective accession of the former socialist economies of eastern Europe, the EU is not in a position to protect such groups from economic change.

Recent developments in OECD labour markets

In identifying the most important recent trends in labour markets there is no better place to start than the United States. Of the developed economies, the US labour market is the most obviously competitive and flexible, the least subject to protection or regulation, and thus an arena in which the workings of market forces are most transparent. Unemployment in the United States, as already noted, has shown virtually no trend increase since the 1950s, yet over the decades, and in particular over the last ten years, the distribution of wages has become wider and wider (see Blackburn *et al.* 1990 or Katz and Murphy 1992). Despite the general improvements in living standards, the real wages of the poorest ten per cent of workers are lower now than they were in 1970.

At the same time there has been in the United States a substantial growth in skilled relative to unskilled employment. The rise both in relative wages and in employment of skilled workers suggests that the main driving force must be on the demand rather than on the supply side. During the past decade or so, there has been a marked increase in the relative demand for skilled as against unskilled labour. Katz and Murphy (1992) have investigated to what extent shifts in the pattern of demand can be attributed to changes in the industrial structure, and to what extent to changes in the proportions of different skills employed within each sector. They find that the main factor has been an increase within each industrial sector in the proportion of more educated and more skilled workers, and of women, despite the rise in the relative wage of these groups. They attribute this shift largely to the nature of technological change in recent years, which has progressed beyond the stage of heavy machinery requiring manual strength or skills for its operation to computers and electronics requiring intelligence in those who work with them.

At the same time, there have been substantial changes in the composition of employment by industrial sector. The share of business and professional sevices and of health, education and welfare have risen, while the proportion employed in manufacturing as well as in agriculture, distribution and the retail trade has fallen. These shifts also serve to raise significantly the demand for skilled relative to unskilled labour and for women rather than men.

The US experience also demonstrates that the present phase of technological development need not be destructive of employment overall. As shown in figure 4.3, in the last decade employment growth has been very much faster in the US than in EU countries, both absolutely and relative to growth in the working population. The introduction of new technologies can coexist with the creation of new jobs, though mostly in service activities, and as already noted, most of the employment growth has been in skilled and relatively well-paid occupations.

These technological developments will have affected the labour markets of the EU countries too, but in contrast to the US, in most EU countries the wage structure has not become more unequal. Only in the UK has inequality increased to any marked degree (OECD 1993). Many US economists, such as Krugman (1994),

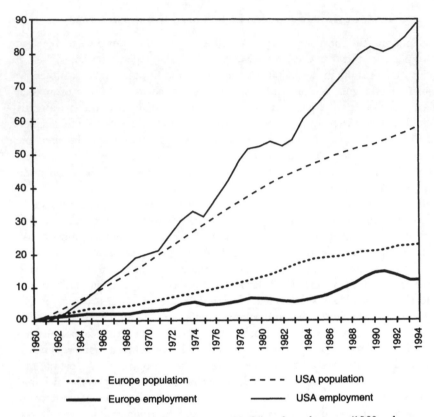

.... Europe population   - - - - USA population

—————— Europe employment   —————— USA employment

Figure 4.3   Total population of working age (15–64) and employment (1960 as base year)
Source: Labour Force Statistics, OECD, table 2, various issues and *Economic Outlook*, OECD, July 1996

have argued that in the face of falling demand for unskilled labour wages have
been held up by a variety of institutional forces, such as benefits, minimum wage
legislation and trade union bargaining rights. The obvious corollary is that the
combination of falling demand and rising real wages has led to widespread
unemployment of unskilled workers in Europe. Thus, Krugman has characterised the EU unemployment problem as 'collision' between, on the one hand,
market forces which are raising the demand for skilled, and depressing the
demand for unskilled, labour, and European welfare state policies on the other.
The basic conclusion is that Europe must become more like America, and permit
greater income equality, which would both sustain more jobs for unskilled
workers and increase incentives to workers to acquire skills and qualifications.

While there is undoubtedly some truth in this line of argument, it has to be
noted that in most European countries, unemployment rates of skilled as well as
those of unskilled workers have been rising. Indeed, the ratio of unskilled to
skilled unemployment rates has shown no systematic increase with more
European countries showing a decline (The Netherlands, Sweden and UK) than

an increase (Italy and Spain) in this ratio (see table 4.1). This suggests that the causes of EU unemployment cannot be attributed exclusively to the effects on the low paid of benefits or trade union rights. Most European countries have strong educational systems and the proportion of new entrants to the labour market with skills and qualifications is rising rapidly. Indeed, the evidence suggests that in many countries the growth in the supply of skilled labour matches, or comes close to matching, the growth in demand (Manacorda and Petrongolo 1996). The rise in European unemployment may more plausibly be linked to the effect of the welfare state and collective bargaining systems on the labour market as a whole rather than just on the unskilled.

The EU labour market as a whole has experienced high wage and low employment growth as compared to the United States, as shown in figure 4.4. The main factors associated with high rates of unemployment in Europe include: first, wage bargaining procedures including the legal rights of unions and workers and legislation affecting the employment contract, such as minimum wage laws or employment protection rights; second, the treatment of unemployed people

Table 4.1 Relative unemployment rates since 1979 (measure ratio: low education/high education[a]

	1979-1982	*1987-1990*	*1992*
France	3.10	4.10	3.10
Germany[b]	2.80	2.60	N.A.
Italy	0.39	0.62	0.60
Netherlands	2.40	1.90	1.80
Spain	1.70	2.00	2.20
UK	3.10	3.40	2.60
Australia	2.40	2.60	2.40
New Zealand	N.A.	4.00	2.70
Canada	3.50	3.30	2.90
US	4.50	4.70	N.A.
Japan	1.80	2.90	2.20
Austria[b]	N.A.	N.A.	3.90
Finland	N.A.	4.90	2.90
Norway	3.20	4.00	3.20
Sweden	3.40	2.40	2.30

Source: S. Nickell and B. Bell, *Oxford Review of Economic Policy*, vol. 11, no. 1, 1995

Notes:
[a] 'Low education' refers to workers with no educational qualifications or with primary school certificate only and 'high education' to workers with at least two years' university education or a further education college or university degree.
[b] In these countries data on education is not available and the ratio is instead of low occupation to high occupation unemployment rates. Low occupation refers to production and related workers, transport equipment operators and labourers. High occupation refers to professional, technical and related administrative and managerial workers. The data are for males only.

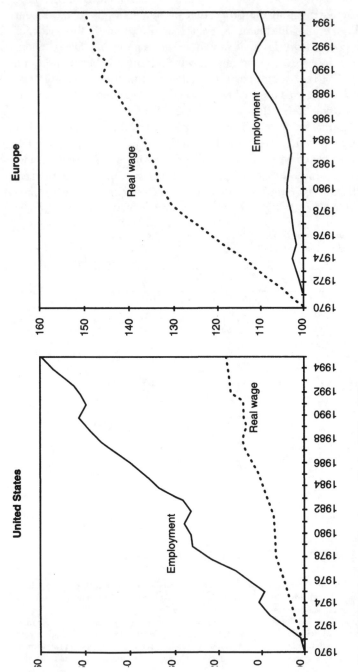

Figure 4.4 Employment and real wages (index 1970 = 100)

Source: Economic Outlook, OECD, annex tables 12, 14 and 20, July 1996.

including the level and duration of unemployment benefits, assistance with job search and other forms of active labour market policy; and third, in the short and medium term, restrictive macroeconomic policy which can increase unemployment not only through its direct effects on demand but also through hysteresis effects (for example, the creation of long-term unemployment) and through possible adverse effects on other areas of government policy (for example, when unemployment is high, governments may be forced to strengthen employment protection legislation or raise benefits).

Macroeconomic management

The idea that macroeconomic management is the key to maintaining full employment has of course been long dead. It is now widely recognised that the rate of unemployment that can be sustained in an economy in the long run depends on structural factors and labour market institutions, and not on aggregate demand. But economies remain subject to macroeconomic, as well as structural, shocks, and it is in this area that EU policies appear to have caused most trouble in recent years.

The problems have revolved around the attempt to create a fixed exchange rate zone, most recently through the Exchange Rate Mechanism (ERM) of the European Monetary System, and ultimately a single currency, for the EU trading area. It should be stressed that the commitment to a single market with free trade in goods and services and free mobility of capital and labour does not of itself logically necessitate a single currency, or fixed or even stable exchange rates. The growth in, and liberalisation of, world trade has continued unabated during the flexible exchange rate era. Similarly, the collapse of the ERM has coincided with, and in no way impeded, the introduction of extensive EU trade liberalisation measures during the last few years. Not only is it possible to envisage a single market with many separate currencies, but calculations of the benefits of moving to a single currency (e.g. European Commission 1990) have found only relatively modest gains. (For example, the transaction costs of converting from one currency to another are estimated to be of the order of 0.5 per cent of GDP.) Even so, the EU has pressed forward in its determination to introduce the single currency within the original Maastricht timetable.

The idea embodied in the Maastricht Treaty of the ERM as a half-way house to monetary union is now in ruins. The collapse of the ERM in September 1992 highlighted two fundamental problems with the management of fixed exchange rate systems which arguably have yet to be solved and could return to haunt a future single currency arrangement. First, a fixed exchange rate system, or a single currency, provides no mechanism of adjustment to macroeconomic shocks affecting member states differentially. This weakness was shown up to disastrous effect by the sharp increase in the German budget deficit following reunification. The macroeconomic adjustment to this deficit required an increase in German relative to other EU prices in EU and world markets. An appreciation of the DM could not be achieved within the ERM, while the Bundesbank was not prepared to see a sharp increase in inflation in Germany. Deflationary monetary policy in Germany was transmitted to the other ERM countries via the fixed exchange rate leading to recessions in the other countries. Speculators in the foreign exchange markets took the view that, rather than attempt to force a decline in money wages and prices, which would have required even deeper and more prolonged recessions, the governments of the other countries would choose to leave the ERM. Speculative pressures thus forced the collapse of the ERM. (Under monetary union, of course, this could not have happened, and governments would have had no choice but to accept a recession of the length and depth required to bring about the requisite relative price adjustment.)

While German reunification was a 'one-off' event, rather the same problems arise where countries are at different phases in their economic cycles. In the first quarter of 1997, for example, the UK was around the peak of an economic cycle with many, including the Governor of the Bank of England, arguing for restrictive monetary policy while France and Germany were in recession. With flexible exchange rates, monetary policy can be expansionary in France and Germany and at the same time restrictive in the UK, but under a single currency that is no longer possible.

The standard 'textbook' analysis of optimal currency areas (Mundell 1961) recognises that when wages and prices are not perfectly flexible an economy can insulate itself from some external shocks by maintaining an independent monetary policy under a flexible exchange rate regime. However, shocks that affect a group of countries in a similar or symmetrical way cannot be dealt with by adjustments in countries' exchange rates relative to one another. Hence, with inflexible wages and prices, countries with similar economic structures and policies, and hence subject to similar shocks, are best placed to form a currency union. Following this line of argument, the European Commission has argued that the economic structures of the EU countries are as similar as, for example, those of the major regions of the United States and the conditions for currency union are thus adequately satisfied. The Commission has also expressed the hope that the single market will of itself bring closer convergence (European Commission 1990), though the permanence of substantial regional disparities within a number of EU countries, such as Italy or the UK, may cast doubt on this prospect. Whether or not one accepts this argument (for an evaluation, see Bean 1992), one may note that the capacity of the United States economy to operate with a single currency may reflect other elements of labour market flexibility not present in many European countries, in particular the much higher rate of internal migration in the United States as compared to most European countries. Thus, for example, Layard *et al.* (1991, ch. 6) contrast the permanence of regional unemployment rate differentials in European countries with the transient character of such differentials in the US. Equally, it is generally believed that wages in the US are more responsive to market pressures than is the case in many European countries. In this sense, labour market flexibility may be seen as an alternative to exchange rate flexibility, which suggests it might be dangerous to give up the one until one has achieved the other.

The second, and perhaps more fundamental problem concerns the convergence of inflation rates. While few people now think there is a permanent trade-off between inflation and unemployment, the output and employment costs of reducing inflation remain heavy, and analysis of the political economy of inflation policy remains an area of active dispute. It seems clear that in a number of EU countries, in particular the UK, France and Italy, inflation has been reduced in recent years at costs which would previously have been judged unacceptable, and that aspirations to European monetary union have provided an explicit objective in this context. But other EU countries, such as Greece, continue to maintain significantly higher inflation rates, and it is hard to envisage that they might be able to join a monetary union. It may be assumed that the more developed the economy, the greater the costs of inflation relative to other forms of taxation, so that the prospects for convergence of inflation may have to await a greater degree of economic convergence than currently exists in the EU.

Historical evidence appears to support the view that countries have different inflation tolerances and that those which have traditionally shown inflationary tendencies cannot easily adjust to the rigours of stable prices. In 1983, France embarked on the *Franc fort* policy and its unemployment rate has been climbing ever since, and is now standing at 12.5 per cent. More dramatically, in 1990 Sweden abandoned its traditional commitment to full employment in favour of price stability. The policy has been successful in reducing inflation to practically zero, but the unemployment rate shot up from two per cent in 1990 to close on ten per cent in 1993 and, despite massive training and job creation programmes for the unemployed, the unemployment rate in early 1997 still exceeded ten per cent.

On fiscal policy, the Maastricht Stage Two proposal that budget deficits be limited to three per cent of GDP – and government debt to sixty per cent of GDP – does not address the requirements of fiscal co-ordination, but is concerned instead with attempting to avoid the situation of a member state government defaulting on its debt which could in turn generate a community wide financial crisis. It is clear that the Maastricht debt condition is impossibly demanding for a number of the EU countries, in particular, Belgium, Greece, Ireland and Italy, and has effectively been abandoned. The deficit criterion, by contrast, which lacks any economic rationale, has been elevated into the critical entry requirement. Attempts by member states to reduce their budget deficits have been to a large extent self-defeating and served to create a recession throughout Europe which only countries opting out of the single currency like Denmark and the UK have been able to avoid.

If the EU were to put in place the preconditions for successful currency integration, it would need to focus on three areas. First, regional and structural policies would be necessary to achieve greater economic convergence. The main mechanism here is the Structural Funds, which exist to promote development in

69

the poorer regions and to assist areas in industrial decline and suffering high unemployment. These Funds are at present relatively small, amounting to only about one quarter of the EU budget. However, the intention is that more of the budget will be shifted into these Funds, and that disbursements from the Funds could amount to as much as five per cent of GDP for the poorer regions (Bean 1992). While this is large relative to other international support programmes (roughly the same scale as the Marshall Plan, and not far short of the total transfer of international support to sub-Saharan Africa as a proportion of GDP today), it will clearly not significantly reduce differentials within the EU within the timescale currently being envisaged for monetary union.

Second, fiscal harmonisation, relating both to the development of rather less arbitrary criteria for determining the size of sustainable deficits, and with the objective of preventing the fiscal policy of one country from creating imbalances between economies, would need to be achieved. Such imbalances with separate currencies destabilise exchange rates, and with a single currency create 'costly pains of adjustment. (These criteria may bear some resemblance to the types of constraints imposed on local government budgets by central governments in federal countries.)

Finally, the development of 'automatic stabilisers', that is mechanisms through which countries hard hit by particular shocks receive automatic fiscal support at the EU level, in the same way that regions do in the event of a decline in the local economy through the workings of the central government budget, is desirable. There is no centralised EU tax system on individuals of the type which provides automatic fiscal transfers in national economies. The only stabilisers to exist at the EU level at present are the Structural Funds, but these are for the finance of specific individual projects, and whatever their other strengths and weaknesses there is no possibility that they can be adjusted sufficiently rapidly in the short run to provide immediate fiscal support to alleviate shocks. What is required is something closer to a 'sliding scale' of contribution rates to the EU budget, whereby a member state suffering an economic downturn automatically receives a rebate in the form of a reduced rate of contribution to the EU budget.

Trade unions, wage determination and employment legislation

It was noted above that trade unions and government legislation continue to play a major role in wage and employment determination in many EU countries. It was argued that this might constitute a possible cause of high unemployment in Europe, not just for unskilled and manual workers, but throughout the labour market as a whole. The argument is that the social criteria which influence wage setting, in conjunction with taxes and other non-wage labour costs, are resulting in 'excessive' labour costs. In a closed economy, the share of wages in national income might be regarded as a policy issue. But the argument now is that the opening up of international trade and capital mobility means that labour in each country is in competition with labour in every other country, with the implication that labour costs in each country can differ only in line with differences in labour productivity.

Most EU countries are reluctant to abandon the principle that people should be able to earn a decent living, to support themselves and their dependents, from their work, and that the structure of wages plays an important role in maintaining social equity. This contrasts with the position of 'liberal' economists, which underpins economic policy in the Anglo-Saxon countries, who argue that wages should reflect market forces, while social objectives should be the responsibility of governments and implemented through the tax and social security systems. The approach in 'corporatist' systems is instead that the 'social partners', employers, unions and government, share responsibility for economic welfare.

There are obvious difficulties in tying economies where wages are set on social principles with those where they are set by market forces into a single trading bloc, such as the European single market. While we examine these problems in more detail below, it must always be recognised that international trade and capital mobility are increasing all the time throughout the world, and the globalisation of world trade constitutes a more fundamental challenge to European labour markets than any effects of the European single market.

As present constituted, the European single market operates across nation states each with their own legislation on wages, employment and working conditions. There is, however, clearly pressure within the EU for some harmonisation of wages and working conditions, on the grounds that differentials could distort competition between firms located in different member states. For example the CEC 1989 report, *Employment in Europe*, argues that 'if differences in working conditions (wages, social protection, social benefits, etc.) are not to lead to distortions of competition, these standards may need to be brought closer in line across the Community' (1989: 67). While various aspects of wage and employment legislation may be 'brought closer in line', it is hard to see how wages themselves can be harmonised given that existing wage differentials reflect different levels of skills and productivity in the workforces of the different member states. As a rough order of magnitude, labour productivity in the most prosperous parts of the EU is about twice as high as in the poorest parts, so wage equalisation is not a practical possibility. Any attempt to impose uniform wages in the single European market can only create mass unemployment in the low productivity regions, exactly as happened in East Germany after unification. Competition within the single market will create pressure towards the equalisation of unit labour costs within each industry across countries, which in turn requires that wages differ across countries to take account of differences both in productivity and in nonwage labour costs.

A second implication of increased competition is that firms are likely to be vulnerable to larger shocks. Where a market is highly competitive, small changes in non-labour costs, or in preferences can have a large effect on a firm's competitive position and hence on its demand for labour. A corollary is that 'solidaristic' wage policies within countries, according to which workers in different sectors receive the same wage, or at least the same wage increase, may no longer be feasible. Employers may need to be able to adjust wages in line with market conditions in their own sector. Thus, for example, Freeman and Gibbons (1993) argue that centralised bargaining broke down in Sweden because it was unable to accommodate the adjustments in relative wages being forced on the Swedish economy by increased international competition during the 1980s.

It is frequently argued that centralised wage setting arrangements have been a force for wage moderation in many countries, and it follows that the gradual disintegration of such systems can be expected to create problems of economic management. In particular, it may oblige countries seeking price stability both to accept higher average rates of unemployment and to introduce institutional changes to weaken the bargaining power of unions given that this is no longer effectively neutralised through centralised bargaining systems. As it takes time to change institutions, this may be another argument for postponing the introduction of the single currency until economies are adjusted to the consequences of the single market.

The single European market, set up to encourage competition across national boundaries, may in fact prove to be as hostile an environment for unions as has been the great continental market of the United States. In America, the unions have been effectively eliminated in the private sector (with only around 10 per cent of workers belonging to a union), and wages are set locally in accordance with market conditions and adjust flexibly as conditions change. These developments obviously run counter to the traditions of involving unions in economic management and of the ideal of the social partnership including representatives of employers and workers taking responsibility for economic affairs, which is part of the traditional mode of government in many continental European countries.

As noted above, there has also been pressure for harmonisation of labour laws and practices across the EU countries in the name of 'fair' competition. Many of the provisions of the social chapter of the Maastricht Treaty were motivated by the concern that different legal standards relating to employment could affect (particularly non-wage) labour costs and thus the competitiveness of firms located in different states. The objectives of the social chapter have been endorsed by all EU countries except the UK.

Numerous aspects of the employment contract are subject to laws or regulation. The main concern in the present context, however, has been the coverage of legislation on workers' rights, including employment protection and working conditions. More specifically, the fear has been that firms operating in more tightly regulated EU countries will relocate to countries with less regulated markets, where they can take advantage of unprotected part-time, temporary or casual workers to reduce not only their wage costs but also their legal obligations with regard, for example, to sick pay or in some cases their need to make contributions to workers' pension funds. The process whereby firms in less regulated markets can undercut their competitors by virtue of not providing supporting social services for their workers has sometimes been described as 'social dumping' (see chapter 5 in this volume). The 'Action Programme' supporting the social charter contains various directives and other instruments designed to bring a degree of consistency to the labour market rules and regulations of the various member states.

An example of this process, which has been a cause of much concern to the UK government, has been the support given by the social charter to the principle of a minimum wage. Here the objective is that each member state ought to have a minimum wage, though it is accepted that the level at which the minimum is set should be defined at the level of the member states. (Many EU countries have statutory minimum wages and in most of the others minimum wages are set in collective bargaining and workers not covered are entitled to have their wages set by reference to such agreements. Only the UK and Ireland at present have no general minimum wage provision.) Where a minimum wage is enforced, its practical impact varies from the substantial – in France, for example – to the insignificant – for instance, in The Netherlands.

It may seem illogical to seek to introduce EU provisions on the principle of a minimum wage if there is no attempt to influence the level at which that minimum is set. In part, the reason may be that minimum wages are one instrument by which organised labour can fight off the threat of being undercut by part-time, temporary or casual labour whose employment falls outside the scope of standard collective bargaining agreements. Similar principles apply to directives governing the wages, overtime pay, holiday entitlements and employers' social insurance contributions for part-time workers. The directives require only that such working conditions for part-time workers be aligned with those of full-time workers, and that employers' taxes are levied on part-time workers on an equivalent basis to those levied on full-time workers.

But is such harmonisation required for economic efficiency? If labour is immobile between countries, heavier uniform taxes on labour in one country than another do not create competitive distortions, but simply depress the post-tax wage of workers in countries where taxes are high. Similarly the imposition of other uniform costs (for example, provision of paid holidays) will not distort competition, but will tend to be associated with compensating wage differentials (for example, lower annual wages in countries with longer holiday entitlements).

Where distortion arises is if taxes are not uniform across sectors, and differ across countries. For example if country A taxes the X industry and country B taxes the Y industry, and workers can work in either industry in their own country, and the products of the two industries are internationally tradeable, then production of X will be located in country B and of Y in country A, for reasons having no economic rationale except to avoid taxes. This relocation also means that neither country collects any tax revenue. A similar point may be made in relation to taxes on different types of labour: if country A taxes only full-time workers and country B taxes only part-time workers, then the industrial structure in A will tend to favour sectors and production technologies employing part-time workers while in country B sectors intensive in the use of full-time workers will be at an advantage. Again such specialisation has no economic rationale but is simply the outcome of tax avoidance.

The provisions in the social chapter, insofar as they concern the imposition of uniform treatment of different types of workers within each country with regard to taxes and regulatory requirements, rather than the level of such taxes, appear thus consistent with the principles of non-distortionary taxation. However, such arguments do not carry over from taxes to direct interventions such as a minimum wage. While it is economically sound to argue that a minimum wage, if one exists, should apply equally to unionised and non-unionised workers, as well as to those in part-time work, a minimum wage necessarily affects some sectors more than others and if set at different levels relative to productivity in different countries will tend to distort competition between them. (The fact that low-wage workers tend to be concentrated in domestic service sectors such as household services or hairdressing means that concerns over international competition may not be not too important a consideration in practice.)

Even if economic theory suggest that taxes on a fixed factor, such as labour within one country, are borne by that factor and do not undermine the competitive position of an industry, this perception is often not shared by industrialists and politicians. Competition in the single market can then be expected to be associated with competitive tax-cutting and deregulation policies on the part of national governments. This development is clearly of concern to a number of national governments and to the European Commission, but it is difficult to achieve agreement in an area where national governments have different views on taxes and regulations in terms of their effects on internal economic efficiency and social welfare.

Unemployment benefits and income support

The experience of severe and persistent unemployment in many EU countries has meant that many unemployed people have suffered long spells out of work. In many countries, the proportion of long-term unemployment has risen to fifty per cent or more of total unemployment while many others experience repeated spells of unemployment interrupted only by brief spells in temporary jobs. Many long-term unemployed people, particularly older workers, appear to have given up looking for work and become resigned to life on the dole.

The persistence of unemployment and the build-up of long-term unemployment have led many to question the design of income support programmes for the unemployed. It has sometimes been suggested that the root cause of unemployment in Europe is the 'generosity' of unemployment benefits, while others have been more concerned about benefits being in some systems available indefinitely and unconditionally. This latter concern has led to a redirection of policy towards 'active' measures to encourage unemployed people to search more widely, to go on training courses or take temporary work in the hope of addressing structural imbalances in the labour market and of preventing the emergency of an 'unemployment culture' associated with long-term unemployment.

In most EU countries, the level of unemployment benefit is higher than in the United States or Japan, but lower than in Sweden or the other Nordic countries (table 4.2). What distinguishes the EU countries is not so much the *level* as the *duration* of benefit entitlements. In the United States and Japan, people can draw unemployment insurance for six months only (subject in the US to local variation) and there is no unemployment assistance except for universal programmes, such as AFDC in the States. In low unemployment European countries, such as Switzerland and Sweden, unemployment insurance terminates after about a year, but the system in both these countries is characterised by severe job search and work test requirements.

There is a clear correlation in the data between the extent of long-term unemployment and the duration of benefit entitlement (figure 4.5). This could in part be a statistical artefact, in that entitlement to benefit gives people an incentive to register as unemployed. In the Figure, unemployment is measured on the ILO definition, i.e. people who are out of work available for work and actively looking for work, and the data is derived from national Labour Force Surveys. It is possible that people who are registered as unemployed and entitled to benefit, but not looking for work, may answer 'yes' to these questions, in case the survey is crosschecked with their benefit claim.

There is little doubt that the main cause of the correlation between the duration of benefits and the proportion of long-term unemployment is that people become accustomed to being unemployed and adjust to it. Thus active labour market policies in many countries have involved both obligations on the unemployed to attend interviews, to apply for jobs, and to accept jobs that they are offered, as well as advice and assistance with job search and the provision of training and temporary work placements. The evidence (OECD 1993) appears to suggest that, of these activities, assistance with job search is the only type of policy to have systematically beneficial effects. The inability of more direct interventionist policies to solve the unemployment problem is a further factor which may encourage labour market deregulation.

At present, the rules and regulations covering unemployment insurance and assistance in the EU are entirely at the discretion of the member states. It is not clear that national autonomy in this area would be at all logical in the context of free mobility of labour between the member states, and a case could be made for harmonisation of various dimensions of unemployment benefit systems much along the lines of the treatment of other non-wage dimensions of the employment contract. Although the numbers are not large, the treatment of citizens of one country becoming unemployed while resident in another raises delicate problems in the context of the notional free mobility of labour.

The UK government is clearly moving most rapidly in the direction of limiting the entitlement to unemployment benefit to established workers who lose their jobs, as against the situation where unemployment benefit is a sort of

Table 4.2 Replacement rates[a] for single-earner households, 1994

| | Replacement rates in the first month of unemployment: no social assistance | | | | | 60th month of unemployment: including social assistance | |
| | Gross replacement rates (before tax) | | Net replacement rates (after tax and other benefits) | | | Gross replacement rates (before tax) | Net replacement rates (after tax and other benefits) |
	Single	Couple, no children	Couple, no children	Couple, 2 children	Couple, 2 children housing benefits	Couple, no children	Couple, 2 children, housing benefits
Australia	34	61	66	76	78	61	78
Belgium	60	60	75	76	76	55	91
Canada	55	55	64	66	67	0	61
Denmark	86	86	92	93	95	86	95
Finland	60	60	67	83	89	37	100
France	65	65	79	81	88	54	83
Germany	40	44	60	70	77	39	80
Ireland	35	66	67	70	70	66	70
Italy	30	30	36	45	45	0	14
Japan	43	43	49	48	48	0	86
Netherlands	70	70	79	78	84	0	95
New Zealand	38	64	70	80	86	64	86
Norway	62	62	66	75	75	0	100
Spain	70	70	74	78	77	0	66
Sweden	80	80	82	85	89	0	121
Switzerland	70	70	75	87	87	0	97
UK	24	39	52	67	90	38	90
USA	50	50	66	60	60	0	19

Source: OECD, *Employment Outlook* (1996), table 2.1, p. 32.

Note:
[a] Replacement rates are the ratio of a person's income if wholly unemployed and eligible for unemployment benefit to the wage the person might expect to receive if in work. The latter is calculated as two-thirds of the average level of earnings of production workers.

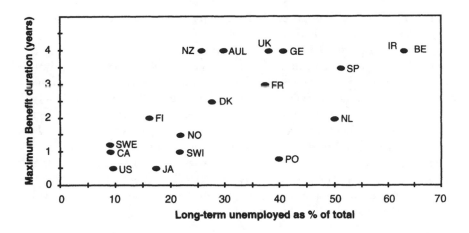

Figure 4.5 Benefit duration and incidence of unemployment

Source: Long-term unemployment: *Employment Outlook*, OECD, various issues. Benefit duration: R. Jackman, R. Layard and S. Nickell, 'Combating unemployment: is flexibility enough', Centre for Economic Performance, Discussion Paper no. 293.

Note: AUL – Australia; BE – Belgium; CA – Canada; DK – Denmark; FI – Finland; FR – France; GE – Germany; IR – Ireland; JA – Japan; NL – Netherlands; NO – Norway; NZ – New Zealand; PO – Poland; SP – Spain; SWE – Sweden; SWI – Switzerland; UK – United Kingdom; US – United States.

universal income support system. Whatever one's views on this approach, it could quite clearly lead to the labour market in the UK developing very differently from in the other EU countries, in particular with regard to the availability of part-time or casual work, which may generate continuing difficulties with regard to harmonising wage and employment legislation.

Conclusion

The economies of the EU countries are having to adjust both to very major changes in the world economy brought about by technical change and trade liberalisation, but also to the requirements of the single European market. Their labour market institutions appear ill suited to this task. EU policy has often appeared more concerned with strengthening workers' rights than with enhancing labour market flexibility. The attempt to improve the pay and conditions of workers irrespective of the demand for them has been a major factor behind the rise in unemployment in many EU countries.

Not only do these problems remain, but there are new difficulties to be faced. The EU has to date responded in a timorous way to the liberalisation of the economies of eastern Europe, but to the extent that its main policy reaction has been to postpone rather than refuse market access to these countries it is obviously storing up problems for the future. The combination of high levels of education and low wages in eastern Europe presents a serious additional threat to the privileged position of the EU worker.

It seems likely that, as far as the employment prospects of the majority of workers is concerned, the main hope must lie in the development of new private sector activities. These may or may not involve work patterns different from the traditional, but it would seem ill advised to put obstacles in the form of legislation or otherwise in the way of those seeking to develop new businesses with non-traditional employment arrangements. Likewise the wage aspirations of the unskilled cannot be allowed to continue to rise in the absence of any growth in the demand for them. Insofar as some EU countries have built up systems looking to the employer to provide a 'social safety net' for their workers, it may be time to consider whether such responsibilities might now be returned in part to individuals themselves and in part to the state.

References

Bean, C.R. (1992) 'Europe 1992: A Macroeconomic Perspective' *Journal of Economic Perspectives*, vol. 6, no. 4 (Fall) 31–52

Blackburn, M., D. Bloom and R.B. Freeman (1990) 'The Declining Economic Position of Less-Skilled American Males' in G. Burtless (ed.) *A Future of Lousy Jobs?*, The Brookings Institution, Washington: DC

Commission of the European Communities (CEC) (1989) *Employment in Europe*, Luxembourg: Office of Offical Publications of the European Communities

—— (1993) 'Growth, Competitiveness, Employment: The Challenges and Ways Forward into the 21st Century', *Bulletin of the European Communities*, Supplement 6/93

European Commission (1990) 'One Market, One Money' *European Economy*, (Oct.) no. 44

Freeman, R. and R. Gibbons (1993) 'Getting Together and Breaking Apart: The Decline of Centralised Collective Bargaining', NBER Working Paper no. 4, 464

Katz, L.F. and K.M. Murphy (1992) 'Changes in Relative Wages in the United States, 1963–87: Supply and Demand Factors', *Quarterly Journal of Economics*, 107, Feb., 35–78

Krugman, P. (1994) 'Past and Prospective Causes of High Unemployment' in *Reducing Unemployment: Current Issues and Policy Options*, Jackson Hole, Wyoming: Symposium, Federal Reserve Bank of Kansas City

Layard, R., S. Nickell and R. Jackman (1991) *Unemployment: Macroeconomic Performance and the Labour Market*, Oxford: Oxford University Press

Manacorda, M. and B. Petrongolo (1996) 'Skill Mismatch and Unemployment in OECD Countries' Discussion Paper no. 307, Centre for Economic Performance, London School of Economics

Mundell, R.A. (1961) 'A Theory of Optimal Currency Areas' *American Economic Review*, no. 51, Sept., 657–65

OECD (1993) *Employment Outlook*, OECD: Paris

5

SOCIAL DUMPING WITHIN THE EU

David Goodhart

Social dumping first entered the UK political vocabulary in 1993 when the US multinational Hoover decided to close a plant in eastern France and shift production to Scotland, where the workers made significant concessions on labour costs. The British government subsequently held up the Hoover case as justification for its job-creating opt-out from the social chapter of the Maastricht Treaty, while the French government complained bitterly about the dangers of unfair competition from the 'Taiwan of Europe'. If social dumping is the idea that capital will flow to areas where labour is cheapest and least protected, dragging down the labour standards elsewhere, the Hoover case seems a classic example – at least of the first half of the equation. Good illustrations of *both* elements are harder to find, although one rather unusual case emerged in Germany at the same time as the Hoover affair. In the early 1990s Mercedes Benz toyed with the idea of building a new plant for its A-class mini-car in Britain or the Czech Republic. Eventually it stayed in Germany but only after concessions on operating costs said to estimate DM200m were wrought from I G Metall, the German metal union.[1]

For a period after the Hoover case the issue of social dumping dropped down the political agenda in Europe. But elsewhere it started to attract more attention. In the US it became a concern thanks to the North American free trade agreement (NAFTA), and the associated fear of job losses to Mexico – a fear which the first serious analysis of the employment effects of Nafta published by the National Bureau of Economic Research in 1996 did not bear out. A little later the debate in the World Trade Organisation about a minimum labour standard social clause and the supposed threat to jobs and wages posed by regions like southern China and eastern Europe also helped to make dumping a genuinely global issue.

In the mid to late 1990s the issue surfaced again in Europe and the UK. Hoover-type headlines accompanied several more Anglo-French incidents. A fast-growing French software company relocated to Kent in 1996. In the same year a Rotherham-based company, Hotel & Catering Staff Supplies, attracted the attention of Michel Barnier, the French European Affairs minister, when it began offering to recruit seasonal staff in the French alps at half the cost of a normal

French worker by paying British rather than French social security rates. More generally, the arrival of the single currency may well heighten anxieties in the hard-currency/high labour-cost countries that Britain and others could unfairly benefit from a softer currency and lower cost labour. Indeed, many continental European politicians began to ask whether 'fair' trade in an increasingly integrated European economy requires considerably more harmonisation of labour and welfare systems.

This chapter deals primarily with the issue of social dumping within the context of the EU. It first seeks to ascertain how widespread social dumping is. Attempts to guard against social dumping through the social dimension of the EU are then considered. More than 90 per cent of labour regulations relating to the cost of flexibility of employment within Europe currently arise from within national labour markets. As Padraig Flynn, the Social Affairs Commissioner for most of the 1990s, has put it:

> There is much nonsense talked about both the volume and nature of social legislation at the European level. In fact the quantity is limited and most of it covers the key areas of health and safety, the free movement of workers and equal opportunities between men and women, which are not controversial.[2]

Nevertheless the EU social dimension has now established a small but significant Europe-wide foothold not only in those fields but also in the wider regulatory territory represented by the controversial directive on working time which became law in November 1996. Much of the original justification for establishing these Europe-wide minimum labour standards was to prevent labour standards being driven down as capital flows more freely between EU member states.

Dumping: how big a problem?

Social dumping is as old as the free market itself. In a competitive market, capital will usually seek out the best long-term return within the constraints set by technology, politics and prevailing morality. It thus demonstrates a preference for low-cost and flexible labour where productivity and other factors affecting the real return from labour are equal. Hence the preference for female over male labour in some industries at the time of the industrial revolution, something which is reappearing in parts of the service sector today. The debate over the Ten Hours Bill in Britain in 1846 (and subsequent debates about the Factory Acts and unionisation) prefigures much of today's argument about social dumping: should capital be free to drive down the price of labour or should there be a regulatory floor? Macaulay's 1846 speech in the House of Commons defending restrictions on the employment of women and children had to combat the argument that business would be lost to German factories if the Ten Hours Bill was passed. He also makes an early defence of the economics of high-cost/high-productivity labour against low-wage sweated labour by arguing that over a twenty-year period a man working a six-day week will produce more than a man working a seven-day week.

A large part of the economic history of industrial countries in the late nineteenth and early twentieth century was about establishing national rules for employment and, to a lesser extent, narrowing pay differentials between regional labour markets. This restricted the opportunity for domestic social dumping while the limited mobility of manufacturing capital meant that dumping across national borders was not yet a major issue.

With the growth of world trade, the opening up of national markets, and the growing internationalisation of business during recent decades, the dumping issue has returned. But, focusing on Europe, how it is possible to establish whether social dumping really exists? It is not sufficient to establish an increase in international investment in lower-wage countries. Rather it is necessary to show that it was the lower wages, or non-wage labour costs, which was the primary incentive for establishing or shifting production there. It is also then necessary to show that downward pressure on labour standards or wages in higher-cost countries came as a result of the investment flow to lower-cost countries.

It is difficult to provide hard evidence of the existence of social dumping in the EU on the basis of any of the above questions. Even on international investment flows the *higher-wage* EU economies have attracted considerably more investment than the lower-wage economies over the past twenty years, and inward investment in low-wage Ireland actually fell between 1973 and 1980 and 1981 to 1990 according to OECD figures. The truth is that within a developed part of the world like the EU the dumping trend is rather muted and difficult to disentangle from the ebb and flow of investment between countries caused by a host of factors which have nothing to do with the price or flexibility of labour. Even the case of Hoover is more complex on closer examination.

Hoover and the limits of dumping

The Hoover example appears, *prima facie*, to be a straightforward instance of a relatively deregulated country, namely Britain, benefiting from the investment decisions of a footloose and cost-conscious US multinational. The transfer cost 650 jobs in Dijon and created 400 in Glasgow, albeit on two-year contracts. More importantly, Hoover used the competition between the two sites to force a significant erosion in the terms and conditions of employment in Glasgow. The president of Hoover Europe, William Foust – pronounced Faust, as union leaders were eager to point out – said that non-wage labour costs of only 10 per cent in Scotland compared with 45 per cent in France was a factor in the company's decision to move.

However there are also reasons for believing that the Hoover case is neither typical nor purely driven by labour costs. Foust also claimed that the decision to opt for Scotland was strongly influenced by the fact that the Scottish plant had spare capacity. Hoover, which has a history of mobility outside America, had decided in 1992 that it needed to concentrate its European activities on one site and for reasons of capacity as well as cost Scotland was the most appropriate.

There are many more general reasons why low-labour costs are not on their own an attraction to mobile capital. If they had been, Africa would have experienced huge inward investment flows. Firstly, in the high technology industries which increasingly dominate international trade, labour costs often made up only a small proportion of total costs. In the UK computer industry, for example, total wage costs represent only 15 per cent of production costs. In electronics they represent 34 per cent and in aerospace 33 per cent. Manual workers account for only 4 percent of production costs in computers, thirteen per cent in electronics and 23 per cent in aerospace. Secondly, differences in labour productivity tend to more or less match differences in wages, leaving unit labour costs at rather similar levels across the EU. Calculations made in 1992 by the *Financial Times*[3] suggest that when measured in DM unit labour costs in manufacturing are very similar between Germany, France, Italy and the UK. Even nominal wage rates appear to be converging quite rapidly. According to a study by Doug as McWilliams the standard deviation of European wage levels fell from 46 per cent in 1974 to 31 per cent in 1991 and are expected to fall further still to 24 per cent by the beginning of the next century.[4] Thirdly, differences in employers non-wage labour costs across the EU differ sharply – from 45 per cent plus in France and Italy to less than 3 per cent in Denmark – but these differences are not necessarily reflected in final costs. As the European Commission's 1993 *Employment in Europe* report states:

> Where social systems are funded from general taxation whether through taxes on income or expenditure, the net wages of employees in terms of purchasing power will correspondingly be reduced and they will accordingly need to earn a higher gross wage in order to achieve a given level of real income. Businesses in such countries will therefore end up paying more in wages – direct labour costs – than in countries where employers, contributions are larger.[5]

Finally, companies are not interested only in labour costs and productivity, but in a whole package of labour costs, flexibility and skill levels. When all these factors are taken into account pluses and minuses often cancel each other out. While Britain has a relatively deregulated labour market, but a patchy record in education and training, Germany is expensive and highly regulated, but has highly skilled workers. Some of the southern European economies, such as Spain, are in theory cheaper than most of the northern European economies, even when productivity is taken into account, but they also tend to be more tightly regulated than most northern European countries in areas such as temporary and part-time work, and making employees redundant.

Taken together the above points suggest that labour cost differences inside the EU are much less significant than they seem. Indeed, given that the cost of closing a plant in country A and moving to country B is quite large, especially within the EU, it will rarely make sense to do so, unless the labour package provides some special comparative advantage such as peculiarly high productivity or the availability of a skill in a particular sector.

What do companies say?

If it is hard to show that differential labour costs are a key factor in determining investment flows, it is going to be harder still to show that these flows are causing downward pressure on labour standards. But what do companies themselves say? The evidence from companies about why they invest in different countries can reinforce such scepticism about dumping, but it does not dismiss the labour factor completely. One authoritative survey on location decisions by European and non-European multinationals placed labour quality in second place and labour costs in fourth. The full ranking in the survey – for the Invest in Britain Bureau – is as follows:

1 Proximity to markets
2 Labour quality
3 Air transport
4 Labour costs
5 Financial incentives
6 Labour availability
7 Site/premises availability
8 Road transport
9 Transport costs
10 Overall costs

Another investment location survey by Ernst and Young concluded: 'For a few projects there was a single factor that stood out as the key influence on the decision. However for the majority of decisions, the outstanding attribute of a winning region was that the region had a particular combination of characteristics.' This survey had a similar ranking to the first, and while the cost of labour and premises were the two most important direct cost factors neither was identified as either a critical or important factor by a majority of respondents. Responses from investors about individual countries were far more positive about the higher-cost countries. Responses to Greece and Portugal were particularly dismissive talking about the difficulties of doing business in countries with a small industrial base. Hugh Stirk, Head of Personnel at Unilever, the Anglo-Dutch consumer goods company, also points out that in the consumer sector the freedom to choose where to site an export base is often constrained by the need to be physically close to customers.

A problem for the future?

Nevertheless, the labour package is obviously important in some location decisions, especially where brand new investment is involved and also in labour-intensive sectors. Why, after all, is computer programming being done in Bombay for London Transport or keying in for the London telephone directory being done in Jamaica? The case of the US – with significant cost and labour regulation differences between regions – also provides some support to those who argue that social dumping is a real menace. According to Douglas McWilliams,[6] there was until the early 1980s faster growth of investment in the lower southern states despite a consistent trend for the wage differentials between north and south to be squeezed. Some economists have also claimed to spot an advantage accruing to 'right to work' states which ban the closed shop.

Even in Europe the labour cost factor may be more significant than companies are prepared to admit. As David Shonfield of Incomes Data Services writes: 'Few companies want to advertise the fact that they make choices on the basis that labour is cheap or legal protection is limited'.[7] And as Hugh Stirk, remarks: 'If it costs twice as much to employ a senior manager in Germany as in Britain it will eventually have some effect.'[8] In the mid-1990s Germany was, indeed, the target for advertisements from the Invest in Britain Bureau, which stated that British wage costs were on average more than one-third lower than in Germany. Presumably the organisation would not have wasted public money without some evidence that the differences are both real and attractive to German investors. Furthermore, however correct the Commission economists may be in theory in claiming that non-wage labour costs affect only the mix of labour costs and not their level, employers seem to take the more straightforward view that non-wage labour costs are an addition to costs. US employers, for example, are said to be particularly happy about investing in Britain because compared with their home base or continental Europe their employee health costs are low.

OECD figures on direct inward investment flows over the past fifteen years do suggest that, adjusted for GDP, the real winners in the EU have been cheap Spain and deregulated Britain. The flow into Britain from 1981 to 1990 was $122bn and the flow into Spain $46bn. Britain also claims the lion's share of investment from both the US and Japan. In 1991 the stock of Japanese investment in the UK was $26bn, with Germany the next highest at $6bn. The stock of US investment was $68bn, with the next highest Germany on $33bn. Indeed, in 1990 the share of foreign-owned companies in gross UK manufacturing output was more than 25 per cent. There is, perhaps, a special Britain effect when it comes to mobile international capital within the EU, however. The poorer southern European economies – with the possible exception of Spain – have done less well than might be expected because of poor infrastructure and relatively highly regulated labour markets. Britain though has an attractive mixture of relatively low-wage and non-wage labour costs (the latter thanks in part to the NHS), good communications and a workforce which seems to respond better to foreign management. The main losers appear to have been France and Germany.

Indeed, some groups of German workers might find the above view of social dumping as a distant threat rather too sanguine. It is the Germans who have felt most uncomfortable about Japanese car plants in Britain. And, under the threat of seeing new plants located abroad, it is the Germans who have already had to make significant concessions in at least two recent location decisions. When Bosch recently decided to build its new components plant at Reutlingen in Germany it was on the basis of an agreement to seven-day working. Even more significantly, Mercedes-Benz comtemplated building the new plant for its A-class mini-car in Britain, France and the Czech Republic, before deciding to stay in Germany at Rastatt. By so doing the company won concessions on operating costs from I G Metall worth a claimed DM200m. General Motors Germany had struck a similar deal for a 475-job diesel engine line to be installed in Kaiserslautern in preference to any of the nine options being considered outside the country. This is probably the closest one gets to real social dumping in the EU.

The above discussion leads to the tentative conclusion that the growing ebb and flow of international capital is only sometimes influenced by the labour package above all other factors. Beggar-my-neighbour industrial restructuring within the EU, such as occurred in the Hoover case, is the exception. But it *is* a possible danger in the future as productivity rises ahead of labour costs in poorer countries and as Britain moves further in a different direction from continental Europe. Also, as it becomes easier to buy in high-quality components from low-cost countries, social dumping may spread through trade rather than direct investment. There will be no need to close plants in high-cost countries but trade-based dumping will reduce the labour standards of the dwindling band of workers sticking the components together.

The European Commission, the social dimension and dumping

At the end of the 1980s the social dimension of the EU was relaunched by Jacques Delors with the strong support of François Mitterrand, largely for political reasons. Delors and other senior figures in the Commission believed that the single market project had become a business technicality. The social charter, drawn up in 1989, was designed to give the single market some populist appeal. It certainly had its desired outcome in Britain where, combined with Delors's famous visit to the TUC, it helped to convert organised labour and much of the political left to the European cause. There is also a broader political justification for the renewal of the social dimension, as has been identified by Robert Lindley:

> Combine the rigours of the single market with those of free capital movement and there arises a situation in which financial markets have apparently been handed much greater power to impose their judgements

of performances and priorities upon the workings of the other constituents of the EU economy.[9]

The measures contained in the revived social dimension were an attempt to ensure that the judgements of one of those constituents, namely labour, did not go unheard.

Delors's original social charter of 1989 was not a radical document. It drew together several measures, many of which were already established in national legislation, while others helped to make up a rather vague wish list. Wary of interfering in such sensitive and domestic matters as employment rules, the Commission did not originally intended to convert the social charter into the directives of the Social Action Programme, but found itself under pressure to do so after Margaret Thatcher refused to sign the charter.

Even prior to the legislation which flowed from the Social Action Programme there was a well-established corpus of European labour law dating from the 1960s and 1970s. This had two main dimensions and two justifications. The first was to help ease labour mobility between EU countries in the hope of creating, eventually, a single European labour market; the second was to ensure a minimum European-wide floor beneath which companies could not be tempted to compete. (Related but somewhat distinct from both of these is the drive to create a European model company with certain common features, such as European works councils.)

The important pieces of EU legislation to encourage mobility have concerned the right to work in other countries, the right to continue receiving benefit from your own country for a limited period while in another EU country, the right to become part of the social security system in another EU country, and, most recently, the mutual recognition of qualifications. Another measure to encourage mobility – easier transferability of occupational pensions – has made little progress. This mobility legislation may have made some difference at the margin to encourage EU citizens to work in other EU states, especially close to borders. But, historically, it is large differences in average rates of pay that have caused the major labour migrations in post-war Europe, primarily southern Europeans moving to northern European countries. Aside from a few professions, such as airline pilots, where there is relatively high mobility, most of the movement is still from poorer countries to richer ones and is declining as poorer countries become richer. Currently only about 1.5 per cent of the EU's working population works in another EU country, and the number has been falling in recent years as the southern European economies have become richer. This highlights one of the conundrums of the European social dimension. The more that rates of pay and working conditions become harmonised in a single economic space the less motivation there is for labour mobility within Europe. So the two justifications for interference by Brussels in national labour markets may actually live in tension with one another.

The second justification for labour legislation – to create a minimum floor across Europe – was, until the 1990s, almost as uncontroversial as the mobility legislation. As Padraig Flynn has noted, the first wave of harmonisation in health and safety and equal opportunities enjoyed a broad consensus. More recent legislative proposals concerning such things as regulations on working time have proved more controversial. This is partly because in Britain they are seen to derive from the more regulated labour market norms of continental Europe, and have been resisted on the grounds that they are unnecessary and would increase inefficiency. Britain has now opted-out of some aspects of the European social dimension, while the other member states have used the 'social chapter' procedure to introduce Europe-wide legislation on European works councils and parental leave.

While some of this legislation is more emblematic than practical there is also a small clutch of directives which seek to address directly the fears of some member states about dumping. One is the working time directive with its forty-eight hour week and minimum holiday requirement. This has now been adopted, but was unsuccessfully challenged by the UK before the European Court of Justice. Another is the posted worker directive which requires that workers from other EU countries observe the minimum wage levels of the countries they are working in. This directive, which has been blocked, is aimed at the growing practice of 'labour dumping', especially in the construction industry, where foreign workers are brought in to a country by foreign companies or employment agencies and receive the pay and social security benefits of the country they came from rather than the one in which they are working. Germany has around 200,000 unemployed building workers, while almost 500,000, legal and illegal immigrants work in the building trade, many of them from other advanced economies such as Britain. After the posted worker directive was blocked by Britain (with Portugal abstaining), Germany introduced national legislation (on 1 January 1997) which requires all companies, foreign and domestic, to pay building workers at least $11 per hour.

Despite this renewed interest in the problems relating to social dumping, officials in the European Commission's labour ministry, DG V, concede, in private, that large-scale social dumping is not an immediate threat. It was not mentioned in the 1993 White Paper on 'Growth, Employment and Competitiveness', and is described only briefly at the end of the Green Paper on social policy of 1994. The drive for anti-dumping legislation, as with the posted worker directive, now comes more from member states than from the Commission itself.

But DG V has not abandoned the social dumping argument entirely. While conceding the lack of hard evidence for it so far, they argue that it is a potential danger worth guarding against. They also make a distinction between countries which benefit from a given comparative advantage, such as low wages, which is legitimate, and countries which consciously reduce labour standards and pay rates to attract investors. It is quite acceptable, therefore, for Portugal, for example, to attract investment on the basis that its wages are one-sixth the level that they are in Germany. However, it would not be acceptable for the Portuguese government to force down wages to one-seventh the German level, or to deregulate hiring and firing, with a view to attracting foreign capital. However, introducing *intentionality* as the main criterion for social dumping makes finding clear-cut evidence of the problem even more complicated.

To British Conservatives, this reasoning seems peculiar. Given the principle of subsidiarity, they demand to know the justification for intervening to prevent countries competing on labour flexibility or costs. What right has the Commission or 'Europe' to interfere with measures designed to create more jobs domestically? Why should people not be allowed to trade off lower pay for higher employment? Why should German managers not threaten their workers with moving production to another country if it helps to improve the efficiency of the business? The justification for a minimum floor is that what happens in one region of a relatively open economic space like the EU has a potentially large impact on other areas. But what happens when the Europe-wide minimum floor itself has a large impact on the labour market traditions of one country? Where is the line to be drawn between the perceived interests of the whole and the principle of subsidiarity? Few politicians, even in the most pro-integration European countries, would argue the case for a complete harmonisation of labour standards. A degree of differentiation is considered legitimate in this field where it is not in some others, in industrial subsidies for example. But how much differentiation is permissible before it becomes an unfair competitive advantage?

The real justification for intervening to prevent competition ultimately comes down to the belief that labour markets are special and regulated ones are generally better than deregulated ones. It is natural enough that Britain, which passed through a period of rapid labour market deregulation and has long had less legally regulated workplaces than continental Europe, should be at odds with most of the rest of Europe on this issue. But Britain's advantages are sometimes exaggerated and much of its foreign capital stock has been built up over many decades during which relative labour costs were rather higher and flexibility rather lower. Even now, the wage cost difference in larger plants is relatively low. According to Eurostat, Britain, France and Italy are all very close in the car industry and Britain is ahead of Italy in computers. Long-established factors such as the openness of markets, including equity markets, making it easier to buy companies, and the English language, probably count for more than labour market deregulation in the eyes of potential inward investors from outside the EU. And, as David Shonfield points out, US investment in Britain in the 1980s was distorted by some heavy investment in North Sea oil.

Indeed, the European Commission ought to have more confidence in its own beliefs in the superiority of the high-cost/high-productivity labour market model as opposed to the low-cost/low-productivity model which Britain is said to be pursuing. If Britain is pursuing that model and it is counter-productive as the Commission believes, then Britain is slowly committing economic suicide and will scarcely threaten the economies of France and Germany. Moreover, the Hoover case is rather misleading. Over the past few years there have been many examples of companies *closing* plants in the UK precisely because it is relatively cheaper to do so here than in Spain or Germany. In 1992, for example, Thomson Consumer Electronics, closed its Ferguson TV plant in Gosport and sacked 3,000 workers. The company said it cost £7,000 to sack a worker in Britain compared with £47,000 in Spain. Companies can be locked-in by high firing costs – one of the factors behind the decision by Ford in early 1997 to concentrate production cuts at the Halewood plant in Britain rather than in Germany or Spain. Britain also loses out from its relatively low skill base and poor educational standards, one reason behind Ford's earlier decision to switch more of its R&D work to Germany.

Conclusion

At least over the next few years Britain is unlikely to gain any significant new advantage from its social chapter opt-out. That is partly because the social dimension as a whole is unlikely to try anything very ambitious. Freedom from low-cost measures such as company works councils may encourage some US employers to cling even tighter to their British base. But most British multinationals will find it simpler to implement the works councils for all of their European workers rather than take advantage of the opt-out. Also, more powerful than the forces of divergence such as the British opt-out, and any attempt to follow it, are the forces for convergence in labour markets as the poorer countries gradually catch up with the richer ones. This certainly applies to pay, as Douglas McWilliams has demonstrated (see above). There has also been some convergence on labour flexibility with a greater acceptance of part-time and temporary work, and, now, a growing interest in shifting the burden of non-wage labour costs from employers onto the state.

The fact that reducing labour standards beyond a certain point produces sharply diminishing returns is the best insurance policy against a downward spiral of competition. But minimum standards within the EU do provide governments with protection against parts of the business lobby keen to impose radical cost-cutting solutions. The British model will continue to be a rallying point for such groups, but it is not going to sweep all before it. EU policy makers ought to be happy to allow competition between labour market systems.

Where should the line be drawn on minimum labour standards? Not even the British government questions that there should be some rules, for example on health and safety, and there is already a social clause in world trade agreements which imposes restrictions on prison-made goods. Most companies in the high quality sectors of the economy will be unaffected by minimum standards legislation, except perhaps over something like working hours. So the jobs which stand to benefit most from the protection are, in the long run, likely to be the relatively low-paid and low-skilled ones. But, at least in the traded sector, they are the ones which are most likely to be exported to developing countries, something which regulation will make more likely. So the puzzle is to find a minimum level of harmonisation which affords some protection to the labour market losers of the high quality economies without causing a higher export of such jobs than appropriate for both the developed and developing economies.

Notes

1 *Financial Times,*
2 Speech in Brussels, 28.5.9.
3 Ed Balls, *Financial Times,* . . 92.
4 Douglas McWilliams, 'Will the Single European Market Cause European Wage and Salary Levels to Converge?', *London Economics,* January 1992.
5 Commission of the European Communities (1993) *Employment in Europe,* Office for Offical Publications of the European Communities: Luxembourg.
6 McWilliams, op. cit.
7 Incomes Data Services (1993) *Focus 66 (Social Dumping),* April.
8 Interview with the author.
9 R. Lindley (199?) 'European Integration and the Labour Market', Institute for Employment Research, University of Warwick.

6

PUTTING THE CART BEFORE THE HORSE?

Labour market challenges ahead of monetary union in Europe[1]

Jens Bastian

At its Summit in Essen on 9 and 10 December 1994, the European Union (EU)[2] had two major challenges on its agenda. One reflected the dramatic changes in progress in central and eastern Europe since the end of 1989 and concerned EU enlargement. The other challenge confronting the EU was mass unemployment. Europe's main economic problem displayed worrying characteristics: over eleven per cent of the Union's workforce is, and increasingly looks like remaining, jobless. In comparative perspective, this figure is almost double America's jobless total (5.7 per cent in January 1996) and three times Japan's (3.5 per cent). At present, more than 18.3 million people in the fifteen European Union countries are unemployed. In the course of 1995 more than 1.8 million people in the EU lost their jobs. Short- and medium-term projections foresee no significant change. While some of this unemployment is cyclical, there is good reason to believe that a large proportion of the population that is out of work in Europe is chronically unemployed. Yet unemployment figures tell only part of the story. Jobless rates tend to underestimate the true gravity of the situation. Many OECD countries are faced with substantial disguised or hidden unemployment, represented by discouraged workers and people involuntarily employed in part-time jobs. In 1992 these two categories, in which women predominate, represented more than 13 million people.

The 'black cloud' of unemployment has been a familiar characteristic of EU summits for over a decade. Moreover, even if individual European economies can bounce back from stagnation or recession to predicted growth rates of three per cent and better in the second half of the 1990s, the good news will only apply to those who are in jobs and who can reasonably expect to remain so in the coming years. Turning the corner of recession will not necessarily bring the jobless back into sustained employment. Furthermore, there is evidence to suggest that jobless growth is becoming a feature of contemporary economic upturns in EU countries.

The major challenge for European labour markets, therefore, is to find the institutional and political preconditions that will bring the jobless – or at least some of them – back into the workforce. The response to this challenge has included changes for those already in jobs, and relates to working conditions and wage flexibility. These have taken root in economies across the EU, often initiated by governments and emphatically supported by employers' associations, but also advanced, albeit reluctantly, by trade unions. The reasons for such changes, as well as the objectives which they seek to attain, are manifold and at times contradictory. Nevertheless, the nine-tenths of Europe who have jobs cannot expect that other tenth to remain hidden, nor can they safely assume that unemployment will only affect others or that joblessness can be blamed on the jobless (Bastian 1994a).

The principal impact of labour market policies initiated by the EU on national policy and on the behaviour of, as well as relationships between, national actors has been a bone of contention since the rise of unemployment in the mid-1970s. Apart from summations of what the EU has achieved – or for that matter, failed to carry out – analysis of policy performance frequently falls short of focusing on the real consequences of EU action or non-action for the individual member states. This chapter attempts to contribute towards remedying these deficiencies by investigating three areas: first, how labour market policy has traditionally been made at the national level and what the specific characteristics of this policy area consist in; second, what measures the EU has conceived in this domain; and third, the relative impact of the EU on national policy. Its findings with respect to the latter indicate that the EU influences, while not necessarily determining, national policy making.

The development of labour market policies at the national level

The use of work-sharing as an attempt to address the social and economic problems caused by mass unemployment in western Europe constitutes one of the most controversial policy developments in contemporary labour market debates. After years of failing to create enough jobs through reliance on economic growth alone, some western European governments, a few employers' associations and a number of trade union organisations have increasingly sought new ways to reduce long-term unemployment[3] and curtail mounting budgetary and social problems. Success, however, has proved elusive. Against a background of prolonged labour market problems since the mid-1970s, one innovative approach, namely, work-sharing, has sought to link two elements of policy measures: a reduction in working hours and early retirement provisions. The first implies a large-scale curtailment of the contractual working week to bring about the '35-hour week', while the second attempts to integrate the younger and/or long-term unemployed by withdrawing employees aged 55 or over from the workforce. The underlying argument in favour of linking work-sharing and early retirement is that distributive equity (a more equal distribution of employment) and social welfare (an improved quality of life)

-can be advanced through the reduction of working hours, on either a weekly and/or annual basis.

Work-sharing proposals placed a greater emphasis on active job placement, and thereby attracted the support of governments and the attention of European Commissioners with social affairs responsibilities, notably, the former Greek Commissioner, Vassou Papandreou. Moreover, work/income-sharing places on the public agenda the need to tackle the issue of burden-sharing when searching for remedies to sustained unemployment. The fact that the working time approach served both to create new jobs and safeguard existing ones made it more appealing than traditional job creation policies. The idea was particularly appealing in those countries of western Europe where there was no institutionalised commitment to full employment, no flexible wage policy and a degree of centralisation in the institutions of collective bargaining, notably, France and Belgium. In both countries, a substantial number of workers took early retirement during the 1980s (Bastian 1994a, b). However, it could not be said that employment performance in either country was a 'success story' and labour markets in both countries suffered from 'institutional sclerosis'. More generally, the arthritic condition of continental Europe's labour markets has kept the door shut on the unemployed.

Unemployment in Europe today, as much as at the beginning of the 1980s, is to a large extent not cyclical, but structural. As a labour market policy, work-sharing was characterised by its redistributive objectives which ran counter to the constant calls by management theorists for 'streamlining', 'contracting-out' and 'corporate downsizing'. Instead of emphasising the virtue of job changing, the strategy seeks to influence the supply side by altering two parameters in the operation of the labour market, namely, the duration and the organisation of work-time. The advocacy of work-sharing (*partage du travail* in French) through shorter hours envisaged a large-scale redistribution of paid work in the mainstream economy between those in full-time employment and those seeking (re-)entry into the labour market.

Support for work-sharing since the early 1970s has been essentially pragmatic. Some governments, and many trade unions, in OECD countries, including (West) Germany, France, Belgium and Britain, see the approach as a response to the end of the halcyon days of continuous economic growth in combination with (near) full employment. According to governmental and union blueprints outlining the positive effects of work-sharing, the alleviation of employment rested on two interdependent elements: first, the amount by which working time is reduced; and second, the speed of implementation: the more speedily the reduction is made, the more likely that job creation effects will materialise. Job creation is thus perceived not only to be the product of new investment and increased profitability, but also the outcome of redistributing the volume of available work. Consequently, firms are compelled to combine improving productivity potentials and reverting to the external labour market for additional employment (Blyton 1982).

What emerges from the policy performance of the past decade is the acknowledgment, albeit reluctantly among trade unions, that the redistributive effect of work-sharing strategies has been exhausted. To those involved in the policy process and its evaluation it became apparent that a redistributive policy of work-sharing had four effects: firstly, it entailed consequences for income formation and budgetary allocation; secondly, it affected the organisational resources of the state as well as the industrial relations actors trying to mediate the plurality of contending interests; thirdly, it revealed the extent to which strategies have to be modified as a consequence of policy performance with unintended by-products; and finally, it created a culture of new entitlements with high social values and the attendant difficulties in attempting to curtail them. For the time being the work-sharing strategy has been returned to the drawing board.

Work-sharing strategies at the end of the 1970s and beginning of the 1980s took two forms. The first, characteristic especially of the early stages, took the form of reducing working hours by establishing opportunities for early retirement. The second consisted in limiting the working week to thirty-five hours. It is noteworthy that Belgium, for instance, introduced various early retirement schemes before finally deciding to reduce weekly working time. In the French case, both options were implemented simultaneously after the Mitterrand government took office in 1981. By contrast, British governments have steadfastly refused to consider a policy of work-sharing that combined early retirement schemes with measures curtailing weekly working time (Bastian 1994b).

Comparing the ambitious claims brought forward by the supporters of work-sharing at the end of the 1970s with the situation more than a decade later, it becomes evident that, with the exception of Germany, the only comparable development has been the introduction of the 39-hour week on an industry-wide scale in Belgium, France and Britain. In other words, after a first reduction at the national level, demands for shorter hours proceeded no further. The recent history of the issue suggests the general tendency of trade unions, and of the early Mitterrand years in particular, to oversell work-sharing to their rank-and-file and the public. Work-sharing tended to be introduced as a panacea for very different labour market problems which in fact varied greatly. After the decade-long advocacy of work-sharing objectives, it can be observed that small steps in work-time reduction did not reverse long-standing unemployment problems (Bastian 1994a).

If the experience of Belgium and France has not been a good one, what explains the rise of work-share models on public policy agendas in Europe? The salience of work-sharing must additionally be seen in the light of an institutional challenge: recourse to other strategies capable of mastering the labour market crisis were either blocked in various OECD countries or established routines of policy making increasingly became subject to legitimation problems. With the slowing, or even cessation, of economic growth and rapidly increasing unemployment rates, public debate was forced to confront the readjustment of two traditionally salient elements of industrial governance: first, determining appropriate trade-offs in income distribution; and second, the allocation of employment opportunities (Bastian 1989: 323). However, only the first of these is subject to contractual specification; the level of employment does not form part of collective bargaining agreements above the level of the firm. In other words, it is a residual category not subject to specification by legally binding norms for the actors concerned. With economic realities radically changing the expectations of actors involved in collective bargaining, especially regarding wages and benefits, the working class and the middle class were affected. As economic growth decelerated, wage growth was curtailed and even went into reverse for younger and less educated men and women in the workforce.

Two additional points are worth making. Firstly, demands for a reduction of the working week and/or early retirement agreements focused on the adaptation of the organisation of working time to the differentiated needs of society and the changing leisure preferences of individual employees. In other words, the reorganisation of work-time and the modification of time regimes, considered to be overly rigid by employers, trade unions and employees alike, though for different reasons, were regarded as measures supporting economic modernisation and extending social welfare gains. In addition to such viewpoints, which dominated the shorter hours debate during the period 1960–80, a variety of social norms were invoked in connection with the linkage between work-sharing and early retirement. These normative considerations included equality of treatment and fairer divisions. For example, first and foremost, industrial unions would call for a reduction in weekly working hours, and receive instant support from their rank-and-file, because they viewed existing disparities between manufacturing and white-collar staff as an unjustified practice. In particular, engineering unions in Britain, Germany and Belgium concentrated on curtailing, and eventually overcoming, differentials between occupational ranks during the 1970s and early 1980s.

Secondly, advocates of the work-sharing/early retirement approach cannot ignore the so-called 'demographic time bomb'. A recent study by the OECD underscores the looming pension problem, stressing that declining populations and a shrinking workforce are conspiring to put pension provisions under pressure in all its member countries. The OECD cited France, Germany, Italy and Japan as the members with the greatest potential financial problems. The study forecast that in these four countries, state pension obligations would peak at about fifteen per cent of GDP during the first half of the next century, compared with current levels of between five and ten per cent. The OECD based its forecasts on the premise that in all its member countries, except Britain,[4] the ratio of pensioners to workers would double by around 2035.

This observation points to the importance of two institutions, one political and the other social, in determining labour market performance. As a political institution the state has become directly involved in labour markets. However, controversies persist over the extent of active labour market policies shaping employment outcomes or impairing economic performance through interventionist means (Scharpf 1991). The social institution, the welfare state, is relevant in so far as it has influenced national capacities to maintain full employment or whether it has contributed to confronting the unfolding labour market crisis. In light of developments in the past decade, the institutional focus of labour market performance raises the question of whether government money can create jobs. In other words, do Europe's governments absorb too much of what their countries produce?

In 1994 the revenues of the European Union's governments amounted to 46 per cent of their countries GDP. (The figure in America is 32 per cent). Some of the purposes for which this money is spent are commendable; it pays, among other things, for Europe's welfare states. But while the motive is humane – and the results are reassuring for those in jobs – the unemployed are not brought back inside the working economy. Still, the fact that the welfare state has been reformed in a number of EU states should not be ignored. Germany, Belgium[5] and Ireland have cut spending as a share of GDP since 1985, while France, Holland and Finland have held it steady. Only in Scandinavia has social spending risen.

Redistributive labour market policies have received considerable attention not only in individual countries, but have also featured in policy initiatives at the EU level. Examination of recent EU proposals permits an assessment about how significant action by Brussels has been compared with domestic policy developments. It is also important to consider whether EU action has taken the form of legislative measures, adopted collectively by the member states in the Council of Ministers, or of rulings laid down by the European Court of Justice.

Recent developments at the European Union level

The European Commission President, Jacques Santer, has repeatedly called for a Europe-wide employment pact between governments and the two sides of industry. The *1996 Pact for Confidence and Jobs* aimed at curtailing unemployment by keeping wage growth below, or in line with, the rate of inflation in return for job creation measures. Santer's initiative recalls the Delors' White Paper on 'Growth, Competitiveness and Employment' which was adopted at the Essen Council of December 1994. The initiative to combat mass unemployment focused on creating jobs by promoting *inter alia* work-sharing and a reduction of working hours. The employment package further urged wage restraint, the reduction of welfare contributions by employers and tax incentives for training. Delors heralded the initiative making it clear that he hoped it would serve as the same kind of blueprint for policy making in the 1990s that the Commission White Paper of 1985 had been for the Single Market Programme. One of the aims of the 1993 White Paper was the creation of 15 million jobs by the year 2000. It sought to combine a reduction in the price of labour with a new approach to solidarity between those in work and those without, which took into account major developments in the labour market, such as the increase in part-time and temporary work. Consideration of work-sharing and reduced hours has thus been an important theme for discussion within the Commission since the mid-1980s (Bastian 1989: 257).

A striking aspect of the discussion of labour market policy in Brussels is the mixture of pragmatism and effort in cross-national consensus, albeit with Britain standing on the sidelines. Far from the overly ambitious regulatory approach taken in the mid-1980s, the current initiatives seek to transcend the established left–right divide. What matters is unemployment. Thus, the pragmatic Social Affairs Commissioner, Padraig Flynn, was open to measures on working time, and a directive on part-time work formed part of the Social Action Programme unveiled in March 1995. This directive would require part-time employees to receive the same hourly pay and conditions as full-timers. A majority of EU members, excluding Britain, is keen to press the issue because it fits with their domestic labour market agendas of promoting part-time work.[6] In other words, the draft directive impacts on national policy making, not by prompting member states to take action, but rather because it supports existing trends.

By contrast, at a time when employers and employees in Germany, Belgium and France, as well as politicians from both left and right, argue that redistributive working time policies could help solve their structural unemployment problems, the prospects for actually agreeing on such steps on a European level appear dim. Such is the case in the wake of a bitter debate that lasted over three years and represented a far more modest objective than the work-sharing directive, namely, the implementation of a 48-hour working week. The directive, adopted by European Community Social Affairs ministers in November 1993, focuses on the adaptation of working time. The directive covers a number of aspects of work-time organisation, requiring minimum periods of daily rest of at least eleven continuous hours, the provision of rest periods for work days of over six hours, while also establishing a minimum four weeks' paid holidays and imposing conditions for night and shift work. EU member states were given three years to implement the directive.

The working week directive was adopted under health and safety requirements, a procedure which has significant implications. Directives concerning health and safety at work can be adopted by a majority of member states and do not require unanimity. The UK, which has long opposed Community intervention in labour market issues on the grounds that it trespasses on the rights of sovereign states and contravenes the right of workers to work, abstained during the vote and vowed to challenge the directive in court. Britain's then employment secretary, David Hunt, opposed the 48-hour working week directive on the grounds that the directive was a piece of social legislation, and therefore should not have been adopted by qualified majority voting. The government further argued that the law should have been considered under 'harmonisation' procedures. This would have allowed Britain to veto the measure, which then could have taken effect only with a British opt-out.

This intransigent position was maintained by the UK despite the fact that a number of concessions had been won. Thus, the UK government obtained a period of ten years' grace in which to implement the directive. Also, workers were given the option of working more than the maximum 48-hour week, provided that the extra work was voluntary and safeguards were introduced to avoid exploitation by employers. In addition, the 48-hour week has to be averaged over four months, workers such as lorry drivers, the fishing industry, police personnel, trainee doctors and other hospital staff were exempted from the scope of the directive, and with the exception of the annual leave provision, all those whose working time is not 'predetermined' – a category which includes a vast array of managerial posts – are excluded from the directive. In practice this long list of qualifications and exemptions means that the sectors most associated with long hours are removed from the scope of the directive.

However, the UK government was determined to maintain maximum labour market flexibility which it regarded as an essential element in ensuring the competitiveness of its economy. British workers were working by far the longest hours in the Union with nearly a third of male full-time workers working more than forty-eight hours a week. The UK was, moreover, the only member state where the length of the working week had increased over the past ten years.[7] While partly reflecting the exceptionally high levels of overtime in manufacturing, this trend was also the result of the managerial and professional employees working increasingly longer hours. Thus, the UK continued its resistance to the directive by challenging its legality before the European Court of Justice.

In March 1996, the British government lost the first round of its fight. The French Advocate General of Court, Phillippe Léger, argued that the challenge should be dismissed. In his interim ruling he maintained that the number of hours worked was 'clearly' a health and safety matter. The concept of health and safety should be given a broad interpretation to cover the general working environment, 'far removed from an approach confined to the protection of workers against the influence of physical or chemical factors alone'. The Advocate General accepted the contention of the Council of Ministers, with the support of the Commission, Spain and Belgium, that the time spent working and the pattern of working hours influence workers' physical and mental state. The opinion was met by angry reaction in the UK. The then Prime Minister, John Major, argued that: 'It is precisely because of legislation like this and stupidities like this that the EU is becoming uncompetitive and losing jobs to other parts of the world'. The Conservative government pledged to continue the struggle against EU social intrusion and to curb the powers of the Luxembourg Court – an objective that was written into the government's White Paper on the 1996 IGC. However, the UK government could do nothing in the face of the ruling laid down by the Court in November 1996, which found against it and was in line with the Opinion of the Advocate General. Moreover, its efforts to circumscribe the power of the Court at the 1996 Intergovernmental Conference Amsterdam came to nothing.

Since the election in May 1997 of a Labour government, committed to signing the social chapter, there has been a considerable change of climate and an end to the tension that characterised the relationship between the UK and the EU for much of the 1980s and 1990s. However, interestingly, New Labour's emphasis on flexibility may mean that the UK still remains at odds with its European partners over social policy in general and how best to address unemployment in particular.

The decision of the European Court in the above case demonstrates its ability to shape the domestic policy of member states. There are many other examples of how the Court has influenced national policy in the social policy domain. For instance, the guidelines for when companies and citizens can sue member states for damages – labeled 'discrimination manifestly contrary to EU law' – were detailed in a ruling of March 1996 (Rs C-46 and 48/93). In two test cases,[8] the Court set an important precedent by making it clear that governments must pay damages for passing laws that violate the rights of any EU citizen in a 'sufficiently serious' manner. The March 1996 rulings are the first significant follow-up to a 1991 land-mark decision declaring that governments can be liable for failing to put EU laws on their books. In fact, the Court set three conditions for determining whether an individual or a company is justified in taking a member state to court. The judges argued that compensation is due when a government violates rights conferred on individuals, when a government does so in a 'sufficiently serious' manner, and when the victim can show clearly that damages occurred as a result of the state's action(s). The Court's decision marks its first attempt at explaining in detail the issue of government liability. In the landmark case in 1991, the 'Francovich ruling', the Court argued that member states should pay damages to companies and citizens that lose money because the government either fails to adopt EU legis-lation or passes new laws that breach EU prerogatives.

The role played by the European Court of Justice in the social policy domain has been highly significant in bringing about policy change in the member states. However, taking cases before the Court is not the only way in which trade unions and other interest groups have been able to fight, and often win, domestic battles at the EU level. The balance of forces in the Council of Ministers may allow interest groups in some member states to achieve at the European level what they could not have won domestically. For instance, the 48-hour working week directive left the detail of compensation or extra time off for exempted workers to be settled by national legislation or collective bargaining. That spelled in practice a potential, and for many British employers, an unwelcome, new role for trade unions.

Another example concerns the decision in February 1996 by the European Commission to scrap plans that sought to alter worker protection when jobs are contracted out. The focus of the controversy was the 1977 EU Acquired Rights Directive, which ensures that workers keep the same wages and conditions when they are transferred to a new employer after a takeover or merger. The directive also requires employers to deal with worker representatives during transfers, thus bolstering the position of trade unions. Known in Britain as 'TUPE' – Transfer of Undertakings (Protection of Employment) – the legislation has been successfully used by unions to challenge the British government's attempts to drive down costs in the public sector by contracting out and market-testing. The courts in both Britain and the EU have upheld compensation claims by public-sector workers forced to choose between cuts in wages and benefits or redundancy when their jobs were privatised. For years the British government had been manoeuvring to get the European legislation changed. Initially, it found allies among other EU govern-ments, especially in France and Germany, and within the Commission, in support of exempting certain types of contracting-out from the TUPE protection – a situation which reflected concern that the European Court of Justice was interpreting the legislation too broadly. In a surprise ruling in April 1994, the Court ruled that TUPE applied to contracted-out services, even if only a single worker is involved.

Commissioner Flynn's response was to propose restricting TUPE to the transfer of 'an economic entity that retains its identity'. This example of Euro-speak would have meant in practice, for example, that workers transferred without any equipment or machinery would not have been covered. Ignoring the Commission's position, British unions sought to sink the plan. As is so frequently the case, the objective was made considerably easier by the UK government's isolated position in the social field. Given the UK's repeated efforts to block the adoption of EU measures relating to labour, its partners are often rather reluctant, to say the least, to offer it any concessions. The British TUC, working closely with and through the European TUC, lobbied extensively against the Commission's proposed changes. The campaign won support not just from the TUC's socialist allies in the European Parliament, but also Christian Democratic politicians from the European People's Party. By securing this cross-party support, the British unions ensured the adoption of a resolution calling on the Commission not to undermine the 1977 legislation. In consequence, the Social Affairs Commissioner withdrew the proposed amendment. Thus, the development of transnational alliances at different institutional levels between domestic interest groups and the European Parliament against the Commission won the argument. A significant, and not at all predictable, coalition was established in order to safeguard existing social policy.

Despite the fact that some issues are now being fought at the EU level, the importance of the domestic policy arena must not be underestimated. Indeed, trade unions have been able to win battles against governments on a national terrain. An example of the continued importance of the domestic arena comes from March 1994 when the House of Lords laid down a ruling that delivered a substantial setback to the UK government's flexible labour market policy. The Law Lords ruled that UK laws on part-time workers' rights concerning redundancy pay and unfair dismissal were in breach of European law. The Major government was thereby compelled to draw up legislation which gives part-timers rights equal to those in full-time employment. The Employment Protection Act of 1978 had restricted the rights of those working less than 16 hours a week. Under the Act, part-time workers were covered by unfair dismissal and redundancy pay provisions only after completing five years of continuous employment. Full-time employees qualify for such entitlements after two years. According to the Law Lords the government had failed to prove that the use of the 16-hour threshold had resulted in an increase in part-time employment. As a result, the UK government found itself having to introduce legislation to bring UK law in line with EU legislation, although it was seriously concerned about the impact on part-time employment through the extra costs that would be imposed on employers, especially given that this was the single most important area of growth in the British labour market.

Questions still searching for answers

What implications does the above discussion have for work-sharing as a strategy to enhance labour market effects? As indicated above, redistributive measures aimed at job creation were at the heart of debates about labour market policies during the past decade. By contrast, current debates turn around defining the organisational features of working conditions. Achieving temporal flexibility has become the new order of the day, and reduced basic hours are being considered as a possible trade-off element in collective bargaining. This suggests that the notion of enlarged flexibility options in working time organisation has gradually been accepted by the unions and their membership. However, their commitment to enhance flexibility in the areas of working conditions, job profiles, rationalisation of bargaining procedures, and new-style pay systems constitute the controversial compromise dimensions. In short, distributional objectives have been replaced by concerns over the allocation of time and its influence on revised working practices.

Within this context, flexible production patterns, highly differentiated working conditions and new-style bargaining procedures constitute transformations that connect with trends in individualised employment conditions, multi-skilling and moves toward greater employment mobility. These features constitute what career management consultants call the growing world of dejobbing. The extent and nature of the 'dejobbed' future is contentious to say the least. Some commentators, including Bridges (1995) and Rifkin (1995), claim that in today's workplace 100 per cent of jobs are temporary,[9] and that the old idea of a 'job for life' is disappearing. The result is a workforce made up of so-called 'vendor workers' who sell their services to a variety of clients and work for them on projects on a short-term basis. This model holds out the prospect of a future which increasing numbers of people are hunter-gatherers, hungry freelancers foraging for work and moving from project to project. While people are working within organisations as full-time employees, their arrangements are too fluid and idiosyncratic to be called permanent jobs. Such a perspective makes dejobbed workers seem the downtrodden victims of economic necessity, an ideal workforce for companies which want to limit their investment in the practice of offering a job for life. The new buzz words of 'dejobbing' or 'delayering' have long been regarded as a feature of manual work but only took off as a debate when it began to affect white-collar workers, in particular in software firms across the US.

According to the Institute of Employment Studies in Britain, the UK is already dejobbing. About 57 per cent of the workforce remain in what can be classified as 'traditional' employment and only 22 per cent are 'traditional-looking' employees (Kent 1995: 2). Temporary work, defined as working on a contract with shorter than standard duration of hours, is carried out by 10 per cent of women and 7 per cent of men in 1991 in the EU labour force. However, national differences in employment markets remain strong. The recent annual report from the European network for small and medium-sized enterprises highlights the wide diversity between workforces across western Europe. In Spain 22 per cent of men and 28 per cent of women were employed in temporary work. In Italy, the proportion was reported at 3 per cent of men and 8 per cent of women respectively. The fastest growth in temporary employment was in France where it rose from 3 per cent for both men and women in 1983 to 7 per cent for men and 10 per cent for women eight years later (Observatory Report 1995). What these figures show is that the employment market is in flux across the EU, subject to a turbulent economic environment. But this also illustrates that sweeping talk of 'dejobbing' belies the detailed variety of the employment scene from one country to another. The tenacity of custom and practice in employment are too easily and frequently underestimated by generalisations such as 'dejobbing'.

These developments in flexible working in various European labour markets not only bring new issues on the policy agendas, but also demand conceptual answers that invariably call to attention the strategies to be adopted in the future. Measures to improve the flexibility of industrial relations, wage negotiations and employment conditions merit a prominent place on the political agendas until the end of the millennium. This is a large and uncharted subject where questions are still searching for answers. As a first step, long-term trends need to be distinguished from the short-term changes resulting from the fluctuating economic cycle.

In this context, the question of who is to achieve the changes, formulate the necessary compromises and monitor their implementation inevitably arises. This question is even more pertinent when it is considered that while the environmental pressure group, Greenpeace, and the human rights association, Amnesty International, both enjoy a high level of respectability, and can mobilise large numbers of the population across continental Europe within a short period of time,[10] the moral standing of trade unions, political parties and (some) churches is subject to considerable criticism, and exercising the 'exit' option out of such mass organisations is becoming increasingly prevalent. At the EU level the directive to form works councils is seen by some as the catalyst for corporate change, and by others as the new arena for consultation and information at the firm level. The form of employee involvement outlined in the directive lays out a range of possibilities, including employee representatives in a European-wide consultation system, company-based joint management/employee works councils, and primarily trade union representatives informing each other about developments in their European-based multinational companies.[11]

There is no single pattern for works councils. Countries like Germany and The Netherlands with a tradition of employee representation at the firm level and codecision-making enshrined in their respective constitutions, interpret the EU directive differently from, for example, France and Italy, where the idea of joint councils with management runs counter to the definition of decentralised trade union action (Bastian 1994a: 115). Furthermore, although the UK is not subject to the works council directive as a result of the 1991 Maastricht opt-out, many British companies are in fact setting up consultation and information committees. At present, most companies that established European works councils appear to be favouring joint management/employee forums, however, without holding negotiating power. The areas of consultation cover training, questions relating to production techniques and the introduction of new technologies. Other subjects for the consultation agenda involve health and safety, work organisation and the external environment. In two noteworthy cases the agenda does go further. The German car manufacturer, Volkswagen, allows working time and wages to be discussed in its company-wide works council, while the French food conglomerate, BSN, permits issues of sexual equality to be debated.

The significance of these European works councils should not, however, be overestimated. The temptation to over-sell them is apparent in some trade union statements. It will take time to discover whether the works councils are capable of transforming European-based multinationals. For example, how will such companies conduct their corporate strategies in providing wide-ranging consultation and information disclosures of their business activities to their employees? The supporters of the directive, and they are not exclusively from the trade union camp, see works councils as a catalyst for much needed corporate reform. But questions remain and gaps persist. Europe's single-market legislation is still without a European company statute, for example. Moreover, the effectiveness of the councils will depend on a number of factors such as the willingness of companies to develop an open and co-operative policy towards their employees and interest representatives and the abilities of trade unions to press their agendas at company level. Only then will it be possible to determine whether the European works council directive is a marginalised irrelevance in the exercise of corporate governance or an important step in the evolution of a more representative form of European-based company where employees exercise rights like shareholders (Transfer 1995).

The demands on the agenda of collective bargaining and industrial policy during the 1990s include the dismantling of labour market regulations, performance-related pay systems, access to training and qualifications, just-in-time production and breaking through demarcation lines of the working day and the five-day working week. The working time issues include weekend working, annualised hours schemes, round-the-clock working schedules, non-standard working time schemes, and part-time work.[12] In short, changing temporal flexibility is considered to be a vehicle for changes in the way labour markets operate. Placed in a broader context, it can be argued that the dynamic of change points to the 'modernisation' of the regulatory framework of the labour market. Such is the terminology being utilised by the conference of the Group of Seven leading industrial countries (G7) on achieving job-creating growth in Lille, France, in April 1996. For the European participants, the principal aim was to identify policies that not only reduce Europe's soaring unemployment in the short term, but that allow labour markets to adjust to economic changes in future, within the requirements of European Monetary Union.

The fundamental question that arises from considering issues surrounding flexibility relates to the extent to which a society wants to push the argument of labour market deregulation. Answers will require imaginative thinking, but will also reflect the nature of the social fabric of EU democracies. Jobs that are provided at hourly rates, often at or below minimum wage levels,[13] not only mean increased insecurity, but also reinforce absolute poverty, as reflected in the terms the 'working poor' and 'work poor' households. Moreover, product-market restrictions[14] may be as important as labour market rigidities in explaining unemployment and influencing future job creation. However, no magic formula is available to confront the jobs crisis afflicting European economies. If economic growth cannot create jobs, then new solutions must be sought.

The new commitments included in the Amsterdam Treaty concerning employment should be welcomed. However, doubts remain about the consistency across the member states of the political will required to support meaningful EU initiatives. Differences in the traditions and approaches to market issues between, and among, existing and prospective EU members are still marked, while most employment policy tools remain in the hands of national governments. Moreover, labour and especially business are sceptical about the usefulness of EU action. For these reasons, it would be unwise to expect the Union to implement radical measures to combat unemployment.

Notes

1 For her unending inspiration and concern, I wish to thank Calliope Spanou.
2 The term 'European Union' is used to refer to the fifteen member states. However, for the collectivity to become a union in institutional and political terms, much remains to be achieved in the realms of legal, social and economic integration.
3 Defined as those who have been unemployed for more than a year, the long-term unemployed make up roughly 40 per cent of the total jobless pool and their number is rising. During the last year for which comparable pan-European data are available, namely 1992, the long-term unemployment rate stood at 35.4 per cent of all unemployed.
4 The British government introduced generous tax breaks to encourage saving in private pensions during the 1980s. More than half of the $2 trillion in private pension assets in Europe are held in Britain and The Netherlands.
5 The Belgian government has started experimenting with workfare schemes. The long-term unemployed are now required to accept small jobs offered to them. The state employment agency lines up the jobs, offering the services of unemployed workers at modest rates, made more attractive by tax breaks. If the jobless person repeatedly turns down offers, unemployment benefits are suspended. But if he or she takes the job, the income supplements the check from the agency.
6 In the same area, for ten years Britain successfully blocked attempts to institute parental leave for a three-month period after childbirth for mothers and/or fathers and special leave of undefined duration for pressing personal reasons. However, in March 1996, under the first agreement to be reached by means of the Social Dialogue (see chapter 7 in this volume) parental leave for at least twelve weeks on an unpaid basis was granted to both men and women. In order for British workers to benefit from the agreement, however, British multinational companies located in the UK will have to decide to start voluntary negotiations with employee organisations. In consequence, they would thereby circumvent the government's veto and Maastricht opt-out. On another matter, the UK won a four-year exemption from an EU law restricting work by children and adolescents to a maximum of twelve hours a week.

7 At the time of writing 6 per cent of British employees were working seven days a week, 16 per cent put in more than forty-eight hours a week compared with an EU average of 7 per cent and 20 per cent were entitled to less than four weeks off a year.

8 In the first case, the UK was ordered to pay compensation to Spanish fishing companies that had been denied the right to register their vessels in Britain. The second decision concerned a German law that restricted the sales of beers brewed in other EU member states.

9 Having to 'kick the job habit' is the credo of such pessimistic forecasts. In Bridge's own words, 'the reality is that what is disappearing today is not just a certain number of jobs, or jobs in certain industries or in one country – or even jobs in the developed world as a whole. What is disappearing is the very thing itself: the job' (Bridges 1995: 6).

10 The success scored by Greenpeace in June 1995 against the sinking of Shell's oil rig 'Brent Spar' off the coast of Scotland was a remarkable example of mobilisation and organisational flexibility. Within days the boycott of Shell's filling stations spread across continental Europe, and was particularly closely followed in Germany, creating an unprecedented coalition that extended from the churches, trade unions and employers' associations, to political parties, governments as well as EU institutions.

11 It was estimated in early 1996 that the directive covers more than 1,500 European companies and 61 works councils have been signed. Companies employing over 1,000 workers with more than 150 in at least two member states are required to establish European works councils.

12 Equal treatment for part-time workers is the order of the day, strongly pushed by European legislation, and gradually making governments change direction. A recent example from Britain serves to illustrate this trend. The Major Government proposed in April 1995 that part-time employees should henceforth be able to take full part in a variety of share plans such as profit sharing and employee share ownership trusts.

13 Temporary and part-time work is especially low paid. According to Business Strategies, a private, independent consultancy in London, no more than a quarter of women in part-time jobs are earning more than £6 an hour (Business Strategies 1996).

14 For example, in the controversial area of biotechnology, appeal is constantly made to the job creation potential in order to overcome the legal and moral concerns raised by policy makers and the public.

References

Bastian, J. (1989) '1992 im Visier – der Europäische Binnenmarkt als Herausforderung für gewerkschaftliche Handlungsstrategien: das Problem der Arbeitszeitpolitik', *Zeitschrift für ausländisches und internationales Arbeits- und Sozialrecht*, 3 (4), 257–87

—— (1994a) *A Matter of Time: From Work-sharing to Temporal Flexibility in Belgium, France and Britain*, Aldershot: Avebury

—— (1994b) 'Modern Times: Institutional Dynamics in Belgian and French Labour Market Policies', *West European Politics*, 17, 34–56

Blyton, P. (1982) 'The Industrial Relations of Work-sharing', *Industrial Relations Journal*, 13, 6–12

Bridges, W. (1995) *Jobshift: How to Prosper in a Workplace Without Jobs*, London: Nicholas Brealey

Business Strategies (1996) *Labour Market Flexibility and Financial Services* London: Business Strategies

Kent, S. (1995) 'Old Job, New Job – No Job?', *The Guardian*, 4 March

Observatory Report from EIMI, *Report on Temporary Work*, Zoetermeer, 1995

OECD (1994) *Economic Outlook*, Paris: OECD

Rifkin, J. (1995) *The End of Work*, New York: G.P. Puttnam and Sons

Scharpf, F.W. (1991) *Crisis and Choice in European Social Democracy*, Ithaca: Cornell University Press

Transfer (1995) *European Review of Labour and Research*, 1:2, April

7

SOCIAL PARTNERSHIP AT THE EU LEVEL

Initiatives, problems and implications for member states[1]

Michael Gold

Introduction

On 14 December 1995, a framework agreement on parental leave was signed in Brussels by representatives of European-level unions and employers' organisations. The significance of this event lies not only in its substance – the setting out across Europe of minimum standards on parental leave – but also in its procedure. For the first time under the terms of the social protocol of the Treaty on European Union (the 'Maastricht Treaty'), employers and unions had arrived voluntarily at an intersectoral agreement covering all member states, except the UK (under the 'opt-out' provisions of the social protocol). The Commission had first attempted to introduce a draft directive on parental leave in 1983, but little or no progress had been made since. The topic had proved too controversial, with the then Conservative government in the UK repeatedly stressing its opposition to the proposed legislation. However, once the Treaty on European Union had come into force in November 1993, a new procedure became possible.

Article 4 of the agreement on social policy (contained in the social protocol) allows employers and unions at EU level to conclude agreements through 'social dialogue' which may then be implemented either in accordance with normal practices in each member state or else through a Council decision following a request to that effect from the signatories and the Commission. In this way, the Commission can pass responsibility for certain areas of EC-level labour market regulation from itself on to employers and the unions (the 'social partners').

Negotiations on parental leave, which had begun in July 1995, accordingly reached a successful conclusion five months later, thereby baptising a new regulatory procedure with important implications for member states. The social partners duly requested the implementation of their framework agreement through the Council, whereupon the Commission proposed a Directive to achieve this purpose. This Directive was subsequently adopted by the Council on 3 June 1996: the social dialogue had achieved its first major success in concluding and securing a substantive agreement at intersectoral EC level.

Major questions

From the very beginning, two major questions have dominated debate over the development of social and labour policy in the European Community:[2]

- the first concerns whether or not the terms and conditions of workers in the member states should be regulated by the EC at all, but if so, then the extent to which such regulation should take place; and
- the second concerns the methods through which regulation is best introduced once the principle is conceded in a particular area. For example, it might take the form of either binding legislation through the adoption of a directive, or simply a non-binding recommendation, or else some other measure adopted through 'social dialogue'.

These two questions are, of course, closely linked. The enlargement of the EC has led to the entry of a number of member states whose legal systems are not of the predominant Roman-German type (Due *et al.* 1991), whilst since the 1980s increasing numbers of member states have in any case themselves been adopting or adapting deregulatory labour policies (Ferner and Hyman 1992b: xxvii). Indeed, the concept of 'subsidiarity' – which has been written into the amended EEC Treaty as article 3B – reflects the view that the EC should intervene in a policy area only if it cannot be adequately dealt with at national, regional or local level (Spicker 1991). Overall, such trends towards decentralisation have, as we shall see, induced the Commission to seek out approaches to social policy less centred on legal regulation than in earlier stages of its development.

In the social and labour policy area, the principal alternative to the legislative approach has come to be known as the 'social dialogue', a term which means rather little to most British policy makers (for a historical overview, see Carley 1993). However, it should be borne in mind that the French term *dialogue social* means, in essence, exchange of views or consultation between employer and worker representatives. Furthermore, when applied to EC processes, its meaning narrows to the exchange of views, consultation and – by extension – negotiation at EC level with three distinct scopes:

- intersectoral (that is, covering employers and workers across all sectors in all member states);
- sectoral (covering employers and workers in individual sectors of economic activity across all member states); and
- company or organisational (covering all employees within an individual company in all its various subsidiaries across the member states).

The intention here is to examine the impact of social dialogue on state autonomy and on the behaviour of employers' and union organisations across the member states. However, this poses a major problem. Whilst the impact of EC legislation, particularly directives, on UK social policy has been examined more or less broadly in various places (see, for example, Nielsen and Szyszczak 1991; Bulmer *et al.* 1992; Gold and Matthews 1996), the impact of the social dialogue has not yet been subjected to such a thoroughgoing analysis.

There are several reasons for this. One is undoubtedly that the legislative approach to the creation of the EC social dimension – which dates back to the EEC Treaty itself – has a long pedigree of achievement that has invited comment (particularly in the areas of equal opportunities and health and safety). Another reason is that the social dialogue – as we stress below – had been designed from the outset as no more than a *consultative* process. It was originally intended to encourage and promote the legislative process, not to rival it and still less to replace it. Putting it more fancifully, if legislation was to be the mother of the social dimension then social dialogue was to be the midwife. Its effects have therefore only ever, till recently anyhow, been indirect. The third, and most significant reason, related to the last point, is that until 1993 there was no provision in the social dialogue to result in *binding* agreements at all. Until then, the process of EC-level social partnership had achieved only 'limited development' (Hall 1994: 293). Only when the Maastricht Treaty came into force, along with the social protocol, did the social dialogue consolidate its function as a regulatory mechanism that could initiate binding measures in the social field parallel to the legislative framework of the Commission.

Running throughout this chapter, therefore, is an underlying theme – that of the constraints on the development of the social dialogue that have held back its impact on the course of the integration of European social and labour policies. In order to understand these constraints properly, the chapter begins with a brief analysis of tripartism within the EC since its inception and then schematically reviews the development of the social dialogue at its various levels since its launch in 1985, with particular reference to its evolution since 1993.

Origins of the 'social dialogue'

The social dialogue – as a specific *process* of consultation between the Commission and employers' and union organisations at European level – dates from January 1985, when a series of informal tripartite contacts were inaugurated by Jacques Delors, the then newly appointed President of the Commission. These meetings brought together representatives of the Union of Industrial and Employers' Confederations of Europe (UNICE), the European Centre of Public Enterprise (CEEP) and the European Trade Union Confederation (ETUC). They culminated in a meeting the following November at Val Duchesse, where discussions took place on economic growth and employment. A more formalised system of working parties was then set up covering areas like new technology and macroeconomic policy. These working parties have been collaborating ever since on a series of issues; for example, in May 1995 the macroeconomic group issued a joint Opinion on job-creating growth which examined the problems of high budget deficits and labour market reform. There was renewed emphasis too on sectoral social dialogue – that is, EC-level consultations focusing on a particular sector like construction, energy supply or retail.

However, social dialogue can also be identified as an *approach* to social and labour policy as distinctively enshrined not only in the EEC Treaty itself but also in a series of tripartite conferences, meetings and committees that have waxed and waned over the years. Whilst the prospect of the Single European Market undoubtedly threw the spotlight on Delors' Val Duchesse initiative in 1985, this was certainly no radical departure from earlier attempts to foster a consultative approach towards social and labour affairs based on tripartism. Indeed, the Commission, in pursuing the social policy objectives laid down in articles 117 to 128 of the EEC Treaty, is required to act by 'making studies, delivering opinions and arranging consultations' (article 118). And, bearing in mind the sheer range of social policy areas in which the Commission is required by article 118 to promote 'close co-operation' – including employment, labour law, working conditions, social security and the right of association and collective bargaining – consultation is clearly the guiding principle for any progress. Without the full consent of employers' and employees' representatives there would be no *implementation* of social policy, no matter how boldly or imaginatively it might be formulated. No wonder, then, that: 'Within the institutions of the European Community there are dozens of committees, joint committees, specialised working parties, etc. composed of representatives of labour and management. Some are directly provided for by the Treaty. . . . Still others were instituted in the course of integration to assist the Council and/or the Commission in carrying out their tasks' (Commission of the EC 1988).

Undoubtedly the most well-known consultative body of this type is the Economic and Social Committee (ESC), which was established under articles 193–8 of the EEC Treaty. It now has 222 members drawn from employers' organisations, unions and 'other interests' including farmers, small- and medium-sized businesses, consumers, the professions and so on, nominated by national governments. The ESC must normally be consulted when the Commission initiates a social policy measure, though its influence has tended to decline with direct elections to the European Parliament since 1979. Other consultative forums that should be noted include the six tripartite conferences that took place between 1970 and 1978 on mainly macroeconomic issues and the Standing Committee on Employment, an enduring legacy of the conferences. The Standing Committee on Employment brings together employers' organisations, unions, the Commission and the Council of Social and Labour Ministers, which presides. Since 1970 when it first met, the Committee discusses and helps to clarify labour market questions (for example, by advocating and defining the social dimension to accompany the completion of the Single European Market in 1992).

However, the role of these bodies, along with that of the many other *ad hoc* consultative forums set up over the years, has been constrained by their status within the EC's constitution as purely consultative forums for the social partners. And as we see below, other factors have also constrained the broader scope of the social dialogue. These include the uneven involvement and legitimacy of the social partners within the process and the great divergences between the industrial relations systems across the member states in relation to implementation of the terms of any joint Opinions or agreements that might be concluded at EC level. Taken together, these factors have ensured that EC 'social partnership' has traditionally had very little impact on the autonomy of member states, a situation that has only very recently begun to change with the evolution of an enhanced role for social dialogue.

This is because the constitutional setting for the social dialogue has changed dramatically since 1993, and steps have been taken to open up and democratise the role of the social partners concerned. Yet its impact on the member states will continue to depend on the most intractable constraint of all – enduring variations in the social and legal frameworks of industrial relations systems across the member states.

Intersectoral developments

So far, we have been reviewing the social dialogue in its broadest sense within the EC – the range of bodies designed to bring employers, unions and EC institutions together for the purposes of consultation, as well as the EC-level organisations through which national employers and unions channel their efforts. Now, however, we turn to the social dialogue in its narrower sense, as a specific process of consultation launched by Jacques Delors in January 1985. What objectives did the Commission hope to achieve? What results have there been? What impact have they had on the member states? And what of sector- and company-level social dialogue?

During the period 1980 to 1987, successive social and labour policy instruments proposed by the Commission were either blocked by the Council or else watered down. The reasons for this deadlock are complex, but include a general questioning of labour market regulation across a number of EC member states, notably in the UK (Hall 1994: 292). In response, attention came to focus on two principal remedies. The first was to extend qualified majority voting on the Council of Social and Labour Ministers to prevent the ability of just one country from blocking moves that had the support of the overwhelming majority of other member states (extensions of this kind were indeed subsequently achieved through both the Single European Act and the social protocol). The second remedy – which is of concern to us here – was to focus increasingly on non-legislative approaches to regulation, of the tripartite kind that already been tried and tested over the years. What they required, however, was a new impetus.

In 1982, a joint meeting of Finance and Social Affairs Ministers advocated 'close consultation' between the social partners in an attempt to improve the economic situation (Commission of the EC 1984: 9) whilst the social action programme adopted by the Council in June 1984 also stressed the need for social dialogue. The programme required the Commission to improve dialogue within the existing institutional framework and to 'work out appropriate methods for encouraging, whilst scrupulously respecting the autonomy of, and responsibilities peculiar to, the two sides of industry, the developments of joint relations at Community level' (Commission of the EC 1988: 110). This requirement was later written into article 118B of the EEC Treaty under amendments introduced through the Single European Act.

Jacques Delors, on his appointment as President of the Commission in January 1985, rapidly made the social dialogue one of his own personal projects. Indeed, in his first statement to the European Parliament, he drew attention to the 'need for a balance between justice and efficiency' and explicitly linked social dialogue with the process of negotiation, declaring:

> Let me then ask this: when will we see the first European collective bargaining agreement? I would insist on this point. A European collective agreement is not just an empty slogan. It would provide a dynamic framework, one that respected differing views – a spur to initiative, not a source of paralysing uniformity.
>
> (Delors 1985: 9)

Stage I

As a first step, Delors convened a series of informal meetings for EC-level employers' organisations and unions throughout most of 1985, culminating at a formal session at Val Duchesse – a palace just outside Brussels – on 12 November attended by representatives drawn from UNICE, CEEP, ETUC and the Commission. The parties adopted two joint declarations: one broadly supported the Commission's 'co-operative growth strategy for more employment' whilst the other, on the social dialogue and the new technologies, advocated the establishment of a working party to investigate the issues further.

The following spring, the Commission duly set up the two working parties, one to investigate implementation of the growth strategy and the second to cover new technology. They issued their first, non-binding Opinions in 1986 and 1987 respectively.

The European Council, meeting under the Belgian Presidency in May 1987, reaffirmed its commitment to the new social dialogue, and the working parties continued to meet throughout the following year, though no more Opinions were agreed.

One of the major problems over the social dialogue, which had been left unresolved, was its exact purpose. UNICE was prepared to discuss social and labour policy but was emphatically opposed to entering into any kind of binding agreement. It therefore insisted that the outcome of the two working parties should be known as 'Opinions' – that is, general statements which do not constrain the parties on either side. The ETUC, on the other hand, believed that these discussions could or would eventually lead to the conclusion of European-level agreements on selected issues. The Commission hoped that the process would at least define the contours of the social dialogue, not least in relation to which areas would, or would not, require legislation. As we have seen, Jacques Delors clearly also favoured the development of European-level collective bargaining.

This lack of clarity over objectives led a couple of commentators, writing in 1988, to maintain that the idea of a social dialogue as a cornerstone of the social dimension appeared to be 'in ruins', though they added that one tangible benefit of the process had been 'the restoration of good working relations between the social partners' (Brewster and Teague 1989: 97).

However, at the same time that confusion appeared to be damaging the social dialogue process, other developments were – at least in the eyes of the Commission – demonstrating its importance. The 1985 White Paper on completing the internal market (Commission of the EC 1985) led to the Single European Act which, coming into force in July 1987, was intended to provide the constitutional means for realising the '1992' programme. This included the promotion of the social dimension, both through the extension of qualified majority voting to matters concerning health and safety and working conditions (article 118A) but also through insertion of social dialogue as a specific responsibility of the Commission. Article 118B of the amended EEC Treaty runs: 'The Commission shall endeavour to develop the dialogue between management and labour at European level which could, if the two sides consider it desirable, lead to relations based on agreement.'

Furthermore, the Belgian Presidency, which in May 1987 had welcomed the social dialogue process, was also laying the foundations for the Social Charter. The Social Charter, which was eventually adopted by all the member states except the UK at the Strasbourg Summit in December 1989, and its accompanying social action programme were the results of pressure from the legislative side, but the Commission was aware that, with the legislative deadlock already alluded to, a voluntaristic approach was equally important if it was to achieve its objectives. Indeed, the social dialogue can be seen very much as a 'twin track' approach to social policy running alongside the legislative one. For this reason, article 12 of the Social Charter states: 'The dialogue between the two sides of industry at European level which must be developed may, if the parties deem it desirable, result in contractual relations in particular at inter-occupational and sectoral level.'

Stage II

In this general context, Jacques Delors believed that the restoration of good working relations between the social partners resulting from Stage I of the social dialogue should serve as the basis for a relaunch. Indeed, the relaunch of the social dialogue took place on 12 January 1989, timed to coincide with the beginning of the new Commission's term of office.

This time, a more formal structure was adopted, with the creation of a steering committee consisting of representatives of UNICE, CEEP, ETUC, the Commission and certain other EC institutions designed to ensure progress in the social dialogue. One of its tasks was to monitor achievements in the priority areas, which included education and training and problems surrounding the evolution of a European labour market. The Commission also committed itself to publishing an Annual Report on employment within the EC which would first be discussed within the social dialogue process prior to submission to the Standing Committee on Employment (the first was duly submitted in July 1989). In addition, the range of issues covered by the social dialogue was broadened to include the allocation of structural aid programmes in individual member states and – most notably – consultation over the contents of the Social Charter and the draft European Company Statute (published in August 1989).

So the 1989 relaunch appeared to strengthen both the form and content of the social dialogue. In due course, both the revamped working parties, which focused on education and training and labour market issues, delivered a series of Opinions covering questions like access to training and the formation of a European geographical and occupational mobility area.

Yet despite all this activity, there was some criticism of its lack of impact on the behaviour of the social partners and member states. Commenting in 1990, the European Trade Union Institute (ETUI) declared that at this pan-European or intersectoral level the social dialogue had 'so far achieved too few tangible results' (European Trade Union Institute 1990: 51). Fundamental disagreements persisted over its aims and objectives, and it was clear that the more recent Opinions reflected no movement towards the kind of agreement advocated by the ETUC. Yet the ETUI continued to maintain that: 'The social dialogue between the inter-occupational federations and at sectoral level could represent an important means of further developing the social system of Europe', adding that a prerequisite for such a dialogue was 'a change in the negative attitude adopted by UNICE . . . with regard to the conclusion of European agreements' (European Trade Union Institute 1990: 51). And changes were indeed shortly to take place.

The breakthrough in this respect came in the context of the Inter-governmental Conferences held throughout 1991 prior to the European Council which took place that December in Maastricht. UNICE had become increasingly concerned at the prospect of amendments to the EEC Treaty that would further extend qualified majority voting and allow (what it saw as) the imposition of statutory European works councils on multinational companies operating across the member states. For defensive reasons therefore, and under pressure from the Belgian, French and Italian employers' organisations, UNICE sought to negotiate a compromise that would permit it to influence or delay EC-level social policy through framework agreements. This was because it believed that compliance with such agreements at national level would provide greater flexibility and room for manoeuvre than compliance with binding directives (Hall 1994: 300).

On 31 October 1991, UNICE, CEEP and ETUC duly agreed to a series of proposals for amending the existing provisions of the EEC Treaty. These proposals later formed the social chapter, which was subsequently downgraded to become the social protocol which itself came into force on 1 November 1993 along with the Treaty on European Union. Articles 3 and 4 of the social protocol deserve special mention.

Article 3 focuses on the promotion by the Commission of 'consultation of management and labour at Community level'. The Commission is required to consult the social partners 'before submitting proposals in the social field' and again on the proposal itself once formulated. Even more significantly, the social partners are granted the right to inform the Commission that they wish to negotiate an agreement on the area covered by the proposal, normally within a nine-month period (which is extendable), thereby shortcircuiting the need for immediate legislation.

Meanwhile, article 4 fosters 'contractual relations including agreements' at EC level. It lays down that agreements should be implemented: *either* 'in accordance with the procedures and practices specific to management and labour in the member states' (for example, through further negotiation on the details at sector or company level); *or* through the Council to which it grants powers to issue binding decisions enforcing such agreements provided that such a move has been requested by the signatories.

Such an article could clearly have a major impact on the conduct of industrial relations across the member states, but it also raises many difficult questions, including how the decisions themselves could be enforced in the context of such widely varying systems of collective bargaining across the member states. For example, to which parties would the decisions be addressed? Would the agreements negotiated within their framework cover all workers? And for what duration? These questions are examined in greater detail below, but in any event the first proposal to be tested under this procedure – for European works councils – did not reach a stage that required any answers.

In October 1993, Padraig Flynn – the Commissioner responsible for social and labour policy since the previous January – launched an appeal for negotiations between the social partners on European works councils to begin as soon as possible under the terms of the social protocol. He stressed the need to have a 'new consensus in Europe on how to make the many changes we know are coming', towards which purpose 'a climate of mutual confidence between the social partners would contribute enormously' (Agence Europe 1993: 7). In the event, negotiations eventually collapsed, and the Directive was adopted by the Council of Ministers in September 1994 under the 'opt-out' procedures that then exempted the UK (Gold and Hall 1994).

Nevertheless, the impetus behind the social dialogue continued to build up.

115

The Commission's Green Paper – its consultative document on the future of European social policy (Commission of the EC 1993) – contained a section entitled 'Reinforcing the Social Dialogue' and subsequently, in December, the Commission adopted the text of a communication outlining its understanding of the practical implications of the social protocol and its accompanying agreement on social policy. It emphasised that the social partners had the right to consultation both on the direction of Community social policy and on its content. These points were later consolidated in the White Paper on social policy published in July 1994 (Commission of the EC 1994a and 1994b).

With such a level of expectations aroused, it then became only a matter of time before an agreement was signed. The issue selected for this purpose was parental leave, on which the Commission had been attempting to legislate since 1983. After five months of negotiations, ETUC, CEEP and UNICE concluded a framework agreement on parental leave on 14 December 1995. It set out minimum requirements and provisions for parental leave with article 1.9 referring it back 'to member states and social partners for the establishment of the conditions for access and modalities of application in order to take account of the situation in each member state' (*European Industrial Relations Review* 1996b: 35). The social partners then submitted the text to the Commission, which later published its draft directive on parental leave that was subsequently adopted by the Council on 3 June 1996. The directive left the terms of the framework agreement intact and applied across all the EC member states except the UK (which was then still subject to the opt-out).

The agreement and accompanying directive mark a major advance for the social dialogue not least because they have demonstrated the willingness of both sides of industry to adopt a legislative model at EC level that transcends existing national systems. The model adopted is loosely derived from Belgian practice where national intersectoral agreements concluded on the bipartite National Labour Council form the basis for subsequent negotiations at sector level which may then be rendered legally binding (Vilrokx and Van Leemput 1992: 374, 377–9).

Major questions are raised in the process, however. First, the social partners had not voluntarily chosen to negotiate an agreement on parental leave, since the subject had been selected for them by the Commission. It might be claimed that, in such circumstances, employers are brought to the bargaining table more by a negative concern to avoid legislation than by a positive concern to negotiate an agreement (certainly a major factor, as we have seen, in explaining UNICE's change of heart over negotiating the social chapter/protocol).

Second, the implications for member states are also highly contentious. On the one hand, the use of the social dialogue to generate directives has arguably conferred a greater deal of openness on the EC legislative process than had been achieved before. It is, after all, appropriate to involve the social partners centrally in negotiating workplace regulations since they bear greater direct responsibility than governments in carrying them out and ensuring their enforcement. On the other hand, the Economic and Social Committee and the European Parliament have had no democratic input into the process at all. Transposition of the directive into national legislation required, as appropriate, new legislation across the fourteen member states affected 'basically at the behest of the three social partners. The term "corporatism" inevitably raises its head' (*European Industrial Relations Review* 1996c: 23). There are, of course, counterarguments: the terms of the social protocol were themselves agreed democratically by the member states which, acting on the Council, had the right either to adopt or reject the directive. Nevertheless, through the social dialogue the role of the social partners has now been dramatically enhanced in relation to national governments and some of the further questions raised – such as the degree of their own legitimacy – will be analysed below.

Sectoral developments

Progress, though less striking, has also been made at EC sector level. In a number of industries joint declarations have been concluded by employers' organisations and unions in areas of mutual interest.

Sectoral social dialogue, in its broad sense, has taken place since the 1950s on formal joint committees within the EC institutions covering areas like coal and steel (1955), agriculture (1963) and road transport (1965), amongst others. Results include two recommendations on working time for agricultural workers adopted by employers and unions in 1978 and 1980. Many of these committees fell into disuse as a result of employer resistance and problems ensuing from enlargement of the EC. Greatest success, however, occurred where the EC had formulated an integrated policy for a sector such as in agriculture and fisheries and then later in transport, where joint committees were set up in inland navigation in 1980 and railways in 1984. A specialist unit to promote sectoral social dialogue was set up in Directorate General V of the Commission in 1990 (unit A/2).

Since 1988 joint declarations or guidelines have been agreed by the social partners across a range of sectors at European level. These include: retailing (1988); construction (1990); rail transport and energy supply (1990); woodworking (1994); industrial cleaning (1994); commerce (1995); hotels and catering (1995); and even local and regional government (1995) (*European Industrial Relations Review* 1997: 24–9).

These joint declarations generally focus on 'win/win' issues like vocational training (retailing, construction, rail transport/energy supply, cleaning), health and safety (construction) and violence at the workplace (commerce). Some cover more controversial issues, such as working time (cleaning) and labour flexibility (hotels and catering). The memorandum of understanding in woodworking forms the basis for further structured social dialogue on all topics except pay and pay-related topics.

Company-level developments

However, it is at the level of individual multinationals that there has been the greatest and most remarkable movement towards EC-level agreements. These have focused on the formation of information and consultation arrangements at group level within multinationals.

Voluntary arrangements

This process had been underway for some years. Indeed, many of the international trade secretariats have established world company councils designed to monitor the operations of selected multinationals worldwide. The International Metalworkers' Federation, for example, set up the earliest ones in 1966 to cover General Motors, Ford, Chrysler and Volkswagen/Daimler Benz, and by now there are several dozen more in existence (Rehfeldt 1992: 51).

However, the creation of the Single European Market and the progressive Europeanisation of company-level operations gave a significant impetus to these developments, and induced a number of multinationals in the mid-1980s to recognise European works councils (EWCs) or rather less formal arrangements at their centre. The earliest examples were located principally in French multinationals, such as Thomson, Bull and BSN (Northrup *et al.* 1988), but by September 1994 – when the European works councils directive was adopted by the Council – there were already at least thirty-five voluntary agreements in place, including some in household-name companies like Grundig, Renault, United Biscuits and Volkswagen (Bonneton 1994).

The great majority of these pre-directive EWCs were based on written agreement between management and employees' representatives but some had been established less formally, for example on an exchange of letters or unilateral management initiative.

Companies across several member states were involved, covering a wide range of sectors (including aerospace, chemicals, insurance, information technology, metalworking, motor manufacturing and so on). Despite the variations in circumstances, a basic framework emerged which was to serve as a model for EWCs in the directive itself: joint meetings, between European-level directors and works councillors/trade unionists drawn from the various European countries where the company has subsidiaries, are held normally once a year to discuss group-level issues. These meetings are informational in character, and generally have rights neither to consultation nor negotiation (Hall *et al.* 1995: chap. 4).

Management, for its part, has cited a series of benefits from such meetings, including the chance to explain corporate strategy and company restructuring, whilst employee representatives find that they can improve their own international contacts and gather information direct from head office (Gold and Hall 1992: 47–51). The scale of this activity has been substantially boosted by the provision of some 79 million ECU (approx. £66 million) through the Commission to help fund transnational meetings of employee and employer representatives over the five years 1992/96 inclusive.

Research reveals that these developments did not begin in random companies. The earliest cases were in the French nationalised sector, encouraged through the active involvement of the then Socialist government, but it is now clear that these factors were irrelevant to their far wider subsequent evolution in the private sector across other countries. According to Marginson (1991):

> Management–trade union relations are more likely to emerge where companies have a single management structure within Europe; have not engaged in a rapid wave of recent acquisitions; produce similar products and services in different locations or integrate production across locations; where unions are able to create an encompassing organisation covering all affiliates in an enterprise; where enterprise organisation already exists at national level; and where significant groups within the workforce are potentially mobile across borders.

This analysis, which has since been further developed (Marginson 1992; Marginson and Sisson 1994), suggests that strong structural pressures had been mounting behind the extension of these arrangements, though not evenly across all kinds of company structure. Conglomerate multinationals, for example, fall well outside the 'ideal type' profile outlined by Marginson above.

European works councils directive

Since the adoption of the EWC directive in September 1994, an additional factor has played a major part in promoting the recent growth of European works councils: article 13 of the directive itself. The directive is not a focus for this chapter since it is a legislative measure and not – as events transpired – the result of the social dialogue. Nevertheless, the directive, which had to be transposed into national legislation by September 1996 across all member states of the European Economic Area (excluding the UK), exempted from its terms any *existing* European works council voluntarily agreed by that date, provided that it covered the entire workforce and allowed for transnational information and consultation of employees on group-level issues. The flexibility permitted under this provision, contained in article 13, prompted growing numbers of companies to take advantage. Some UK companies, for example, found it easier and more acceptable to integrate their UK employees into the arrangements by voluntary agreement than by waiting to negotiate them under the framework of the directive as transposed into the legislation of another member state that excluded UK employees from involvement owing to the UK opt-out. A notable company in this category is National Westminster, which signed an agreement setting up its worldwide NatWest Group Staff Council with the unions in January 1996. Other UK companies with EWC-type agreements include BOC, BT, Coats Viyella, Courtaulds Textiles, Pearson, United Biscuits and Zeneca.

Indeed, an initial overview of article 13 agreements conducted after the September 1996 deadline listed 173 companies, of which 29 (16.8 per cent) were UK-based. However, total confirmed figures are likely to be much higher, possibly around the 250 mark (*European Works Councils Bulletin* 1996b: 11).

These developments clearly illustrate the limitations of the UK opt-out from EC social and labour policy under the social protocol. Whilst it may have proved possible through the opt-out for the UK government to avoid the impact of *legislation* resulting from the transposition of a directive on some employment matter (such as parental leave), UK employers are inevitably drawn into any issue – procedural or substantive – where such innovations are freely supported, negotiated and implemented by the social partners themselves.

With the EWC directive now in force – and eligible companies without voluntary arrangements consequently required to negotiate an EWC or information and consultation procedure on request – opinions vary over the number of companies that might be affected. The TUC estimates that it covers 1,234 multinational companies employing some 15 million workers across the European Economic Area (Trades Union Congress 1995: 59), whilst the ETUI has listed 1,152 companies with headquarters based across 25 countries worldwide. Of these, 274 companies are based in Germany, 187 in the USA, 122 in France and 106 in the UK (European Trade Union Institute 1995). The UK companies are covered as they have sufficient employees in other member states to trigger the required thresholds despite the opt-out.

Under the terms of the directive, such companies must delegate responsibility for negotiating a European works council to one of their subsidiaries elsewhere in the EEA. That also helps to explain why an increasing number of UK employers, though not necessarily convinced of the merits of EWCs, sought to retain control of developments by establishing UK-based arrangements in advance of the directive. The decision of the Labour government, elected in May 1997, to 'sign the social chapter' will now dramatically increase the number of UK companies involved. The TUC which had estimated that 113 UK companies with 1.4 million employees in the UK would be covered under the opt-out, now adds a further 127, with 800,000 UK employees, once the social chapter has been signed (that is, a total of 240 UK companies with 2.2 million employees) (*European Works Councils Bulletin* 1996c: 1–2). The CBI, by contrast, is less conservative, calculating that 160 UK-based companies were covered under the opt-out, with up to an additional 200 once the social chapter were signed – a total of 360 (Confederation of British Industry 1996: 1).

Prospects for social dialogue

This overview of social dialogue leads to a consideration of its prospects as a regulatory measure. We have already acknowledged the constitutional limitations of bodies like the Economic and Social Committee that restrict its competence broadly to consultative status. However, the Maastricht Treaty accorded a more central, dynamic role to the Delors-inspired intersectoral and sectoral social dialogue and we now turn to examine the constraints on its further development.

Representational status of the parties

One serious constraint on the development of EC social dialogue is the degree to which the organisations of the social partners involved enjoy genuinely representational status, and hence legitimacy, in the eyes of their members and other social agencies.

Broadly speaking, the contours of employers' organisations and union structures at European level are familiar enough. As noted above, there are separate employers' organisations for the private, public and agricultural sectors (UNICE, CEEP and COPA respectively) whilst on the union side most national union confederations affiliate to the ETUC, which also recognises a number of European Industry Committees (for all the main sectors like metalworking, food, chemicals, education and so on).

However, in no sense do employers' and union organisations mirror one another at this level. There are, for example, a number of significant contrasts between UNICE and ETUC. Firstly, there are numerous organisations at EC level that represent business and industry, such as the European Round Table, the American Chamber of Commerce EC Committee, the European Community Services Group and the UEAPME, which represents the interests of small- and medium-sized companies. However, the ETUC is effectively the sole body representing the European labour movement (though not professional and managerial employees or CGT, the French Communist-oriented union confederation which still remains outside its sphere). Secondly, the relationship between the EC and UNICE on the one hand and the ETUC on the other is quite distinct. The ETUC is funded in part by the EC and operates its own research arm, the European Trade Union Institute (ETUI) and other specialist bodies on training and health and safety as well as its own College. In addition, within Directorate-General X a separate department is responsible for trade union affairs. UNICE does not possess such research facilities, nor does it benefit from such a close relationship with the Commission, though the new European Centre for Industrial Relations in Florence is jointly run by UNICE, CEEP and ETUC. Finally, the ETUC recognises and acts on behalf of fifteen European Industry Committees (which group sector-level unions across Europe), but European-level employers' sectoral organisations do not belong to UNICE. Larger sectoral organisations, such as CEFIC (chemicals) or CEDC (retail), make their own representations as appropriate, but usually follow the lead of UNICE because they are primarily trade or industry associations.

This lack of structural 'fit' at EC level has provoked a crisis of legitimacy which will undoubtedly worsen unless addressed. The Commission recognises

UNICE, CEEP and ETUC as 'social partners' but both UEAPME, on behalf of small- and medium-sized enterprises and CEC, on behalf of professional and managerial employees, have protested against their exclusion from the social dialogue. Furthermore, they announced in consequence that they were not bound by the terms of the framework agreement on parental leave, whilst EuroCommerce, for businesses in the European commercial sector, does not feel represented by UNICE and labelled the agreement 'undemocratic' (*European Industrial Relations Review* 1996a: 4). Indeed, UEAPME submitted a petition in September 1996 to the European Court of Justice seeking an annulment of the subsequent directive on parental leave on the grounds that it was 'systematically disregarded' at all stages of consultation under the social policy agreement (*European Industrial Relations Review* 1996d: 3). The progress of social dialogue is bound to be held up until such basic questions of legitimacy are resolved. To assist, the Commission published in 1996 a communication on the development of social dialogue at Community level. It believes that the question of 'representativeness' must be determined on a case-by-case basis and calls on the social partners to propose solutions (*European Industrial Relations Review* 1997: 29).

Implementation and enforceability

As we have seen, article 4 of the social protocol outlines two ways in which EC-level agreements could be implemented and enforced. The first is 'in accordance with the procedures and practices specific to management and labour and the member states'. The second – which is restricted under article 2 to certain areas like health and safety, information and consultation and equal opportunities – is through a Council decision on a proposal from the Commission, by request from the signatory parties. Parental leave was the first topic to be dealt with under this procedure and the second was part-time work, the subject of a framework agreement signed in June 1997 by UNICE, CEEP and ETUC.

However, these procedures raise a series of questions that have been concisely summarised by Hepple (1993: 26–31). First, member states are under no *obligation* to ensure the implementation of EC-level agreements. The Declaration on article 4(2) of the social protocol declares that member states are under 'no obligation ... to apply the agreements directly or to work out rules for their transposition, nor any obligation to amend national legislation in force to facilitate their implementation'. Clearly such an agreement – unlike a directive – cannot be relied on to guarantee minimum standards across the EC, even though the legal status of the Declaration appears to be unclear.

Second, there is a wide divergence between member states in relation to the nature of collective bargaining structures and the means to make them generally binding across a given sector. In Belgium and the Netherlands, for example, national procedures exist for the negotiation of national, intersectoral collective agreements that may then be proclaimed generally binding by due process of law. By contrast, in France, Germany, Spain, Portugal and Greece such a centralised approach is not the practice. Agreements in those countries are generally concluded at sector level and extension procedures (sometimes known as *erga omnes*) may be invoked through the Ministry of Labour to ensure their application to non-organised employers and employees throughout a given bargaining unit (the conditions for extension naturally also vary from country to country). In Italy there is also sector-level bargaining, but extension procedures are likely to be considered unconstitutional (Treu 1991: 95–6). And unlike their Danish counterparts, Irish unions and employers have little influence over their members who fail to comply with agreements. This is the situation also in the UK, where provision for the extension of collective agreements under Schedule 11 of the 1975 Employment Protection Act was abolished by the 1980 Employment Act (Salamon 1987: 377).

Weiss, too, in a more general discussion on the problems facing the development of EC-wide collective bargaining, refers to similar impediments. There is, for example, wide diversity between the states over the subjects that can be negotiated and the criteria for establishing the representativeness of the domestic negotiating partners. Differences also exist between states over the legal regulation of strikes and lock-outs as well as implementation of the terms of agreements, such as recourse to labour courts and the *erga omnes* aspects referred to above. These factors, amongst others, 'show clearly that there is no homogeneous legal pattern of collective bargaining and collective agreement throughout the Community' (Weiss 1991: 64).

Third, there are further problems involved if the parties requested the Commission to submit their agreement to the Council for implementation through a decision. The subjects are restricted by article 2 of the social protocol and it may prove difficult to 'squeeze framework agreements, intended to lay down principles or minimum standards for the whole Community or a particular sector into the mould of an EC "decision" in this limited sense' (Hepple 1993: 31). Interestingly, Hepple also queries whether the term 'decision' is used in the strict legal sense defined in article 189 of the EEC Treaty and suggests that the Council could decide on any appropriate means to enforce an EC-level agreement, including a directive (Hepple 1993: 31). Events have proved him correct: the Commission did indeed choose the means of a directive to implement the terms of the framework agreement on parental leave.

Social dialogue and collective bargaining

So far, in analysing developments within the social dialogue, we have been, in effect, focusing principally on developments within the process of information disclosure and consultation at European level. We turn now to the prospects for collective bargaining at European level (though many of the basic issues relating to representation and implementation are similar). Much has been written on this subject over the last twenty years or so (for example, International Labour Organisation 1973; Roberts 1973; Blanpain et al. 1979), and first we have to be clear about what is meant by the term 'collective bargaining at the European level'.

Broadly, it can refer to two quite distinct processes (Trades Union Congress 1992). The first is the process through which the results of collective bargaining in other member states are brought to bear on domestic negotiations at intersectoral, sectoral or company level (so, for example, unions may prepare demands based on best terms and conditions across other member states, whilst employers may counter by comparing relevant international productivity indicators). The second is the process through which employers' organisations and unions actually conduct negotiations face to face at European level in an attempt to conclude binding agreements.

These agreements may themselves be of two sorts: procedural and substantive. For a procedural agreement employers and unions negotiate 'an operational mechanism which details and regulates the manner in which a specified issue is to be handled' (Salamon 1987: 387). To this extent, a number of such agreements have already been concluded at European level. We have already observed, for example, that the social chapter itself – subsequently the social protocol – was the result of negotiations between ETUC, UNICE and CEEP which concluded in October 1991, a few weeks before the Maastricht Summit. At sectoral level, procedures relating to training and other issues have been agreed whilst, most notably, some 250 multinational companies have already established European works councils in some form or other, mostly following detailed negotiations.

Substantive agreements, by contrast, refer 'to those terms of employment, such as wages, hours, holidays, etc. which can be converted into monetary terms' (Salamon 1987: 289–90). At intersectoral level, the framework agreement on parental leave and the agreement on part-time work are so far the only examples. There are very few substantive agreements at European sectoral level, whilst the case of Danone is significant at company level. In April 1996, this French multinational signed an agreement with the unions for a Joint Information and Consultation Committee, covering all its subsidiaries across Europe. Provision is made for this Committee to 'negotiate joint statements and measures, including with respect to employment, training, information, safety and working conditions, as well as to the exercise of trade union rights'. It has been commented that this experience is 'widely seen as the closest European works councils have yet come to some form of collective bargaining at European level' since the agreement is 'the first to accord an explicit negotiating role to the European works council' (*European Works Councils Bulletin* 1996a: 1).

Since procedural agreements already exist at EC level, what we need to establish here is whether EC-level collective agreements on *substantive* issues will just remain a vision, or whether they too could become a significant reality. Is the experience at Danone merely a blip, or could it represent the start of a more significant process? Some would argue, for example, that European Monetary Union, in making pay levels across the member states more transparent, could act as a catalyst for the gradual evolution of EC-wide agreements covering pay and other conditions.

The answer depends initially on the degree to which recognition rights are extended to unions and employee representatives to bargain collectively at EC intersectoral, sectoral or company level. This in turn assumes that the problems of representation, implementation and enforceability analysed above can be satisfactorily resolved and, indeed, that the unions themselves actually demand it (Marginson and Sisson 1994: 44–5). These points are well summarised by Weiss:

> The secret of the legitimacy of a collective agreement is the support it is given by the workers and employers, in whose name it is being concluded. This implies involvement which – at least until now – has not been reached for negotiations taking place at European level. In addition there is no doubt that the member organisations on both sides would hesitate very much to give a mandate for the conclusion of European collective agreements to their umbrella confederations at European level.
>
> (Weiss 1991: 65)

Developments at all three EC levels in relation to information disclosure, consultation and the negotiation of procedural agreements have been patchy and opportunistic, but that is scarcely surprising. The spread of recognition of employee representatives for these purposes over the last hundred years or so within any national economy has been equally patchy and opportunistic (see, for example, the chapters on various industrialised countries in Bamber and Lansbury 1993).

So clearly, when we come to consider the development of EC-level collective bargaining we must bear in mind that it is not an all-or-nothing affair as is sometimes implied. Teague, for example, asks why European collective bargaining did not emerge during the evolution of the social dimension, with very little consideration for the stages through which it is likely to have to develop (1989: 95). Union recognition – the process by which management formally acknowledges the legitimacy of a union's right to determine jointly terms and conditions – is indeed 'perhaps the most important stage in the development of an organisation's industrial relations system' (Salamon 1987: 408). But it is important to take into account the fact that recognition too may proceed in stages: the literature identifies the right to representation, the right to consultation and the right to negotiation.

> First time recognition can take three forms: first, the right to representation, that is the right of the union to represent employees usually through union representatives on individual grievances at work; second, the right to consultation, that is the right of the union to be consulted on

non-negotiable matters; and third, the right to negotiation, that is the right to represent members fully both in procedural and in substantive matters such as pay and conditions.

(Farnham and Pimlott 1988: 347)

On this basis, we can appreciate that the central theme of the preceding sections on social dialogue has been to trace the progress made by unions to gain the initial stages of recognition at EC level. However, to be strictly accurate, we need to qualify the above quotation slightly to adapt it for EC-level purposes. The right to representation is perhaps best exemplified at EC level not through the right to represent employees in individual grievances (an illustration more appropriate to workplace recognition) but through the right to information – in other words, the right of unions at EC level to receive relevant information about events likely to affect their members across the member states and to represent their views accordingly in the light of it.

In addition, recognition is not static; once recognition has been granted by employers for certain defined purposes, it may become relatively easier for its boundaries to be spread further. For this reason, the mere fact that social dialogue has taken place at all is an encouraging sign for those who believe that labour market regulation should proceed on a voluntary, flexible basis. The problems encountered so far, including employer resistance, inadequate structures, lack of resources and economic recession, are not different in kind from those encountered during the process of *national* recognition.

Developments so far are presented in table 7.1

Insofar as *representation* is concerned, we have covered intersectoral, sectoral

Table 7.1 Union recognition at EC level for purposes of social dialogue

LEVEL	Intersectoral	Sectoral	Company
STAGE			
Representation	conceded	conceded	growing rapidly
Consultation	limited	limited	limited
Negotiation			
i)Procedural agreements	Procedural agreement October 1991 (Now enshrined in social protocol)	limited but growing	growing
ii)Substantive agreements	Framework agreement on parental leave, 1995 (now a directive)	limited	potential through EWCs
	Framework agreement on part-time work, 1997		

and company levels in preceding sections. The ETUC represents the views of its affiliated unions – a total of some 45 million employees – in relation to UNICE and CEEP on a variety of issues in a variety of forums, including the Standing Committee on Employment and the social dialogue steering committee and working parties. National union confederations, like the TUC, are represented on the Economic and Social Committee. In addition, there are around 250 multinationals in which works councils or unions, through some form of European works councils arrangement, are recognised for the purposes of information disclosure, and this figure is growing rapidly.

Consultation is considerably more limited, though the Economic and Social Committee is consultative and the relaunched social dialogue – particularly through the provision of working parties on key issues – promotes the exchange of views between the social partners. At company level, however, there is virtually no consultation yet, with only the agreements at Bull and Volkswagen having so far a consultative element. Yet it is also true that unions and employee representatives are keen to extend existing information rights to embrace consultation as well, as part of their strategy within multinationals.

Negotiation or *collective bargaining* remains, however, the most controversial area. Sectoral agreements have been concluded at European level covering, for example, training (rail transport and energy supply) and working time (cleaning), and formal information disclosure procedures have been established in numerous companies through EWCs.

Furthermore, there are now two agreements at intersectoral level on substantive matters, those on parental leave and part-time work. The most significant step prior to this was undoubtedly the agreement concluded in October 1991 by UNICE, CEEP and the ETUC on procedures to promote and enforce EC intersectoral and sectoral 'contractual relations' which subsequently formed the basis for the social protocol to the Treaty on European Union.

Unless recognition is granted – unless, that is, employers see recognition as serving their own longer term interests – it seems likely that the social dialogue will be generally restricted to little more than 'social monologue' on the side of the employee representatives. The nature and timing of recognition will themselves be moulded by deep-seated structural factors that must also be considered when weighing up future prospects for the social dialogue. Yet it must be stressed that over the last ten years major steps towards recognition at all levels have already been taken.

Future prospects for EC-level collective bargaining

The debate on the future of the social dialogue in general and EC-level collective bargaining in particular has tended to be couched very much in the style of 'on the one hand this, on the other hand that'. Optimists have tended to emphasise pressures towards the emergence of collective bargaining on the one hand, whilst the pessimists tend to emphasise the barriers on the other. Though an understanding of these pressures is, of course, important, analysis needs to focus more critically on the levels at which social dialogue is most likely to take place and the forms it could take.

Foremost amongst the optimists has been Peter Coldrick, who has argued that 'European collective bargaining will be here sooner than later' for three principal reasons (1990a). First, he points out that 'in some areas European industrial relations already exist'. He cites the social dialogue as an example, as well as the fact that large companies already follow the kinds of deals their competitors are reaching with their workforces. However, we have already analysed the limitations of the social dialogue, and European performance comparisons have been used by employers and unions for many years. Throughout the 1970s, for example, the Ford pay claim was drawn up on behalf of the Transport and General Workers' Union by the Trade Union Research Unit at Ruskin College, Oxford, making full use of relevant international comparisons (Gold *et al.* (1979): chap.1). And although European-level union campaigns for the 35-hour week, for example, adumbrate closer union cooperation, the success of the campaign, from the unions' point of view, still relies on national, not European, bargaining strengths. Secondly, Coldrick maintains that European legislation – such as the draft European company statute and the contents of social action programmes – will bring employers and workers together, especially at the company level. However, as we have seen, requirements to disclose information or even to consult do not necessarily lead to recognition for the purposes of collective bargaining on substantive issues. And thirdly, Coldrick believes that European Monetary Union (EMU) will not be realisable or sustainable unless collective bargaining becomes 'European'. Elsewhere, he argues that before long, 'everyone will be paid in ECUs instead of in DM or francs or pounds. Workers – and managers – are bound to make comparisons between what they are being paid and what similar people a few miles away across a frontier in another country are being paid' (Coldrick 1990b: 4). Such comparisons will, he claims, promote the Europeanisation of bargaining within countries, and then pave the way for European collective agreements within the larger multinationals under pressure from public authorities, both national and European, eager to make EMU a success.

This is, of course, a highly contentious view. Even if a common currency were in general use this does not, in itself, constitute a sufficient basis for the emergence of cross-border collective bargaining. Indeed, in the context of monetary union, opposite pressures might develop: since devaluation would no longer be possible as a way of combating inflation, greater flexibility and decentralisation in pay bargaining may be required to prevent loss of competitiveness and rising unemployment. Marsden argues that:

> the social partners and governments in member countries should concentrate on mobilising awareness of the constraints of the new macroeconomic environment and on developing national pay forums to

discuss pay in a wider economic context. They should also seek controlled decentralisation to company level, and should develop policies designed to weaken the linkages in wage structures and boost productivity.

(1992: 601)

The question then becomes not whether EMU will spawn European-level collective bargaining, but rather whether inflexible or overcentralised pay structures – characterised by wide variations in labour costs between the member states – may themselves undermine EMU. In other words, the development of EMU might have exactly the opposite effect to that envisaged by Coldrick. Far from promoting EC-level collective bargaining, EMU could well encourage the introduction of greater flexibility into pay structures of a kind required to reduce inflationary pressures across the member states.

However, whatever the eventual fate of EMU, Teague points to three sets of barriers that have already impeded the development of European-level collective bargaining: the economic recession, employers' opposition and trade union shortcomings (1989: 95). Economic recession has forced a defensive reaction on to the unions which have 'frequently' tried 'to persuade multinationals to transfer their closure programmes to another country' (1989: 96). Employers' resistance, as articulated through UNICE, has focused on the possible loss of competitiveness which could result from European-level collective bargaining. And organisational and political shortcomings on the part of the unions, as well as lack of resources, have also hampered moves in this direction. In this respect, improvements have resulted in the 1990s from the financial support granted by the Commission to help unions meet and develop joint policies for the purpose of setting up European works councils.

Teague distinguishes between 'maximalist' and 'minimalist' views of the social dimension. Broadly speaking, these contrast such 'co-operationist' views as expressed by Coldrick on the one hand with the deregulatory views as expressed by UNICE on the other. He concludes: 'since the gap between these two models is so wide it is hard to see how a compromise solution can emerge' (1989: 113).

One possible result would be consolidation of a 'two-speed' Europe with the fifteen existing members pursuing a redefined maximalist strategy but new members, in the context of enlargement into eastern Europe, pursuing a minimalist line. But even so, the maximalist strategy is itself undergoing redefinition under pressure from serious levels of unemployment – acknowledged by all the EC institutions and member states – and the Labour government's indication that it will continue to cast a sceptical eye on further regulation of the employment market. Signing the social chapter clearly does not imply wholehearted endorsement of maximalism. In any case, further major practical problems remain for the UK, not least because of the wide divergences between its own voluntaristic system of industrial relations and the more prescriptive, regulatory-based systems in most of the other member states. These divergences – if left untouched – would continue to impede the chances of an even-handed implementation of EC-level collective agreements across all member states. Finally, it may be that the emphasis on even-handedness is misplaced. In their recent analysis of framework agreements, joint opinions and the diffusion of 'best practice: at EC level, Marginson and Sisson (1996:20) suggest that these looser arrangements are more appropriate in a rapidly changing environment. If so, the gap between maximalist and minimalist views of the social dimension becomes less problematic.

Conclusions

It is quite clear then that there will be no sudden breakthrough into European-level collective bargaining like a kind of industrial relations 'big bang'. It is more likely that information disclosure, consultation and negotiation will evolve in an opportunistic way, within the context of an eventual EMU, whenever they favour the mutual interests of the parties. Indeed, this is how they evolved in domestic settings throughout the last 150 years or so, as unions across Europe gradually established recognition for a variety of purposes.

In this respect, some likely spheres of development can be identified:

- Article 118B of the EEC Treaty gives a clear legal base for the Commission's endeavours in this area, to which articles 3 and 4 of the social protocol lend further support. If the political will exists, then we might expect over time that the various obstacles to more intensive use of social dialogue may be gradually overcome, especially given a more sympathetic attitude adopted by the UK government.
- The social dialogue process will continue at intersectoral and sectoral levels, and further framework agreements in areas like sexual harassment at work may well be concluded. Nevertheless, their implementation and enforcement will remain highly problematic.
- At multinational company level, the establishment of information/consultation arrangements will accelerate under pressure from the Directive on European works councils. It is perhaps at this level that the mutual benefits are easiest to perceive as companies, faced by the challenges of the single European market and the need to restructure and remain competitive, find it expedient to explain their strategies in European-level forums.
- The principal level for determining pay and conditions will remain for the time being the individual profit-centre within the company or, where unions are recognised, the relevant bargaining unit.

So whilst there are identifiable pressures within the EC to maintain the interest of both social partners in the social dialogue at all levels, the emergence of a genuine EC-level industrial relations area characterised by common information, consultation and negotiating procedures will be a slow and opportunistic process.

Notes

1   I should like to thank Duncan Matthews and David Mayes for their comments on a much earlier draft of this chapter which was published as a working paper by the National Institute of Economic and Social Research. I should also like to thank the editors of this book for their helpful suggestions on refining and improving this version.

2   The term 'European Community' is used throughout this chapter except in relation to specific references to the Treaty on European Union (the Maastricht Treaty).

References

Agence Europe (1993) 'Mr Flynn invites social partners to begin negotiations immediately on European works councils – UNICE willing?', 15 October

Bamber, G.J. and Lansbury, R.D. (1993) *International and Comparative Industrial Relations*, London: Routledge

Blanpain, R. *et al.* (1979) *Relations between Management of Transnational Enterprises and Employee Representatives in Certain Countries of the European Community*, International Institute for Labour Studies Research Series No. 51, Geneva: International Labour Organisation

Bonneton, P. (ed.) (1994) *Voluntary Agreements on Information and Consultation in European Multinationals*, Working Paper No. WP/94/50/EN, Dublin: European Foundation for the Improvement of Living and Working Conditions

Brewster, C. and Teague, P. (1989) *European Community Social Policy*, London: Institute of Personnel Management

Bulmer, S., George, S. and Scott, A. (eds) (1992) The *United Kingdom and EC Membership Evaluated*, London: Pinter

Carley, M. (1993) 'Social Dialogue' in Gold, M. (ed.) (1993), pp. 105–134

Coldrick, P. (1990a) 'Collective Bargaining in the New Europe', *Personnel Management*, October, pp. 58–61

——— (1990b) *Project 1992. EMU and European Collective Bargaining*, November, Brussels: ETUC

Commission of the EC (1984) *Social Europe*, No. 2, Brussels

——— (1985) *Completing the Internal Market*, COM(85)310 Final, June, Brussels

——— (1988) *The Social Dimension of the Internal Market*, special issue of *Social Europe*, Brussels

——— (1993) *European Social Policy: Options for the Union (Green Paper)*, Communication by Mr Flynn, COM(93)551, 17 November, Brussels

——— (1994a) *European Social Policy – A Way Forward for the Union. A White Paper*, COM(94) 333 Final, 27 July, Brussels

——— (1994b) *White Paper on European Social Policy – Key Proposals*, Memo 94/55, 27 July, Brussels

Confederation of British Industry (1996) 'An Informed Choice – the European Works Councils Directive', *Human Resources Brief*, July

Delors, J. (1985) 'The Thrust of Commission Policy', Statement to the European Parliament, Strasbourg (14/15 January), *Bulletin of the European Communities'* Supplement No. 1

Due, J., Madsen, J.S. and Jensen, C.S. (1991) 'The Social Dimension: Convergence or Diversification of Industrial Relations in the Single European Market?', *Industrial Relations Journal*, summer

European Industrial Relations Review (1996a) '"Outsider" organisations dispute partners' parental leave deal', No. 264, January, p. 4

—— (1996b) 'Framework Agreement on Parental Leave', No. 264, January, pp. 35–36

—— (1996c) 'Into the unknown: implementing the parental leave directive', No. 267, April, pp. 19–23

—— (1996d) 'UEAPME challenges parental leave directive', No. 274, November, p. 3

—— (1997) 'Commission sets out options for the future of social dialogue', No. 276, January, pp. 24–9

European Trade Union Institute (1990) *The Centenary of May Day: Portrait of the European Trade Union Confederation*, Brussels

—— (1995) *European Works Councils: Inventory of Affected Companies*, Brussels

European Works Councils Bulletin (1996a) 'Danone EWC's negotiating role confirmed', No. 2, March/April

—— (1996b) 'Voluntary EWCs – the final picture', No. 5, September/October, pp. 11–15

—— (1996c) 'UK "opt-in" would extend Directive to 127 new UK companies', No. 6, November/December, pp. 1–2

Farnham, D. and Pimlott, J. (1988) *Understanding Industrial Relations*, London: Cassell

Ferner, A. and Hyman, R. (eds) (1992a) *Industrial Relations in the New Europe*, Oxford: Blackwell

—— (1992b) 'Industrial Relations in the New Europe: Seventeen Types of Ambiguity' in Ferner, A. and Hyman, R. (eds) (1992), pp. xvi–xlix

Gold, M. (ed.) (1993) *The Social Dimension: Employment Policy in the European Community*, Basingstoke: Macmillan

Gold, M. and Hall, M. (1992) *Report on European-level Information and Consultation in Multinational Companies -an Evaluation of Practice*, Dublin: European Foundation

Gold, M. and Hall, M. (1994) 'Statutory European Works Councils: the Final Countdown?' *Industrial Relations Journal*, September, Vol. 25, No. 3, pp. 177–86

Gold, M., Levie, H. and Moore, R. (1979) *The Shop Steward's Guide to the Use of Company Information*, Nottingham: Spokesman Books

Gold, M. and Matthews, D. (1996) *The Implications of the Evolution of European Integration for UK Labour Markets*, Research Series No. 73, March, London: Department for Education and Employment

Hall, M. (1994) 'Industrial Relations and the Social Dimension of European Integration: Before and After Maastricht', in Hyman, R. and Ferner, A. (eds) (1994), pp. 281–311

Hall, M., Carley, M., Gold, M., Marginson, P. and Sisson, K. (1995) *European Works Councils – Planning for the Directive*, London: Eclipse/Coventry: IRRU, University of Warwick

Hepple, B. (1993) *European Social Dialogue – Alibi or Opportunity?*, August, London: Institute of Employment Rights

Hyman, R. and Ferner, A. (eds) (1994) *New Frontiers in European Industrial Relations*, Oxford: Blackwell

International Labour Organisation (1973) *Multinational Enterprises and Social Policy*, Geneva

Marginson, P. (1991) 'Bargaining in ECUs? European Integration and Transnational Management-Union Relations in the Enterprise'. Paper for the International Industrial Relations Association European Regional Congress, Bari (23–25 September 1991)

—— (1992) 'European Integration and Transnational Management-Union Relations in the Enterprise', *British Journal of Industrial Relations*, 30, pp. 529–45

Marginson, P. and Sisson, K. (1994) 'The Structure of Transnational Capital in Europe: the Emerging Eurocompany and its Implications for Industrial Relations', in Hyman, R. and Ferner, A. (eds) (1994), pp. 15–51

—— (1996) *European Collective Bargaining: A Virtual Prospect?*, Brussels: European Trade Union Institute

Marsden, D. (1992) 'Incomes Policy for Europe? or Will Pay Bargaining Destroy the Single European Market?', *British Journal of Industrial Relations*, 30, pp. 587–604

Nielsen, R. and Szyszczak, E. (1991) *The Social Dimension of the European Community*, Copenhagen: Handelshojakolens Forlag

Northrup, H.R., Campbell, D.C. and Slowinski. B.J. (1988) 'Multinational Union-Management Consultation in Europe: Resurgence in the 1980s?', *International Labour Review*, 127, pp. 525–43

Rehfeldt, U. (1992) *L'expérience des comités de groupe européens*, February, Paris: CNRS

Roberts, B.C. (1973) 'Multinational Collective Bargaining: A European Prospect?', *British Journal of Industrial Relations*, 11, pp. 1-19

Salamon, M. (1987) *Industrial Relations: Theory and Practice*, Hemel Hempstead: Prentice Hall

Spicker, P. (1991) 'The Principle of Subsidiarity and the Social Policy of the EC', *Journal of European Social Policy*

Spyropoulos, G. (1990) 'Labour Law and Labour Relations in Tomorrow's Social Europe', *International Labour Review*

Spyropoulos, G. and Fragnière, G. (eds) (1991) *Work and Social Policies in the New Europe*, Brussels: European Interuniversity Press

Teague, P. (1989) *The European Community: the Social Dimension*, London: Kogan Page

Trades Union Congress (1992) 'The European Collective Bargaining Agenda', Workshop Paper presented by the Trades Union Congress to the TUC Conference, *After Maastricht – the Challenge of Social Europe*, 27 February, London

—— (1995) *European Works Councils*, London: TUC/Labour Research Department

Treu, T. (1991) *European Employment and Industrial Relations Glossary: Italy*, London: Sweet and Maxwell/Luxembourg: Office for Official Publications of the European Communities

Vilrokx, J. and Van Leemput, J. (1992) 'Belgium: A New Stability in Industrial Relations?' in Ferner, A. and Hyman, R. (eds) (1992a), pp. 357–92

Weiss, M. (1991) 'Social Dialogue and Collective Bargaining in the Framework of a Social Europe' in Spyropoulos, G. and Fragnière, G. (eds) (1991) pp. 59–75

8

THE EUROPEAN UNION AND WOMEN'S RIGHTS

From the Europeanisation of national agendas to the nationalisation of a European agenda?[1]

Sonia Mazey[2]

The introduction of equal opportunities legislation on behalf of working women throughout the European Community (EC) during the 1970s was a direct consequence of EC-level judicial and legislative activity. Whereas in other areas, discussed elsewhere in this volume, established, national policies have become progressively 'Europeanised', the EC was a major catalyst in the generation and extension of national sex equality laws to protect the rights of working women. In short, the EU delivered a 'shock' to national policy systems and helped to create a new policy area at the national level. The origins of these policies lie, however, in the activities of second-wave feminism during the late 1960s and early 1970s. Feminist ideas, values and policy demands constituted a major, new challenge to long-established, cultural attitudes and traditions regarding the socio-economic and political status of women. European feminists were therefore key members of a new 'advocacy coalition' (Sabatier 1988), which emerged during the 1970s and which sought, and continues to seek, to 'reframe' (Rein and Schön 1991) the way in which policy issues and problems which affect women are addressed by governments. In particular, women have sought to persuade policy makers of the need to address the socio-political causes of sex discrimination against women.

This chapter focuses upon just one aspect of this campaign, namely the demand for sex equality within the workplace. As argued below, the EC constituted an important, alternative policy making arena or venue for European feminists in their campaign for equal pay and equal treatment between male and female employees. The European Commission in particular, backed by the European Parliament and women's networks, has been a 'purposeful opportunist' (Cram 1994: 198) in this sector. The principal policy developments at the EC level in this sector are outlined and their impact upon national policies is evaluated. This analysis highlights the crucial role played not only by the European Commission, but also by EC law and the European Court of Justice (ECJ) in supporting the rights of working women and forcing national policy change. As several commentators have observed, the overall, material impact of the EC equality policies has been limited: women's pay as a ratio of men's has remained at about 75 per cent in the EU as a whole; occupational segregation of the labour market by gender is still the norm; and 'indirect' discrimination against women workers continues to be widespread. However, application of the EC equality Directives has undoubtedly benefited working women, by providing them with a legal means of redress in cases of sex discrimination. Moreover, politicians and civil servants can no longer afford to ignore the gender implications of welfare and labour market policies. Thus, this case study provides a good illustration of the power of European institutions, such as the Commission and the ECJ, to construct new national agendas and to force national political systems to attend to new problems. Incorporation of the equality Directives into national law has also generated a whole new area of bureaucratic and political activity at EU and national levels. Notwithstanding feet-dragging by some member states, the past twenty years have witnessed the development of a formal, institutional framework at EU and national levels, associated with the implementation and monitoring of EC legislation and positive action programmes. Several transnational women's networks and Brussels-centred interest group coalitions have also developed around this policy issue. As Hoskyns (1996) and Warner (1984) point out, feminist groups played an important catalytic role in the development of EC equal opportunities legislation during the 1970s. Twenty-five years later, a much wider range and number of women's organisations, trade unions, employers associations, local authorities and firms throughout the Community are routinely involved in the formulation and implementation of sex equality policies. Regularly consulted by Commission officials, many of these organisations are also associated with the official European Women's Lobby (EWL) in Brussels, the European Network of Women (ENOW) and the Committee for Women's Rights in the European Parliament. Thus, at the very least, the EU has changed the 'stakeholder' (Richardson 1996: 4) map in this sector. The EU has thus played a key role in the creation and legitimation of new policy actors with whom national governments now have to deal. Moreover, as women have become more sophisticated policy actors, so their interest and participation in a whole range of policy issues such as health, the environment, education, citizenship and political representation has increased. Women's rights can no longer be contained by policy makers within a single sector. Just as the environmental movement became a significant cross-sectoral policy actor (at both the EU and national levels) during the 1980s, so the women's movement seems now to be following a similar trajectory (though some way behind).

Notwithstanding the significance of the above developments, national governments remain influential in this sector as EC sex equality policies are affected by and adapted to suit national policies and policy traditions. Even in *dirigiste* EU policy areas such as competition policy there is much cheating, slippage and re-steering by national and regional governments (Richardson 1996: 278–94). Such an implementation gap is particularly apparent with regard to EC sex equality policy, not least because it is very much an adolescent policy area in the early stages of development. In addition, as argued below, the juridical basis for EC invention in this sector is relatively weak and narrow. In consequence, Commission attempts to expand the scope of EC sex equality policies beyond the narrow confines of article 119 have invariably been contested by some 'minimalist' member states (notably the UK). It is also the case that policy responses and outcomes in this sector remain, for the moment at least, largely anchored at the national level. National political traditions and ideology have been influential 'filters' in the sense that they have determined the manner in which national governments have complied with EC legislation and, by implication, its impact. More importantly, national governments continue to enjoy autonomy over policies which fall beyond the legislative scope of article 119 (for example, childcare provision, welfare and taxation policies, education), but which nevertheless affect the position of women within the labour market. In short, EU initiatives in this area have been mediated via often strong national 'policy styles' and the 'policy hinterland' created and shaped by particular policy traditions and ideas. Forbes (1996), for instance, argues that the ideological commitment of successive UK Conservative governments since 1979 to the minimal state has brought about the 'privatisation of sex equality policy'.

Equally important in this sense is the impact of factors exogenous to the policy sector at both EU and national levels. There can be little doubt that the impact of EC equality policies has been limited by recent international developments and changing, transnational policy fashions. In particular, globalisation and increasing international competition have persuaded many EU heads of government and employers of the need for greater labour market flexibility, more deregulation and lower labour costs. Meanwhile, EU member governments generally are seeking to reduce welfare expenditure levels, a trend reflected in recent welfare reforms in France, Germany and the UK, which have reduced the level of social protection provided to workers and their families by the state. In short, the social democratic/welfare consensus which prevailed among EC member states during the 1970s – and which facilitated the introduction of EC equality legislation – no longer exists. In its place, there now exists among EU national governments and employers' lobbies a new policy fashion based upon market-oriented, socioeconomic policies and minimal state intervention. The policy-making environment generally throughout the EU has therefore become less supportive of policies specifically aimed at women which increase employers' social costs or which increase state welfare expenditure levels. Thus, though the issue of women's rights is now – thanks largely to the EU – on national agendas, the future development of sex equality policies seems somewhat uncertain as the 'window of opportunity' (Kingdon 1984) seems to be closing.

The traditional policy frame: gendered national welfare and labour market policies

The position of women in the labour market – the central concern of EC sex equality policies – is linked to, and mirrors to a considerable degree, their status within national family and welfare regimes. As illustrated below, such policies have traditionally been based upon a policy 'frame' within which women are assumed to be primarily dependants and mothers rather than economically independent workers. All public policies are a product of the relationship between ideas, values, interests and the manner in which issues are 'framed'. Rein and Schön define framing as a way of selecting, organising, interpreting and making sense of a complex reality in order to provide guideposts for knowing, analysing and acting. Thus a frame provides a perpective from which an amorphous, ill-defined and problematic situation can be made sense of and acted upon (Rein and Schön 1991: 263). Influential in this process are advocacy coalitions, defined by Sabatier as comprising interest groups, administrative agencies, journalists, analysts and researchers with an interest in the policy sector (Sabatier 1988: 138). Members of the advocacy coalition have the potential capacity to create new policy frames and to transpose their ideas and values from one policy arena to another. This dynamic, conceptual framework is particularly helpful in understanding how and why the issue of sex equality, initially raised as a national policy problem in the 1960s, rapidly became an EC policy issue. This approach also highlights the crucial role played in this process by influential policy entrepreneurs in transmitting new policy frames from the national to the supranational arena – and back again to national policy makers.

As illustrated below, national welfare and labour market policies prior to the 1970s were underpinned by long-established cultural values, traditions and assumptions. Moreover, they were held in place by an effective constellation of interests, including governments, employers, (some) trade unions, and even middle-class women who believed women's proper role to be that of homemaker. Thus, policies for working women, such as they were, were an artefact of much broader societal developments, not the product of 'women's' policy. So, the fact that France formally adopted provisions on equal pay much earlier (in the 1950s) than other European countries owed much to the wartime resistance role played by women, the post-war programme of the French Left and the preamble to the 1946 Constitution, which guaranteed women equal rights 'in all domains' (Hoskyns 1996: 55). Major policy change in this sector was, therefore, dependent upon the emergence of some new and important actors, developments and issues capable of challenging this dominant, but increasingly anachronistic and therefore increasingly unstable policy settlement. In short, policy change was largely a consequence of the emergence in the late 1960s of a new, feminist 'advocacy coalition', which exposed the sexist nature of the traditional policy frame.

In general, the concept of sex equality played little role in the design of post-war, state family and welfare policies. Indeed, such policies were based, albeit to varying degrees, upon the assumption of a male breadwinner and a dependent wife and children. The gendered division of labour which characterised post-war European welfare regimes has deep historical roots. As Lewis points out, at the turn of the century 'social investigators, philanthropists and policy makers shared the view that the traditional division of labour between adult family members was crucial to social stability and personal welfare. Thus, 'the concern was not so much to maximize the welfare of working women as mothers, but to minimize their labour market participation, a position that was shared by male and female trade unionists and by middle-class women social reformers' (Lewis 1993: 16). Influential public policy instruments used to achieve this objective were taxation and welfare regimes, which with few exceptions penalised married, working women via high marginal tax rates and low benefits. As such, these policies constituted a major barrier to women seeking to enter the labour market. Inadequate publicly funded childcare provision constituted an equally important obstacle to working mothers. Since the 1970s, some modification of welfare and labour market policies, often in response to pressure from EC law, has improved the situation for working women somewhat (for example, the introduction in the UK in the 1980s of individual taxation for married women). However, as recent research undertaken by the European Network of Experts on the Situation of Women in the Labour Market confirmed 'welfare state reform in Europe still does not include a rethinking of the male breadwinner systems on which many countries base their welfare system' (European Commission 1996: 8)

In Britain, for instance, under the post-war Beveridge settlement, women were treated as dependants for the purposes of social security entitlement. Until the mid-1970s, married women were even offered the 'married women's option' of paying lower national insurance contributions in return for a lower entitlement. British governments have also provided little support for working mothers: maternity rights granted in 1975 were actually eroded in the 1980s and the number of publicly funded childcare places was reduced.[3] In similar vein, the German tax system continues to be heavily weighted in favour of married, single-earner couples, while German family law has served to underpin the ideal of paternal authority. Indeed, until 1977, a (West) German husband was legally empowered to prevent his wife from taking paid employment if he felt this to be detrimental to family life (Ostner 1993). However, adherence to the male breadwinner model has been strongest and most long-lived in Ireland where a marriage bar prevented women from working in the civil service until 1977 and where the tax system subjected married working women to high marginal rates and low tax-free allowances. In addition, until the mid 1980s (and pressure from EC law), married women received lower rates and shorter lengths of benefit and were not eligible for unemployment benefit (Lewis 1993: 17). At the other end of the spectrum, the Nordic countries may be described as weak male breadwinner states, since here the welfare state has provided for women as workers as well as dependants. In Sweden, for instance, government policy in the early 1970s actively encouraged the entry of women to the labour market and the creation of a dual breadwinner family norm via the introduction of separate taxation, the expansion of publicly funded childcare provision and the introduction of a generous parental leave policy. In France also, women have historically been recognised as paid workers. There were no early-twentieth-century attempts to push women out of the labour market and paid maternity leave was introduced as early as 1913. Since the 1970s, governments have provided both generous family allowances to those families with a single earner and a high level of publicly funded childcare. Nevertheless, as Hantrais (1993) argues, the attitude of the French state towards women's welfare has been ambivalent, resulting in contradictory policies, some of which treat women as workers while others view women as dependants and mothers. Thus, as in Germany, until 1970, French family law permitted the husband to decide whether his wife should work. Moreover, both the French tax and social security systems (which are household based) continue to penalise married women workers. Thus, European state welfare and labour market policies towards women vary between EU countries, ranging across a spectrum from so-called strong male breadwinner states (Ireland, UK, Germany) to weak male breadwinner states (Nordic countries). The former model (which is consistent with the traditional policy frame identified above) defines wives primarily as dependants and mothers and provides few incentives for married women or mothers to work. By contrast, the latter perspective, which fits more closely with the aspirations of women's groups, expects all adults to be employed and provides incentives through individualised taxation and benefits and through assistance with childcare. In reality, most contemporary EU welfare and labour market regimes exhibit elements of both strong and weak male breadwinner states. However, as the recent report by the European Network of Experts on the Situation of Women in the Labour Market noted, the traditional policy frame continues to exert considerable influence in most EU member states. Moreover, as the report concludes:

> the direction of change [in welfare policies] is towards more means-testing, fewer individual rights and more limited support for parents in their attempts to reconcile work and family life. . . . The progressive integration of women in the wage economy may have highlighted the inequalities associated with the male breadwinner model of organisation, but the pattern of female integration into the wage economy over recent years has continued to be shaped by the gender division of labour in the household.
>
> (European Commission 1996: 6)

Thus, it would appear that national policy traditions and styles have proved quite resilient to the attempts by women's groups and EC policy makers over the past twenty-five years to reframe welfare and labour market policies in order to address some of the key sources of sex inequality within the labour market.

Achieving sex equality in the workplace: the importance of the Brussels policy arena

During the 1960s, the political salience of feminism increased as women's movements throughout western Europe became actively involved in national campaigns for sex equality in all spheres of public and private life. The demand for sex equality within the workplace – notably the demand for abolition of wage differentials between men and women doing the same job – was central to this campaign. Generally speaking, however, national policy makers remained unresponsive to women's material demands. In part, this was due to the nascent and internally divided nature of the European feminist movement at this time, which undermined its political effectiveness. However, lack of policy change was also attributable in part to the overwhelming weight at that time within national policy-making arenas of traditional beliefs and values regarding the relationship between women and the labour market. Powerful socio-economic interest groups including male-dominated trade unions and employers were also reluctant to revise their view of the labour-market value of women employees.

However, as Baumgarter and Jones argue, it is often the case that in a pluralist political system 'there remain other institutional venues that can serve as avenues of appeal for the disaffected' (Baumgarter and Jones 1991: 1,045). As they go on to explain:

> Each venue carries with it a decisional bias, because both participants and decision-making routines differ. When the venue of a public policy changes, as often occurs over time, those who previously dominated the policy process may find themselves in the minority, and erstwhile losers may be transformed into winners.
>
> (Baumgartner and Jones 1991: 1,047)

In short, both the institutional structures within which policies are made and the individual strategies of policy entrepreneurs are important in determining policy outcomes.

For European feminists, the EC constituted just such an alternative venue, not least because article 119 of the Treaty of Rome already provided (in theory) for equal pay between men and women. In a strategic move, women's groups began in the early 1970s to invoke article 119 of the Rome Treaty in national equal pay campaigns and to focus their lobbying activities upon EC policy makers. Significantly, article 119 had been included in the Treaty primarily in response to French concerns over the possible need to harmonise social costs to employers within the common market arising from national variations in differential wage rates for men and women. No attempt had been made by national governments to apply article 119 once the Treaty came into force. However, as Hoskyns (1996) observes, article 119 was rescued from oblivion by two kinds of political activism generated by Belgian women which helped to place the new 'feminist' policy frame on the EC agenda: industrial action taken by women employees of a munitions factory, who sought to use article 119 in support of their claim for equal pay; and the professional activities of the advocate and academic lawyer, Eliane Vogel-Polsky who argued for a strong definition of article 119 in the courts. Indeed, it was Vogel-Polsky who brought the *Defrenne* test case against the Belgian state airline,

Sabena which resulted in the ECJ's landmark ruling confirming the direct applicability of article 119.

Article 119 undoubtedly provided EC policy makers and the women's lobby with a necessary juridical hook on which to hang their demands for further EC sex equality legislation. However, other factors also helped to make the EC a more favourable venue for women's groups. First, EC policy makers, unencumbered by pre-existing policies and vested interests in this sector, were generally more receptive to the new policy frame which underpinned women's policy demands. Secondly, the pluralist and 'open' nature of the EC decision-making process (in contrast to the highly centralised and 'closed' nature of many national political systems) provided the women's lobby with multiple 'acccess points' to decision makers. Thus, as Vallance and Davies (1986) demonstrated, links between women's groups and women MEPs, established during the 1960s proved extremely useful in placing women's rights on the EC's policy agenda. Thirdly, as members of a new political system, EC Commission officials, European judges and MEPs were in the early 1970s generally committed to consolidating and extending the policies and legal authority of the EC. Thus, since its inception, the European Commission has actively cultivated close relations with the relevant policy commuity in an attempt to create 'constitutency' support for EC intervention in a particular policy sector (Mazey 1992). This is a familiar pattern of EC policy development which we and others have have observed in a number of policy sectors (Mazey and Richardson 1995; 1996; Cram 1993; Peters 1991). As argued elsewhere (Mazey 1996), the development of EC sex equality policy constitutes yet another example of a policy area developing critical mass via skilful bureaucratic management of key interests by the Commission. Fourthly, Hoskyns suggests that the general mood within the EC at this time was socially progressive. Thus she cites one of the ECJ judges involved in the *Defrenne* case, who referring to the activities of the Court said 'this was not a Court engaged in conservatism and reaction – the mood was progressive. . . . The events of 1968 did not disturb us very much, we felt we were already acting in the spirit of 1968' (Hoskyns 1996: 71). Moreover, on the specific issue of equal pay, several EC policy makers were influenced by the fact that both the 1951 International Labour Organisation (ILO) Convention (No. 100) and the UN's Universal Declaration of Human Rights contained a commitment to the principle of equal pay between men and women. Finally, as Meehan (1990) has argued, during the early 1970s EC political leaders were anxious to enhance the popular legitimacy of the Community and so decided to strengthen EC social policy. Following the 1972 Paris Summit the European Commission was asked by EC heads of government to draw up a Social Action Programme. Adopted by the Council of Ministers in 1974, this programme listed as a priority 'the undertaking of action to achieve equality between men and women as regards access to employment and vocational training and advancement, and as regards working conditions including pay'. Thus, at the EC level, women encountered a somewhat more favourable policy-making venue to that which prevailed in most national capitals.

SONIA MAZEY

EC action designed to eliminate sex discrimination: policy and institutional developments

In contrast to other policy sectors, the Treaty basis for EC competence with regard to sex equality is relatively weak. This fact has necessarily influenced the type of EC policy instrument used in this sector. Commission proposals for EC legislation in this sector have been based upon either article 119 or, as in the case of the 1992 maternity Directive, upon article 118 (Health and Safety at Work). Commission attempts to introduce legislation on related issues which affect the labour market position of women, notably childcare provision, sexual harassment in the workplace and parental leave, have been challenged in the Council of Ministers on the grounds that they lie beyond the narrow confines of article 119. Checked, the Commission has nevertheless sought to extend the policy debate to such issues by means of 'soft', legally non-binding policy instruments, including recommendations and positive action programmes. Though not legally binding upon member states, there is some evidence that these initatives, combined with other social and political changes, have contributed to greater awareness of sex discrimination on the part of employers, trade unions and the public generally. They have also enabled the Commission to broaden the policy agenda in this sector.

The EC equality Directives

Article 119 of the EC founding Treaties states that:

> each Member State shall during the first stage ensure and subsequently maintain the principle that men and women should receive equal pay for equal work. For the purpose of this article 'pay' means the ordinary basic or minimum wage or salary and any other consideration whether in cash or in kind, which the worker receives, directly or indirectly, in respect of his employment from his employer.

This article constitutes the only legal basis for EC women's policy. In short, it is the hook upon which all subsequent EC legislation in this sector hangs. It came up for interpretation before the European Court of Justice for the first time in 1971 in *Defrenne vs.the Belgian State*. The case was a complex one which lasted five years and involved three separate appeals relating to differential retirement ages, pension entitlements and pay for male and female cabin staff employed by the Belgian state airline, Sabena. The Court ruled that article 119 did not extend to pension schemes or retirement ages. On the question of equal pay, however, the Court's 1976 ruling in the *Defrenne* case was a landmark in the development of Community law on equal pay. Crucially, the Court ruled that article 119 had 'direct effect' in member states; women could rely upon it in national courts irrespective of whether or not national legislation existed on equal pay. The ruling came as a

142

shock to governments throughout the EC who realised they could no longer ignore article 119 (Landau 1985).

The *Defrenne* ruling gave fresh impetus to women's rights campaigners throughout the Community and brought the issues of equal pay and equal treatment firmly to the forefront of the EC's political agenda. The way in which the policy issue was processed within the Commission highlights the policy-making importance of different institutional structures and policy-making arenas. Significantly, within the Commission, debate extended beyond the problem of achieving *proceduralité* equality between women and men within the workplace to include other aspects of the policy hinterland which adversely affected women's position within the labour market, namely tax and social security measures, childcare facilities, and education and training opportunities. Furthermore, key individuals involved in this analysis of the policy problem were women who were prominent members of the 'feminist' advocacy coalition committed to analysing the problem of women's issues within a new, wider policy frame. These included the French sociologist, Evelyne Sullerot, author of the influential analysis of women's importance in the labour market, *Histoire et sociologie du travail féminin*, and Jacqueline Nonon, a French Commission official in DG V who was given responsibility for preparing the equality Directives. Having decided to create an *ad hoc* working group on women's work, Nonon deliberately chose not to consult established 'independent experts' or civil servants from appropriate departments, but sought instead to nominate women with a genuine interest in the issues. Of the eighteen national representatives appointed to the group, only five were men and several women appointed were actively involved in equal pay negotiations. Trade unions active at the EC level who argued that the group should have been set up as a sub-group of the Standing Committee on Employment were also by-passed. Though all members of the group stressed the need for 'positive' intervention, i.e. policies affecting women's rights beyond the workplace, to help women reconcile domestic responsibilities with employment aspirations, Nonon's strategy 'was to expand policy outwards from equal pay and "stretch the elastic as far as it would go"'(Hoskyns 1996: 102).

This strategy is reflected in the six EC Directives adopted between 1975 and 1992 and in the incremental development of this policy sector at the EU level (Mazey 1996). The 1975 Equal Pay Directive (75/117) introduced the principle of equal pay between men and women for 'work of equal value', thereby confirming the provisions of article 119. The 1976 Equal Treatment Directive provided for equal treatment of women and men as regards access to employment, vocational training, promotion and working conditions. The 1978 Directive (79/7) concerned the principle of equal treatment for men and women in matters of statutory social security benefits (excluding retirement ages and survivors' benefits). This was followed by two further equality Directives: the 1986 Directive (86/378) on equal treatment in occupational social security schemes and the 1986 Directive on equal treatment between men and women engaged in an activity including agriculture in a self-employed capacity, and on protection of self-employed women during pregnancy and motherhood. As Cunningham (1992) has argued, these measures were based upon a narrow definition of social policy as primarily concerned with economic concerns. They were also based upon a liberal interpretation of equality: the emphasis was upon removing barriers and on non-discrimination, rather than upon the development of 'positive' or special policies for women, which might entail a redistribution of opportunities from advantaged groups to disadvantaged groups. However, the 1992 Directive on the protection of pregnant women from exposure to hazardous substances in the workplace and on rights to maternity leave was arguably the first Directive based upon an acceptance of the need to treat women differently to men in order to promote a more equal outcome in terms of employment opportunities.

EC positive action programmes for women

The above Directives have been complemented since the early 1980s by a series of pluriannual, EC 'positive action programmes' on behalf of women, intended to increase the impact of EC equality laws, raise public awareness of women's issues and promote equal opportunities for women and men beyond the workplace. Specific initiatives funded have included in-service training for women, women's co-operatives, 'confidence-building' courses for women, the appointment of equal opportunities counsellors in companies and local authorities, creche facilities, and information campaigns on EC equality. More recent programmes have sought to change the image of women portrayed by the media, encourage a more equal division of labour within the household, and improve the representation of women in all spheres of decision making in political, professional and public arenas (Commission of the European Communities: 1991b). Two additional programmes were introduced by DG V for women during the 1980s, which were influential in the creation of new local and transnational women's networks: the Local Employment Initiatives for Women (LEIs); and the Community Programme for Women's Vocational Training Schemes (IRIS). The LEIs programme provides grants for women starting new businesses. The IRIS network, which has now ended, sought to increase the provision of high quality training for women by means of transnational and national partnerships and sponsorships. The programme was co-ordinated by the Centre for Research on European Women (CREW), which works under the direction of the Commission (Commission of the European Communities 1991a). These initiatives were followed by the creation in 1990 of a new Community Initiative Programme, New Opportunities for Women (NOW). Introduced as part of the reformed Structural Funds, the NOW programme was designed to assist the integration of women into the labour market. Unlike the Directives, these programmes, funded partially by the European Social Fund are not legally binding and their impact at the national level has varied considerably between member states depending upon the availability of co-financing. Nevertheless, their existence has enabled the European Commission to extend the policy agenda in this sector to issues such as housework, childcare, political representation, women's health, sexual harassment, all of which lie beyond the juricial scope of article 119. As the former UK Commissioner, Ivor Richards, on leaving the Commission in 1985 argued:

> without the Action programme to use as a lever on the Council, the Commission would have had to justify every step it tried to take in this field [Equality Policy]. We can wave it at governments to justify work in areas where member states might not wish us to be too active.
> (CREW Report January 1985 V.1. Quoted in Rutherford 1989, p. 303)

Institutional developments at the EU level

The past twenty years has also witnessed the gradual development of a number of institutions, agencies and networks at the EU level associated with the formulation and implementation of EC equality policies. This institutionalisation of the policy sector has been important in helping to keep women's issues on European and national policy agendas, thereby maintaining the momentum for further policy change. Women MEPs have, since the 1970s, constituted an important part of the women's lobby at the European level and, since 1981, there has been a standing committee for women's rights within the European Parliament. Within the Commission, some twenty-five full-time officials are employed in the Equal Opportunities Unit, set up within DG V (Employment, Industrial Relations and Social Affairs) in 1976. This Unit works in close collaboration with the Advisory Committee on Equal Opprtunities, established by the Commission in December 1981. This Committee, which meets twice a year, to review policy developments and future initiatives, brings together representatives from the official equal opportunities bodies in the EC member states. The European Women's Lobby (EWL), employers and trade union organisations also have observer status on this Committee. In the European Parliament, women's interests are formally represented in the Standing Committee on Women's Rights.

As an active policy entrepreneur, the Commission has also played a crucial role in promoting the development of EU and transnational policy networks in this sector. For instance, there are now nine European Networks of Experts, each of which comprises between twelve and twenty-four independent experts (one or two from each member state) who monitor the impact of existing legislation and/or collect data which might be used to justify further Community action. The most well-established networks include the Expert Network (of lawyers) on the Application of the Equality Directives, set up in 1982, and the Network (of economists) on the Position of Women in the Labour Market, established in 1983. Four additional networks were created in 1986: the Network for Positive Action in Enterprises; the Steering Committee for Equal Opportunities in Broadcasting; the Network on Childcare and other Measures to Reconcile Work and Family Responsibilities; and the Working party on Equal Opportunities in Education.

These networks constitute influential 'epistemic communities' (Haas 1992), a term invoked by Haas to describe transnational networks of scientific and professional experts who are influential in the policy-making process. In this particular sector, they have played a significant monitoring role. They have also drawn into the EC policy-making process other national, authoritative experts, academics and interested groups (for example in Commission funded seminars and workshops), thereby generating new transnational 'epistemic communities' asociated with EC equality policy.

The Commission has also encouraged the growth of a transnational European women's lobby to support and legitimise Commission initiatives in this sector. As part of this mobilisation process, the Commission established the Women's Information Service in 1976 to publicise EC equality policies in the member states and to organise international conferences for women. The European Women's Lobby (EWL), set up in 1990, is also funded by the European Commission. It co-ordinates the lobbying activites of some forty-eight national and European non-governmental organisations throughout the EC, whose total membership exceeds 100 million. As the 'official' women's lobby in Brussels, the EWL is regularly consulted by the Commission on EC legislative proposals affecting women and on wider EU developments such as the 1996 IGC. As Bew and Meehan (1994) note, as a transnational network, the EWL has also played an important role in communicating downwards information about EU policy initiatives. However, compared to business and industrial networks, the policy community associated with EC equality policies is fragile. In part, this fragility is due to the relative immaturity of the policy sector. However, it is also attributable to the nature of the women's lobby. In particular, the political and cultural diversity of the women's lobby has sometimes resulted in internal divisions within the lobby over strategy and/or policy objectives (e.g. over issues such as abortion). In addition, women's groups, especially at the national level, tend to be loosely organised and poorly resourced. Not surprisingly, such groups find it difficult to be effective EU lobbyists (Bretherton and Sperling 1996). Nevertheless, there now exists at the EU level an established policy community and politico-administrative framework for policy making in this sector. Though based around a relatively small Unit within the Commission, this organisational framework may yet (as occurred in the case of EC environmental policy), become more prominent within the EC policy-making process.

Forcing national policy change: the importance of national policy styles and policy hinterlands.

The legislative impact of the EC equality directives

Adoption of the above Directives prompted a flurry of implementing legislation in EC member states. The precise way in which the Directives were incorporated in each country varied according to prevailing social norms, traditions of labour market regulation and politico-administrative arrangements. In Germany, for instance, civil servants initially decided that the equality provisions in the Constitution and the right of appeal to the Federal Constitutional Court provided sufficient protection for women and no further action was needed. Only in 1980 was a 'compliance law' introduced specifically to ban sex-discrimination in recruitment, promotion and dismissal, a right to equal pay for the same or equivalent work and a strong 'recommendation' against sex-specific language in job advertisements was added to the Civil Code (Hoskyns 1996: 119). Interestingly, the UK was not a member of the Community when it introduced its Equal Pay Act in 1970 or when the possiblity of a Sex Discrimination Act was first mooted. However, as Meehan and Collins (1996) suggest, the very fact that the UK government aspired to EC membership at this time – and that it had been warned that it would fail the test on article 119 – may well have been influential in forcing the UK to be a pioneer in this sector. Member states were also obliged to establish official equal opportunities agencies to monitor the implementation of the Directives and assist complainants. In Ireland, the Employment Equality Agency (EEA) was created to monitor legislation and policies from the perspective of women. Meanwhile, in Germany the working group on women's issues of the Federal Ministry for Youth, the Family and Health was extended and given responsibility for the dissemination of information on women's projects. In the UK, the Equal Opportunities Commission was established, charged with the responsibility of working towards the elimination of sex discrimination, promoting equality of opportunity between men and women and monitoring equality legislation. Thus, both ECJ rulings and legislative initiatives undertaken by the European Commission were influential in forcing policy change at the national level.

Undoubtedly, the Directives have been crucially important in prompting national policy change in this sector, demonstrating the capacity of exogenous developments to force national policy change. Forbes (1996) thus cites Lord Lester's view that in the case of the UK 'Community law has enabled the EOC and individual women and men to win in the courts what we in the mid-1970s could not win in Whitehall and Westminster' (Lord Lester of Herne Hill 1994: 231). The European Court of Justice over the years has been a powerful institutional catalyst of change. Landmark ECJ rulings have been important both in clarifying and – in most cases – extending the scope of the Directives. Cases such as *Worringham and Humphreys v Lloyds Bank* (1981), *Burton v British Railways Board* (1982), and *Barber v Guardian Royal Exchange* (1990 and 1993), for instance, have confirmed that the provisions of article 119 and the Equal Treatment Directive apply to pension and redundancy benefits (irrespective of whether they are paid under a contract of employment, under statute, or on a voluntary basis), private contracted-out and company pension schemes (Honeyball and Shaw 1991; *Financial Times* 21 December 1993). The rights of part-time workers (who are predominantly female) have also been strengthened (albeit at a rather uneven and slow pace) by Court rulings based upon EC equality Directives. In September 1994, for instance, a European Court ruling (in the case *Vroege v NICV and another*) on sex equality in company pensions stated that employers must admit part-time workers to pensions schemes if barring them constitutes an indirect form of sex discrimination. The Court also pointed out that this principle had, in fact, been established in an earlier ruling (*Jenkins v Kingsgate*) in 1976. In view of this fact, the Court ruled that female, part-time workers hitherto excluded from company pension schemes may claim retrospective benefits in respect of employment dated back to 1976. A UK government actuary's report estimated that backdated pension claims from female part-timers could cost UK companies and their pension funds £7 million. In the same month, the UK House of Lords ruled that the application of different qualifying conditions for part-timers compared with full-timers in the UK unfair dismissal and redundancy payments legislation contravened EU equal pay and equal treatment laws, because the hours threshold had a disproportionately adverse effect on women (Department of Employment 1994). Overtly sexist job classification schemes and collective agreements have also been eradicated as a result of the Directives. More generally, in legislative terms, the development of a body of EC equality case law has resulted in the permeation of domestic legislation and company policies with equal opportunities clauses.

The importance of the policy hinterland

However, application of the Directives has also highlighted their limitations. Leaving aside the problems of non-implementation and non-compliance with EU equality Directives, as Hoskyns and Luckhaus (1989) have argued, the flexibility enjoyed by member states as to *how* they implement the Equality Directives may limit their 'positive' impact. For example, as Meehan and Collins (1996) argue:

> UK governments have been ungenerous in the way in which they comply with new requirements stemming from the EC; for example, responding slowly to some key rulings (or ignoring them until forced to do otherwise), being cautious about income taxation, making it more difficult to claim disability allowances, fighting the idea of a Directive for pregnant women workers, and equalising retirement ages upwards instead of downwards.
> (Meehan and Collins 1996: 29)

National policy styles beget a dense 'hinterland' of detailed programmes, policies and institutions and it takes a very long time for EU institutions to permeate and change this hinterland significantly. Meanwhile, national political and cultural traditions, hegemonic values and the characteristics of the politico-administrative system may either reinforce or undermine EC sex equality policies. As Forbes (1996) argues, the neo-liberal, minimal state philosophy of successive Conservative governments has effectively limited the impact of EC policies within the UK. A major policy consequence of this philosophy has been the extension of flexible and part-time working, promoted by the UK government as 'an aid to equality of opportunity' (Forbes 1996: 150). However, as Forbes points out, this trend has, in reality, been accompanied by a reduction in the level of labour market protection for (predominantly women) part-time and low-paid workers (as reflected, for example in the abolition of the wages councils). Meanwhile, EC attempts to increase access to full-time benefits, maternity and childcare provision are all characterised by the UK government 'as socially (even socialist) inspired policies which would detrimentally skew the operation of the labour market and produce results harmful to society's and women's interests' (Forbes 1996: 150). The philosophical commitment of recent Conservative governments to a minimal state is, Forbes argues, also detrimental to sex equality since it allows the government to avoid the gender implications of policies which lie beyond the narrow confines of sex discrimination laws. Thus, policy issues relating to the family, education, welfare and poverty can be left to the market or the voluntary sector. The 'Opportunity 2000' campaign, launched by the Prime Minister, John Major, in 1991 provides a good illustration of this non-interventionist, market-oriented, policy style. Ostensibly, the central objective of this campaign was to increase the quantity and quality of women' participation in the labour market. Significantly, however, it was not a government initiative, but a self-financing campaign set up by an organisation called Business in the Community, operating under the Charities Act. Member firms (which numbered 305 in December 1996 (*The Guardian* 2 December 1996) pay an annual fee for advisory information and network services on issues relating to women's employment. According to the Director of Opportunity 2000, Liz Bargh, the campaign is driven by the needs of business: the aim is to help employers to realise the potential economic value of women employees (Forbes 1996). Though women may benefit from this campaign, this is arguably a secondary consideration to the primary objective of assisting business interests. Thus, in the UK, the gendered analysis of public policy advocated by women which has gradually emerged since the late 1960s has been seriously challenged since the late 1970s by a national policy frame based upon different and opposing values and objectives. Moreover, on those occasions when the UK government has sought to shape the policy agenda on 'women's issues' such as the family, abortion and chidcare, it has directly challenged the values and policy objectives of the feminist policy frame, emphasising instead the importance of women as mothers and the societal importance of the traditional, nuclear family.

In contrast, in France during the early 1980s, the situation was quite different. Here, the election of a Socialist government in May 1981, backed by a socially progressive coalition of interests, provided a far more favourable policy hinterland for sex equality policies than existed in the UK at this time. The ideological commitment of the Mitterrand administration to Keynesianism, democratisation and redistributive social justice provided a sympathetic 'policy frame' for sex equality policies. In terms of specific actions, the new government appointed a Minister for Women's Rights and in 1983 introduced 'the most significant single piece of legislation on women's rights with respect to equality at work' (Hantrais 1993: 123). The *Loi Roudy* (named after the Minister for Women's Rights, Yvette Roudy) legally obliged all firms to produce an annual report on the situation of men and women employees in order to ensure compliance with equal opportunity laws. Companies were also expected to set quantitative and qualitative targets for recruitment, training and promotion of female workers. In those cases where such targets were not met, firms could establish positive action programmes for women (funded partly by the government) or operate quotas for promotion to positions where women were under-represented (Hantrais 1993: 123). More generally, during the period of the first French Socialist administration (1981–4), women's interests were incorporated into policy debates on issues such as political representation, health, poverty, citizenship and welfare. Nevertheless, France provides a good illustration of how quickly such 'windows of opportunity' (Kingdon 1994) can disappear. In 1986, Yvette Roudy's Ministry was downgraded to a *Délégation à la Condition féminine* by the newly elected, right-wing government and was not reinstated by the Socialists when they were re-elected in 1988. Instead, they appointed a *Secrétaire d'Etat chargée des Droits des femmes*. Edith Cresson's 1991 (centre-left) government included a *Ministre délégué aux Droits des femmes* responsible to the Minister for Labour Employment and Vocational Training. As Hantrais observes, the choice of title reflects the policy orientation of the government in power. Whereas the left has tended to be more concerned historically with women's rights, particularly as workers, the right has tended to emphasise women's status as mothers. One important consequence of this ambivalent attitude towards women has been generous family allowances, maternity and parental leave arrangements and publicly funded childcare provision. In contrast to UK governments, French governments of both left and right – in keeping with the French policy style – have been strongly interventionist in this policy sector.

The changing international and European context: a rival policy frame emerges

Implementation of EC sex equality policy has also been affected by international and European-level economic and political developments. By the early 1980s, the fragile combination of circumstances which had facilitated the introduction of the early EC equality Directives was beginning to disappear. During the 1980s, national economies throughout the EC suffered prolonged economic recession and high unemployment levels. Increasingly, at national and EC levels debate has therefore centred upon the need to restore economic competitiveness in order that European industries might be able to compete with Japan and the USA. Central to this debate within the EU during the 1980s was the disagreement over the 'correct' labour market and social policies to be pursued. On the one hand, there were those, such as the UK government, employers and business associations, convinced of the need to deregulate and cut labour market costs, irrespective of the social consequences. Meanwhile, others including the former Commission President Jacques Delors, the French and German governments, trade unions, acknowledged the need to improve competitiveness and restructure European industry, but wished to do this by pursuing 'a European middle way', which would preserve a minimum set of rights for workers. Over time, the deregulators have prevailed, both at the national levels (notably in the UK, but more recently in France and Germany) and at the EU level where, notwithstanding the provisions of the 1989 Social Charter, market liberalisation and deregulation have acquired the status of a new orthodoxy. Moreover, this policy trend has been reinforced by the domestic policy consequences of another major EU policy commitment, namely Economic and Monetary Union (EMU). In order to meet the convergence criteria for EMU membership, national governments throughout the EU have been forced to reduce public expenditure levels and pursue deflationary economic policies. Both developments have resulted in welfare cuts and low wages.

Women workers in particular, have been adversely affected by these policy developments. Though female labour market market participation rates have increased in recent years, women tend to be concentrated in low-paid, part-time and casual jobs. As such, they have been particularly affected by labour market deregulation and welfare cuts (European Commission 1996). Moreover, against this backdrop of economic liberalisation, there is little support within the Council of Ministers for further EC equality legislation, *unless* such legislation is compatible with the needs of the internal market. This may mean that the window of opportunity for EC sex equality policy has all but closed. Certainly, if they are to continue to be influential EU lobbyists, women's groups (and others such as environmentalists and trade unionists) must now adapt their strategy to accommodate the emergence of a new European policy frame which emphasises the needs of a powerful advocacy coalition within Europe, namely that of business and industry. Given the relative immaturity and internal diversity of the European women's lobby, this may prove a difficult task.

Conclusion: EC equality policies at a critical juncture

The foregoing analysis of EC equality policy highlights the capacity of European institutions to force policy change at the national level. It also demonstrates the importance of the EU as an alternative policy arena or venue for interests such as women and environmentalists, who find themselves marginalised at the national level, but who are able to use the EC policy-making process to bring recalcitrant national governments into line. Despite the tenuous Treaty basis for EC sex equality policy, the past twenty years have witnessed the gradual expansion of EU competence in this aspect of social policy. The ECJ and the European Commission, backed by women's groups, have both played a central role in this process. Since the late 1970s, the Commission has also fostered the development of transnational women's networks and set up European networks of 'experts' to monitor and advise on various aspects of equality policy, thereby keeping the issue of women's rights on national agendas.

However, further Europeanisation of this policy area in the near future is likely to be incremental in nature. Given the precarious legal basis for Community action in this sector, the introduction of further legislation will almost certainly require the support of all EU member states. Such support is unlikely to be forth-coming. The changed economic and political climate since the late 1970s has facilitated the emergence of an increasingly dominant 'competitiveness' policy frame (Mazey and Richardson 1997), which has curbed the enthusiasm of EU member states for interventionist, anti-discriminatory policies. Moreover, it would, for instance, be foolish to underestimate the resilience of traditional national policy styles in this sector: though gendered public policy analysis is no longer stuck in a ghetto, it is far from being routine practice among national policy makers. Existing policies are also underpinned by powerful interests and estab-lished socio-cultural traditions which are likely to prove resistant to change and which are likely to endorse the need for competitiveness. Thus, it is unlikely that EC policy makers will be able to penetrate the dense policy hinterland, which lies beyond the legislative reach of the EU, but which affects the rights of working women.

Worsening economic conditions and the resurgence of neo-liberalism in several EU member states has also prompted widespread support for economic deregula-tion within the Union. The further development of EC equality policy raises fundamental constitutional questions of sovereignty inside the Community. As Streek has argued, the supranational European state governing the internal market is likely to resemble a 'pre-New Deal liberal state' characterised by a high level of civil rights and a low level of social rights (Streek 1992: 113). Business support for the SEM was premised upon the assumption that the future European political economy was to be 'less subject to institutional regulation—national or supranational— than it would have been in the 'harmonisation'-minded and social democratic 1970s' (Streek 1992: 110). Anti-discrimination laws constitute a form of state intervention interrupting the functioning of the market. The effec-tiveness of EC equality policies in the future is therefore likely to depend upon whether removal of discrimination is functional to the market, for example, by redressing irrational under-utilisation of women's skills. The UK group, Employers for Childcare, has for this reason supported EC proposals for a Childcare Directive.

Commission officials within the Equal Opportunities Unit acknowledge that present conditions make the introduction of new equality legislation unlikely. The emphasis at present is therefore upon increasing the effectiveness of existing Directives and 'mainstreaming'. This involves the replacement of specific inita-tives for women by the integration of equal opportunities policies into other EC economic and structural policies on the grounds that equal opportunities, just like environmental policy, is no longer a marginal question, but central to all aspects of EC policy making. The current debate within the Commission on flexible working time is cited by officials as a good illustration of how equality issues such as family responsibilities might be incorporated into general EC policies. The logic of this argument is appealing: such a development would help to ensure that women's rights permeate policy making in all sectors at the EU and, by implication, national level. However, in order to be successful, this strategy will also require the support of policy makers in other DGs within the Commission. As Hoskyns (1996: 151) reports, such support has not always been forthcoming in the past from officials. Thus, EC sex equality policy seems to have reached a critical juncture. Important material benefits have been achieved for women in the workplace and a much wider debate on women's rights has been forced onto national political agendas by EC action in this sector. However, the obstacles to further development of this policy sector are now daunting.

Notes

1 The empirical material on EU sex equality policies used in this chapter is drawn from an earlier publication: Mazey 1996.
2 The author would like to thank Jeremy Richardson for his helpful comments on an earlier draft of this chapter.
3 Publicly funded childcare for children aged 0–3 years, percentage of age group covered: UK (age group 0–5 years): 2 per cent; Germany: 2 per cent (W), 50 per cent (E); France: 23 per cent; Italy: 6 per cent; Denmark: 48 per cent; Sweden: 33 per cent (*Bulletin on women and Employment in the EU*, No. 9, October 1996, p. 8.

References

Baumgartner, F. and Jones, B. (1991) 'Agenda Dynamics and Policy Subsystems', *The Journal of Politics*, vol. 53 (4) 1,044–73

Bew, P. and Meehan, E. (1994) 'Regions and Borders: Controversies in Northern Ireland about the European Union', *Journal of European Public Policy*, vol. 1(1) 95–114

Bretherton, C. and Sperling, L. (1996) 'Women's Networks and the European Union: towards and Inclusive Approach?', *Journal of Common Market Studies*, vol. 34(4) 487–508

Commission of the European Communities (1991a) 'Equal Opportunities for Women and Men', *Social Europe*, 3/91, Luxembourg: Office for Official Publications of the European Communities

—— (1991b) 'Equal Opportunities for Women and Men. The Third Medium-Term Community Action Programme – 1991–1995, *Women and Europe Supplements*, no. 34

Cram, L. (1993) 'Calling the Tune without Paying the Piper? Social Policy Regulation: the role of the Commission in European Community Social Policy', *Policy and Politics*, vol. 21, 135–46

—— (1994) 'The European commission as a Multi-Organisation: Social and Information Technology Policy-Making in the European Union', *Journal of European Public Policy*, vol. 1(2) 195–217

Cunningham, S. (1992) 'The Development of Equal Opportunities Theory and Practice in the European Community', *Policy and Politics*, vol. 20 (3) 177–89

Department of Employment (UK) (1994) *Rights of Part-time Workers*, Press Notice, 20 December

European Commission (1996) *Bulletin on Women and Employment in the EU*, No. 9, October

Forbes, I. (1996) 'The Privatisation of Sex Equality Policy', *Parliamentary Affairs*, vol. 49(1) 143–60

Haas P. (1992) 'Introduction: Epistemic Communities and International Policy Co-ordination', *International Organisation*, vol. 49 (1) 1–35

Hantrais, L. (1993) 'Women, Work and Welfare in France', in Lewis, J (ed) *Women and Social Policies in Europe. Work, Family and the State*, Aldershot: Edward Elgar Publishing, 116–37

Honeyball, S. and Shaw, J. (1991) 'Sex, Law and the Retiring Man', *European Law Review*, vol. 16, 47–58

Hoskyns, C. (1996) *Integrating Gender: Women, Law and Politics in the European Union*, London: Verso

Hoskyns, C. and Luckhaus, L. (1989) 'The European Community Directive on Equal Treatment in Social Security', *Policy and Politics*, vo. 17 (4) 321–35

Kingdon, J. (1994) *Agendas, Alternatives and Public Policies*, New York: Harper Collins

Klein, R. and O'Higgins, M. (1985) 'Social Policy After Incrementalism', in Klein, R. and O'Higgins, M. (eds) *The Future of Welfare Policy*, Oxford: Basil Blackwell

Landau, E. (1985) *The Rights of Working Women*, Luxembourg: Commission of the European Communities

Lewis, J. (ed) (1993) *Women and Social Policies in Europe. Work, Family and the State*, Aldershot: Edward Elgar Publishing

Lord Lester of Herne Hill (1994) 'Discrimination: What Lawyers can Learn from History?', *Public Law*, 231

Mazey, S. (1988) 'European Community Action on behalf of Women: the Limits of Legislation', *Journal of Common Market Studies*, vol. 27(1) 63–84

—— (1992) 'Conception and Evolution of The High Authority's Administrative Services (1952–1956): From Supranational Principles to Multinational Practices', in Morgan, R. and Wright, V. (eds) 'The Administrative Origins of the European Community', *Yearbook of European Administrative History*, Baden-Baden: Nomos Verlagsgesellschaft, 31–49

—— (1996) 'The Development of EU Equality Policies: Bureaucratic Expansion on Behalf of Women?', *Public Administration*, vol. 73(4) 591–610

Mazey S. and Richardson, J. (1995) 'Promiscuous Policy-Making: the European Policy Style?', in Rhodes, C. and Mazey, S. (eds)*The State of the European Union, Vol.3: Building a European Policy*, Boulder: Lynne Rienner and Longman, 337–60

—— (1996) 'EU Policy-Making: a Garbage Can or an Anticipatory and consensual Policy-Style?', in Mény, Y, Muller, P, Quermonne, J-L (eds) *Adjusting to Europe*, London: Routledge, 41–60

—— (1997) 'Policy Framing: Interest Groups and the 1996 Intergovernmental Conference (IGC)', *West European Politics*, vol. 20(3) 111–33

Meehan, E. (1990) 'Sex Equality Policies in the European Community', *Journal of European Integration*, vol. 13(2–3) 185–96

Meehan, E. and Collins E. (1996) 'Women, the European Union and Britain', *Parliamentary Affairs*, vol. 49 (1) 221–34

Ostner, I. (1993) 'Slow Motion: Women, Work and the Family in Germany', in J. Lewis (ed.) *Women and Social Policies in Europe. Work, Family and the State*, Aldershot: Edward Elgar Publishing, 92–115

Peters, B. Guy (1991) 'Bureaucratic Politics and the Institutions of the European Community', in Sbragia, Alberta M. (ed.) *Euro-Politics: Institutions and Policymaking in the 'New' European Community*, Washington DC:The Brookings Institution, 75–122

—— (1994) 'Agenda-setting in the European Community', *Journal of European Public Policy*, vol. 1, 9–26

Rein, H. and Schön, D. (1991) 'Frame Reflective Policy Discours', in P. Wagner, C. H. Weiss,

B. Wittrock and H. Wollman (eds) *Social Sciences, Modern States. National Experience and Theoretical Crossroads*, Cambridge: Cambridge University Press

Richardson, J. (ed.) (1996) *European Union: Power and Policy-Making*, London: Routledge

Rutherford, F. (1989) 'The Proposals for a European Directive on Parental Leave: some Reasons why it Failed', *Policy and Politics*, vol. 17(4) 301–10

Sabatier, P. (1988) 'An Advocacy Coalition Framework of Policy Change and the Role of Policy-Orientated Learning therein', *Policy Sciences*, vol. 21, 128–68

Streek, W. (1992) 'From National Corporatism to Transnational Pluralism: European Interest Groups and the Single Market', in Treu T. (ed.) *Participation in Public policy-making: the Role of Trade Unions and Employers Associations*, New York: Walter de Gruyter, 97–121

Vallance, E. and Davies E. (1986) *Women of Europe: Women MEPs and Equality Policy*, Cambridge: Cambridge University Press

Warner R. H. (1984) 'Social Policy in Practice: Community Action on behalf of Women and its Impact in the Member-States', *Journal of Common Market Studies*, vol. 23, 141–67

9

TRAINING POLICY

Steering between divergent national logics

Susan Milner

> Every soil brings forth its own trees. The same can be said for the
> different vocational training systems in Europe. They have adapted
> to their environment.
>
> CEDEFOP leaflet, 1995a

Training policy was the subject of an apparent consensus in the 1980s and 1990s, as EC institutions, governments and opposition parties alike, as well as social actors, proclaimed their commitment to improving the skills of Europe's workers, particularly in the face of unprecedented competition from low-wage but highly skilled labour forces in the fast-growing Pacific Rim economies. But this apparent consensus hides a real division between radically different approaches to training, which is visible in the persistence of nation-specific approaches to training in the pursuit of identical objectives. Thus, while training systems in all member states underwent significant change in the 1980s and 1990s, important differences remain and the EC itself has been largely powerless to influence such change directly. Nevertheless, it will be argued in this chapter that the EC has been able to act as a catalyst for change in the sense that it has accompanied and legitimised changes already taking place and facilitated an exchange of information, creating a menu of choices which national governments have been able to use selectively in their own search for economic competitiveness. Given that the impetus for change comes from the international commercial environment, governments seeking to improve national systems have explicitly compared their performance with that of competitors, and in this context the EU has been able to find a role in compiling information and disseminating best practice.

As will be discussed later, training systems are notoriously embedded in nation-specific institutional settings. As such they represent a nexus of interests and relationships, at the heart of which are business companies. However, although the behaviour of companies to a large extent determines employee access to training and the amount and content of training received, states shape the system as a whole in their relationship with organised interests. This relationship between national governments and organised interests, which has developed over many years if not centuries, explains why EC policy has been slow to take root. Moreover, Crouch (1995) shows that training policies reflect fundamental choices of economic strategy which are also strongly ideological. He describes the difference between the German and UK training systems as that between two rival logics – neo-corporatism and neo-liberalism – which dictate solutions to the central policy question: how can governments encourage companies to invest in training? It will be argued here that the EC's method of working does not allow it to choose between fundamentally divergent ideologies. Rather it seeks compromises between member states, always preferring consensus to majority voting. As a result, it has been unable to shape policy choices in vocational training.

EC initiatives in the field of vocational training

The Rome Treaty gives clear competence to the EC to promote vocational training, whereas there is no mention of common policies on education. Article 128 of the Rome Treaty authorises the Council of Ministers, on a proposal from the Commission and after consulting the Economic and Social Committee, to lay down general principles for the implementation of a 'common policy on vocational training capable of contributing to the harmonious development both of the national economies and of the common market'. Thus in a Decision of 1963[1] the Council established the principle that all individuals should receive adequate training, with particular reference to the need for member states to promote basic and specialised training, and, if necessary, retraining together with opportunities for promotion through higher qualification. Common vocational training policy was to rest on the individual rights of workers to life-long training. However, despite the clear mandate for common training policies given by the Rome Treaty and the 1963 declaration of principles, EC training policy made only slow progress thereafter (see Milner 1992; Rainbird 1993).

In fact, article 128, with its provision for a common policy, sits rather oddly with the accompanying measures in the chapter of the Treaty which sets up the European Social Fund (ESF). Article 125, which lays down the rules for applications to the ESF, makes clear that member- state governments retain responsibility for planning retraining arrangements, including financing training schemes (with costs to be shared on a fifty-fifty basis with the EC). Spending on EC training programmes has overwhelmingly taken place within the ESF's retraining activities (see table 9.1). This effectively leaves the EC as the instrument of member state restructuring. The 1988 reforms of the Structural Funds, which led to a doubling of resources, significantly enhanced the role of the Commission by setting Community-wide objectives and earmarking a proportion of funds for multi-annual programmes, but member states subsequently used the principle of subsidiarity to claw back powers (see Marks 1992; Allen 1996). Anderson (1995: 148) notes that 'the Community has defined the problem, adopted objectives, and employed instruments in ways that, apart from the level of subnational involvement in the policy process, are scarcely distinguishable from national approaches employed throughout Europe'.

Moreover, by placing training policy within the context of the European Social Fund, the Rome Treaty effectively limits training policy to retraining workers threatened by redundancy, although the objectives of the ESF are defined very broadly to include the improvement of workers' employment opportunities and facilitate free movement of labour.

The position within the Rome Treaty of provisions for a common vocational policy undoubtedly explains the confusion surrounding subsequent policy initiatives. First, the emphasis on retraining unemployed workers tended to encourage reactive or compensatory measures at the expense of forward-looking policy initiatives. Second, the distinction between initial and continuing vocational training or retraining has never been clearly made: the Commission's 1991 'Memorandum of Vocational Training', a key document setting out policy after Maastricht, omitted to define vocational training (DGB 1992). This failure to define the respective contributions of initial and continuing training – and thereby the division of responsibilities between the traditional actors within national training systems, notably between the public and private sectors – made it very difficult to develop focused policies. On the other hand, however, the ambiguities surrounding definitions of vocational training allowed the EC to interpret its policy brief widely when it chose to, as for example, in the case of higher education.

A comparison with policy on education, particularly higher education, is illuminating. Despite the omission of education policy from the powers given in the Rome Treaty, in 1976 the first Education Action Programme laid down objectives for co-operation on education policy: the promotion of closer relations between the education and training systems in Europe, increased co-operation between universities and institutions of higher education, improved possibilities for academic recognition of diplomas and periods of study, encouragement of freedom of movement of teachers, students and researchers, achievement of equal opportunity of access to education.

Table 9.1 Expenditure on education and·training programmes/European Social Fund/ R & D programmes

Activity	1987	1988	1989	1990	1991	1992	TOTAL
Education and Training	0.20	0.16	0.27	0.38	0.51	0.57	0.38
European Social Fund	7.30	6.61	7.65	8.77	7.71	8.10	7.74
Research and Development	2.92	2.42	3.26	3.76	2.64	4.03	3.22
CEC TOTAL	100	100	100	100	100	100	100

Source: Commission of the European Communities, *EC Education and Training Programmes 1986–92* (1993)

Undoubtedly, the relative importance of higher education and vocational training reflected the priorities of national governments. It was not until the late 1970s and the growth of mass unemployment that vocational training, traditionally the poor relation of national education and training systems, attracted the serious attention of policy makers. However, even in more recent years it has proved easier to set common programmes in higher education than in vocational training. It is true that national structures of higher education are on the whole more similar than vocational training structures and that in most countries the role of the state is more clearly defined. This clearer division of responsibilities is seen in the fact that the body responsible for making decisions on education and training policy was the Council of Education Ministers. In some member states, both education and training come under the remit of the education ministry, but in other countries the two policy areas are split.

In the absence of a dedicated policy unit, training policy inevitably developed on an *ad hoc*, reactive basis and remained firmly under the control of national government (especially since the ESF depended on national government financial support). It was not until the Task Force for Human Resources, Education, Training and Youth was set up within DG V in 1985 that training became a major policy issue. But the institutional arrangements themselves provide only part of the answer, because they in turn reflect policy priorities. Cram (1993) shows that the Commission acted in an entrepreneurial way to carve out areas of competence in social and environmental policy, using its limited treaty powers to the full. Why, then, was there a lack of political will on the part of supranational actors in the area of vocational training? It may well be that, as in national policy settings, the importance of vocational training became apparent only in the late 1970s. But it is noteworthy that from the start the EC lacked both clear objectives in training policy and a framework in which the central question of how to involve companies in training could be addressed. This reflects a fundamental policy dilemma which can be seen in many of the EC's pronouncements on training: whether to opt for a high-trust, neo-corporatist approach to training or a neo-liberal approach. As Crouch (1995) and Coffield (1992) make clear, the difference between these two alternatives does not simply represent a choice between centralisation and decentralisation, as many politicians would have us believe. In fact, Crouch shows that the neo-liberal approach is strongly statist, since it seeks to prevent organised interests from building up networks of influence.

The EC itself appears to oscillate between these two approaches. Lacking the resources of a state, the EC has sought to promote neo-corporatism in its own methods of working in order to build up a network based on reciprocal trust, necessary to ensure even the most limited policy implementation. Also, in order to legitimise supranational policy initiatives, it points to international competition and argues in its own policy documents in favour of a high-skills economic strategy. According to this argument, Europe's competitive advantage lies in its human capital, in line with Porter's (1990) work on the comparative advantage of nations. The model here is Germany, which, Porter notes (1990: 368), has no great natural resources, but the strength of its economy lies in its highly paid, highly skilled and highly motivated workforce. The 1995 White Paper on education and training (CEC 1995a) stresses that the European dimension of training forms a necessary component of the 'European social model' in which competitiveness, employment, education and training are linked. At the same time, however, the ethos of EC economic policy has largely followed the neo-liberal approach. This apparently schizophrenic approach – the tension between 'market-making' and 'market-breaking' – to most areas of social policy characterises the Single European Market initiative, and has propelled training policy since the mid-1980s. It is typical of the multi-tiered system of governance described by Leibfried and Pierson (1995).

Although the Single Act itself contained nothing in the way of new provisions on training, it opened the way for a new wave of policy initiatives. The Hanover Council of 27–8 June 1988 stated that the Single Market should be accompanied by a commitment to continuing training. The new policy offensive stemmed from four main strands of thinking. First, the new orthodoxy of the 1980s saw economic competitiveness as increasingly dependent on optimum use of human resources, namely skills. Second, implementation of the principle of worker mobility (one of the four freedoms which has proved remarkably difficult to achieve despite a rash of measures in the 1960s which in theory removed many of the barriers to free movement) meant that the Commission could point to a clear 'transnational' element of training policy and thus justify greater Community co-ordination of national policies. Third, the Single Act gave rise to calls for accompanying measures to ensure a 'level playing field', notably in the social field (leading to the adoption of the Social Charter). Fourth, even the optimistic Cecchini report noted that additional measures would be needed to preserve social cohesion, particularly an increased need for compensatory measures (employment and retraining initiatives). Thus the Single Act provided the justification for increased Community action which, it should be added, the new Commission after 1985 was willing to use to the full. The Commission set up a separate policy unit within DG V, a Task Force, to deal with education and training.

The late 1980s saw a flurry of new initiatives (see table 9.2): COMETT was launched in 1986; ERASMUS in 1987; and PETRA in 1988. Youth for Europe, arising out of the Adonnino report on a People's Europe adopted by the European Council in 1985, was established formally in 1988. EUROTECNET, originally set up experimentally in late 1980s, was formalised in 1990, LINGUA and TEMPUS launched in 1990, and FORCE set up in 1991. Here it should be noted that the political will expressed in the Single Act allowed the Commission to develop a Community policy which went beyond previous competence in two significant respects. First, it set up a policy network which to some extent bypassed national government, and it was able to do this because a transnational dimension of policy had been identified. Second, the Community continued to develop its competence in the sphere of education even though it had no constitutional mandate to do so. It was opposed in this by the UK, notably in the cases of ERASMUS and

LINGUA, but rulings laid down by the European Court of Justice allowed the Commission to continue to expand its competence in this area through its generous interpretation of the term 'vocational training' (Nielsen and Szyszczak 1991: 75). This helps to explain why the EC has not sought to clarify definitions of training and the division of responsibilities within training systems.

Table 9.2 EC education and training programmes

Short title	Full title	Duration	Budget execution up to 1992 (MECU)
COMETT	Programme on cooperation between universities and industry regarding training in the field of technology	1986-94	206,6
ERASMUS	European Community action scheme for the Mobility of University Students	1987-	307,5
PETRA	Action Programme for the vocational training of young people and their preparation for adult and working life	1988-94	79,7
YOUTH FOR EUROPE	Action Programme for the promotion of youth exchanges in the Community - 'Youth for Europe' programme	1988-1994	32,2
IRIS	European Network of Vocational training Projects for Women	1988-93	0.75
EUROTECNET	Action Programme to promote innovation in the field of vocational training resulting from technological change in the European Community	1990-94	7.0
LINGUA	Action Programme to promote foreign language competence in the European Community	1990-94	68,8
TEMPUS	Trans-European Mobility Scheme for University Studies	1990-94	194,0
FORCE	Action Programme for the development of continuing vocational training in the European Community	1991-94	31,3

Source: Commission of the European Communities, *EC Education and Training Programmes 1986–92* (1993)

As well as these Community programmes, moves towards a common training policy received a boost from the Social Charter (point 15):

> Every worker of the European Community must be able to have access to vocational training and to benefit therefrom throughout his [sic] working life. In the conditions governing access to such training there may be no discrimination on grounds of nationality. The competent public authorities, undertakings or the two sides of industry, each within their own sphere of competence, should set up continuing and permanent training systems enabling every person to undergo retraining, more especially through leave for training purposes, to improve his skills or to acquire new skills, particularly in the light of technical developments.

This provision is interesting because it echoes the individual rights approach fostered in the 1963 Council Decision. It also gave rise to specific measures outlined in the Social Action Programme for the first time. However, these measures were limited in scope. They concentrated on reorganising training activities within the Commission so as to increase efficiency. In 1990, EC training programmes were rationalised. For instance, the Youth for Europe programme became integrated into PETRA, and the various training initiatives under the European Social Fund were now regrouped into several key programmes, notably EUROFORM. At the same time programmes were extended and given additional, though still very limited, financial support. It was on the basis of these measures that the Commission claimed in its second report on the application of the Social Charter that 'Community action programmes in the field of vocational training have made enormous progress since 1987 in the wake of the adoption of the COMETT programme' (CEC 1992: 19).

Organisational streamlining continued and made a difference. The education and training strands of Community action were grouped together in the Socrates and Leonardo programmes respectively. Also, the Task Force was moved out of DG V and became a fully fledged Directorate-General, namely, DG XII, with responsibilities for Education, Training and Youth, at the same time that a Commissioner was nominated for Education, Training and Research for the first time. The creation of a Directorate-General and a Commission portfolio dedicated to education and training undoubtedly gave a boost to policy. Although not one of the larger DGs, DG XII has a small team that is focused and energetic. It has experience in the field and Edith Cresson as Commissioner keeps a high profile. Moreover, organisational rationalisation can have an important impact. As Marks noted in the case of structural policy, the creation of DG XXII, established to manage the Structural Funds after the 1989 reforms, reflected a shift in power towards supranational actors and away from national government (but he also noted that 'effective co-ordination demands power' and expressed doubts that the small new unit could wield sufficient authority) (Marks 1992: 220). Effective institutional co-ordination is a prerequisite for entrepreneurial action on the part of supranational policy actors; it does not by itself denote policy activism. Table 9.1 shows that neither the reform of the 1988 Structural Funds nor the institutional rationalisation of education and training programmes since the mid-1980s resulted in increased spending on education and training, which still accounts for a small share of the total EC budget.

The Treaty on European Union provided new powers for the European Union in the field of education. The Treaty gives the Council the power to adopt recommendations on 'incentive measures' in the educational field, acting on a qualified majority (using the new co-decision procedure) (article 126). Clearer objectives for vocational training policy are also set out in article 127, which authorises the Council to adopt measures towards these objectives according to the co-operation procedure. Emphasis is now placed on shared cultural values of education and training which will 'provide the basis for the emerging European identity and citizenship' (CEC 1993b: 2).

However, several commentators consider that the new provisions have weakened Community competence in education and training rather than reinforcing it (see DGB 1992: 24), on the grounds that the new articles expressly exclude any notion of harmonisation and pledge respect for national laws and practices, following the principle of subsidiarity. Thus, the new article 127 does not speak of a common policy on vocational training but 'a vocational training policy which shall support and supplement the action of the member states, while fully respecting the responsibility of the member states for the content and organisation of vocational training'. On the other hand, however, the objectives of vocational training policy were widened by the TEU. It is made clear that Community action covers both initial and continuing training, and training is seen as a means of helping businesses adapt to change as well as integrating young workers and the unemployed into the labour market.

In the 1990s, then, the powers of the Community to intervene were strictly curtailed, with responsibility for policy making placed unambiguously in the hands of national government. Harmonisation of the laws and regulations of member states is expressly excluded. But in terms of breadth of policy coverage or issue density, the Community has widened its sphere of action. The recognition of the limits of Community competence, coupled with an expansion of the EC's policy fields, is typical of a new, 'realist' social policy approach. It could be argued that it offers scope for action in new, controversial areas as well as those which have traditionally been uncontested; that is, where a 'European dimension' can be identified, namely transnational exchanges and measures to achieve greater transparency and recognition of qualifications in order to promote labour mobility.

Thus, the new emphasis on the fight against unemployment legitimates Community initiatives on training and gives vocational training a central place in EC policy making. The first document to bring vocational training into the mainstream and suggest a more pro-active training policy was the 1993 Delors White Paper on growth, competitiveness and employment. In particular, the White Paper promoted continuous vocational training as an instrument of economic competitiveness, and adaptation to technological advances and changing market needs. The December 1994 Essen Summit brought employment to the forefront of EC activity and identified five priority fields of action, including vocational training. It thereby opened the way for DG XII to put forward new policy initiatives, which it duly did, contributing a list of proposals for the Action Plan that followed Essen. Many of these proposals resembled earlier Commission statements in that they represented vague exhortations to member states to give greater priority to training. For example, they stressed the need to widen access to training – the subject of a 1991 Joint Opinion between social partners and a 1993 Council Recommendation. However, other proposals were more specific and indicate a potentially more pro-active role for the Commission in co-ordinating national policies and helping to set the agenda for change at national level. These include, for example, the suggestion that member states should set national targets for qualification levels of the whole workforce, the idea of guaranteed training or work placements for young people – an idea which has been floated by the British Labour Party – and the promotion of lifelong learning. The latter proposal in particular was then taken up in the November 1995 White Paper, entitled 'Teaching and learning: towards the learning society', and gave rise to a specific policy initiative, namely, the decision to designate 1996 'The Year of Lifelong Learning' in order to highlight activities such as career guidance and information on continuous training opportunities in member states. In this way, the Essen Summit relegitimised Community action on training and gave a new boost to the principles of EC action which had been laid down in the 1963 Decision.

However, the June 1995 Commission Communication, based on the Essen discussion, defined the role of EC actors as one of co-ordination and information, notably the pooling of information on national practices. This is in line with the provisions of the TEU, which clearly establish national governments as the key policy actors and protect national training systems from Community intervention. Thus, the exchange of issue density for specific policy instruments may in fact restrict the role of EC institutions as independent policy actors.

Nevertheless, the new deal on the division of labour – under the label of subsidiarity – between EC institutions and member states may well suit the former. It allows them to develop a policy brief, administer programmes and acquire legitimacy. It also saves them from making fundamental choices of economic strategy which it is, in any case, beyond their power to enforce. Member states, on the other hand, preserve both their decision making and their financial autonomy, since training programmes could potentially demand a sizeable amount of state spending, whilst retaining the use of Community programmes as an instrument of economic restructuring. Thus, the Council response to the Commission's 1995 White Paper warned of the dangers of adopting a single set of proposals on education and training, emphasising instead the complexity of the issues involved. Rather than seeking to impose a 'single institutional measure', each member state 'will endeavour to introduce and develop such arrangements as it considers necessary' (OJ 96/C 195/01). The Council response stressed that the usefulness of EC initiatives lay in the exchange of information and the funding of experimental projects at a time of change.

National vocational training policies

Training systems are deeply embedded in the relationship between states and national networks of organised interests. States play a crucial role in shaping these systems. Crouch (1993) has shown that fundamental differences between western European countries in the relationship between state, employers and trade unions reflect state traditions which have developed over many centuries. Thus, the neo-corporatist training systems of Germany, Austria and Scandinavia have evolved separately and under different conditions. Austria, for instance, stands out because of the strongly centralising state under the Habsburg empire. However, they have all retained elements of the medieval guild system which elsewhere, as, for example, in France during the French revolution, were dismantled or eroded.

It should be noted, of course, that the situation in all EU member states is dynamic: vocational training has undergone considerable change in recent years. The process of economic convergence which has taken place has meant that training policy has gained importance, as well as becoming the focus of debate and criticism particularly in a common context of mass unemployment, not only in the most developed economies of northern Europe, but also in the poorer countries, which have had to adapt rapidly to the opportunities and risks of the enlarged market. The impact of similar economic pressures in increasingly globalised markets may therefore suggest a convergence of training systems. Moreover, in the continuing debate on ways of improving training systems, much attention has inevitably been paid to comparisons between countries, and some countries have sought to copy elements of other systems which seem to work well. At a general level, it is possible to identify some similar trends. However, these trends can be seen across all industrialised countries, including newly industrialised countries, and are not limited to the EU. It is therefore difficult to argue that convergence is the product of EU policy co-ordination.

In all countries, the nature and purpose of vocational training have been transformed by the shift away from old industrial production methods towards new production methods in industry. New technologies have made old skills redundant and have broken down the generational reproduction of skills that have traditionally been at the heart of initial vocational training, especially apprenticeships. A similar need for rapid adaptation to customer needs and technological change is evident in the growing service sector. These changes have placed great strain on initial vocational training systems, which in most member states have been revised to take account of companies' changing needs and to strengthen the link between business and training institutions. At the same time, they have created a new need for continuous vocational training, since skills learnt in initial training will need constant updating. Continuous vocational training has therefore undergone radical change. From being an instrument of personal development – adult education and 'second-chance' learning – or a means for individual workers to gain promotion, it has become an additional element of companies' drive for competitiveness (see Podevin 1995). In the 1980s and l990s, training came to be regarded as an important indicator of a country's competitive advantage, measured in terms of attainment of internationally recognised qualification standards and expenditure by states and companies on initial and vocational training. In the UK, for example, the government funded a study of changing skill and qualification levels in France, Germany, USA, Australia, Japan, Korea and Japan because of a perceived need 'to improve education and training standards in the UK to meet those of our international competitors' (IES 1996: 1). Finally, training systems have been radically transformed by the introduction of specific programmes for groups affected by mass unemployment, particularly youth and the long-term unemployed, in which training serves social rather than economic ends.

It is little wonder, then, that a comparative study based on continuous training in three sectors – construction, banking and insurance, and electricity/electronics – carried out by CEDEFOP to support the 1991 Joint Opinion on ways of ensuring access to training found a number of transnational trends of this nature. In particular, it identified an increased financial commitment by the state and a search for the appropriate legislative instruments to encourage companies to invest in training. On the other hand, the study found a great range of diversity of methods in each sector, not only between, but within, countries.

Similarly, four main issues emerged from a cross-national study of youth training programmes in six European countries (Germany, Spain, France, Italy, Sweden and the UK). One of these issues – the reproduction of social inequalities in access to training – cut across national borders. But significant differences were found at the level of structures (institutionalised or *ad hoc*) and the economic choices governing the type of programme on offer. Differences were also found between methods used to evaluate training programmes, with some countries such as France providing data on individual career trajectories and others, for example, Sweden, concentrating on the macroeconomic effects of training schemes (CEREQ 1996a).

The Commission's 1995 White Paper on education and training stressed both common trends – lengthening of periods of study, wider access to higher education, a search for more flexible ways of recognising skills, attempts to link training more closely to the needs of business – and the diversity of national situations.

The persistence of underlying features and structures of national training systems, reflecting the historical development of the state in western European societies, confirms the 'societal effect' approach to cross-national comparison developed by Maurice, Sellier, Sorge and others (see Maurice and Sellier 1979), which holds that 'whatever happens in one sector of society is always connected to events or to structures in other sectors' (Sorge 1995: 242). Crouch's analysis goes further in attributing a central role to the state in allowing organised interests into the policy making arena – the neo-corporatist model – or preventing them from gaining a foothold – the neo-liberal model (Crouch 1995). To these two models, we

might also add a third where vocational training has traditionally been less important than state-sponsored formal education routes, and the links between training
and business companies weak. France follows this approach, but it is also seen to
some extent elsewhere, for example, in Finland.

Let us now look briefly at the training systems of Germany, the United
Kingdom and France to see how much they have changed in recent years and
to what extent any changes may be attributed to Community intervention or
influence.

Germany

Germany's training policy has remained relatively stable. Rose and Page (1990)
identify only five new initiatives during the period 1979–89 in response to unemployment (as opposed to forty-three in the UK). Crouch (1995) attributes this
stability to the continued effectiveness of the system, based on apprenticeships or
alternance training. The keystone is the 'dual system' in which school-leavers
receive college-based, certified training in transferable skills (usually for one day a
week) whilst employed on trainee wages within companies. Each year around a
third of young people leaving secondary education commence training within the
dual system. The system ensures a relatively good match between business needs
and the training provided. In the 1980s, the dual system came under criticism for
insufficient attention to labour market supply and demand, but this has been
corrected by recent initiatives which limit the number of apprenticeships in over-
subscribed professions. Initial training is therefore extremely important, and it
dovetails into workplace organisation, while career advancement is based on
attainment of recognised transferable skills (see Sorge 1995).

German businesses also invest relatively highly in continuous training, although
this type of training is likely to be targeted selectively, and to be of short duration
(perhaps 'refresher' courses). In 1993, Germany came top out of seven EU
member states in a FORCE/EUROSTAT survey for the proportion of businesses
(59 per cent) using training courses (CEREQ 1996b).

Among EU member states, Germany has the highest proportion of young
people who at age 18 have followed a vocational education and/or training
programme: 93 per cent as against 45 per cent in France and 16 per cent in the
UK. This may explain why Germany is alone among EU member states in having
lower rates of youth unemployment than for the population as a whole (CEC
1995b).

Impetus for change in the German system has come from two main sources.
First, German reunification added considerably to the already growing need for
active labour market policies for those made redundant or threatened with redundancy in older industries. Already in 1970, West Germany was way ahead of
France and Britain with regard to the number of trainees on special employment
training schemes relative to the total workforce (Balfour 1972: 121) and such
schemes have mushroomed in the new *Länder*. According to some analysts, the

severity of the unemployment situation in Germany's eastern regions created the conditions for policy innovation (see Blancke and Widmaier forthcoming); others, however, criticise such training schemes for failing to attack the roots of the problem, which lie in labour market regulation (see Lange 1993). Second, Germany's 'high skills equilibrium' has come under threat from employers who have complained about high labour costs. On the whole, the social partners remain committed to the neo-corporatist arrangements which hold the initial vocational training system in place, but the consensus is beginning to fray at the edges. Continuous training is more problematic as companies feel the recession bite (Bispinck 1990). However, for the time being at least, Germany's apprenticeship-based system is generally seen as effective in combating youth unemployment and creating a highly skilled workforce able to adapt quickly to changing economic and technological conditions.

The United Kingdom[2]

The UK is generally considered to lag well behind Germany in terms of the skill levels of its workforce. In contrast with Germany, apprentices account for only a small proportion of young workers, many of whom enter full-time jobs with no qualifications. Traditionally, British companies prefer 'on-the-job training'. But they have failed to invest the necessary resources into informal workplace training to bring the skill levels into line with those of their competitors. In 1964, in an attempt to encourage companies to invest in human resources, the UK government introduced Industrial Training Boards to administer sectorally transferable skills training, with the imposition of training levies on firms. The multipartite Manpower Commission, introduced in 1973, was supposedly modelled on Sweden's corporatist training administration (Crouch 1995: 298). However, in the UK it was used as an instrument of deregulation. The 1973 Education and Training Act weakened the powers of the Industrial Training Boards and replaced the levy grant mechanism with a levy-exemption procedure (Rainbird 1993). The Industrial Training Boards were then abolished or privatised in the 1980s, and the apprenticeship system all but collapsed in the recession. In the place of the MSC, eighty-two Training and Enterprise Councils (TECs) were set up in England and Wales. TECs are responsible for the delivery of government-funded training schemes. They are independent bodies, composed of local business people and training providers. In theory trade unions are also invited to join TECS but in practice they are dominated by employers. The TECs were modelled on North American rather than European initiatives and according to many academic observers they represent a further dismantling of the UK training system. Crouch (1995) sees the TECs as continuing the logic of neo-liberalism: they can enforce no sanctions, they have limited resources and they must provide training as cheaply as possible. Many TECs have publicly complained that government finances are insufficient to allow them to provide adequate training. Since they are contractually obliged to carry out government-sponsored schemes for the unemployed, their wider mission of matching training to local company needs is often neglected. According to a survey of TECs in northern England, TECs were unable to change the prevailing company culture 'antipathetic to education, training and enterprise' (Coffield 1992: 15).

In 1988, vocational training was reorganised within the framework of a new system of skills certification, National Vocational Qualifications (NVQs). NVQs represent five levels of skill, ranging from NVQ1 – ability to perform relatively simple work, roughly corresponding to basic general education – to NVQ5 – equivalent to higher education or higher vocational certificates, e.g. recognised professional qualifications. These five levels of attainment correspond to EU-recognised training levels, as laid down in a 1985 Council Decision (OJ L199, 31 July 1985) They reflect a flexible approach to vocational training certification because existing, non-certified skills acquired on the job may be validated at the lower end of the scale. The NVQ approach has been severely criticised because it seeks to validate the existing skills base, often at a very low level, rather than to upskill. More worryingly for the government, take-up of NVQs has been very slow, and traditional vocational qualifications have remained considerably more popular than NVQs.

At the same time, the government regularly revamped training courses for the young and long-term unemployed (over six months), and introduced an accompanying series of changes to the unemployment benefit system.

The 1980s thus saw a series of changes in the UK training system, forty-three new initiatives in total. Rose and Page (1990) attribute this policy activity to the great flexibility of the UK system, but Crouch's (1995) view is more negative. All are agreed that the UK model is based on an economic strategy dependent on flexible labour markets and low labour costs. According to Crouch, this strategy creates problems in that it leads the UK to trade in low-value products which can always be undercut by the newly industrialised economies. This strategy sits uneasily with the UK government's proclaimed desire to invest in skills, as is borne out in comparative surveys of skill levels in the developed world. In 1990 the House of Commons Select Committee on the European Communities concluded that the UK 'does not have a clearly articulated national strategic framework for training' and argued that 'given the gap between the UK and its main industrial competitors . . . and the long history of failure which has marked the voluntary approach to training in this country, the Committee consider that some form of statutory underpinning is needed to act as a catalyst for change' (quoted by Rainbird 1993: 199). The Confederation of British Industry, too, has repeatedly expressed concerns about Britain's dwindling skill base. The CBI's task force on vocational education and training noted that 'the UK still compares unfavourably in a number of sectors with EC competitors', especially Germany (CBI 1990: 109). It expressed a desire for the West German dual system to be emulated in Britain, with the aim of providing training, full-time or combined with employment, for all under-18s. It also called for the establishment of individual career profiles from the age of fourteen.

Prompted by the CBI's criticisms, in 1991 the government set official national training targets for developing workplace skills. Thus by 1997, at least 80 per cent of all young people should have attained NVQ Level 2; by the year 2000, at least half of the cohort should attain NVQ Level 3. In addition, lifelong learning targets were set, in accordance with EU training policy: by 1996, the European Year of Lifelong Learning, all employees should have taken part in training or development activities, and half of the employed workforce should be aiming for qualifications within the NVQ framework, preferably on the basis of individual training plans; by the year 2000, 50 per cent of the employed workforce should be qualified to at least NVQ Level 3 (CEDEFOP 1995a: 391–2).

These targets do not by themselves, however, address the problems of inadequate structural underpinning of training identified by the House of Lord Select Committee and the CBI. Peter Robinson of the Centre for Economic Performance wrote in the *Financial Times* (7 October 1996) that the new vocational qualifications have not led to any appreciable increase in the training available to individuals; take-up of the NVQs is slowing, and indeed the government has been forced to abandon its 50 per cent target. The reforms undertaken in the 1980s and 1990s continued the voluntaristic approach to training. In its 1991 White Paper, 'Education and Training in the 21st Century', the government restated its opposition to a statutory approach: 'The commitment of young people and their employers to training needs to be secured by voluntary means.' It is difficult to see how real improvement in skills can be attained by exhortation alone within the prevailing business culture which sees training solely as a cost.

France

France represents an institutional model of vocational training in which training is essentially provided by schools or colleges. After a period of initial general education (seven to nine years) students move on to vocational courses lasting two or three years and leading to a Vocational Proficiency Certificate (CAP) or Vocational Education Certificate (BEP). After a further two years' study, they may prepare a Vocational Baccalaureate. In France's elitist education system, vocational training is something of a poor relation. Those following vocational subjects are often those who have failed their basic subjects, and employers appear to set little store by vocational diplomas (Caillods 1994). Many young people leave the educational system with no qualifications whatsoever – around 15 per cent, although this has fallen from around a third in the early 1980s – and the proportion of workers without vocational training is double that in Germany. Apprenticeships traditionally do not enjoy high prestige and play a secondary role in the training system, covering about one-seventh of the total number of individuals receiving training (CEDEFOP 1995b: 29).

Continuous vocational training occupies an important place in the French system. The qualifications of French workers result from a combination of on-the-job training, vocational experience and length of service. The relatively dense supervisory layer in French businesses provides an opportunity for individual career advancement (see Sorge 1995).

Employers' investment in training is relatively high. In terms of spending per employee, France comes top of the list in western Europe (CEREQ 1996b). This may be explained by the statutory payroll levy of 1.1 per cent. The French levy system, first introduced in 1971 and increased several times since then, certainly encourages larger companies to invest in training: the actual contribution level increased from 1.3 per cent of the wage bill in 1972 to 2.34 per cent in 1986 (CEDEFOP 1995b: 142). However, the evidence suggests that access to training remains unequal despite the presence of a company training plan in 40 per cent of companies (as opposed to only 20 per cent in Germany). Only around 12 per cent of small companies (with between ten and forty-nine employees) train their employees compared with 46 per cent of French companies in total.

Various attempts have been made to boost apprenticeships, which involve around 60,000 young people a year – around a tenth of those in Germany's dual system. An apprenticeship tax of 0.5 per cent of the total wage bill is levied on companies, in addition to a regional apprenticeship tax. Also, since 1992–3, work-experience placements have been introduced into BEP, CAP and Vocational Baccalaureate courses.

In order to give training to the significant number of young labour market entrants with no qualifications – up to a third of the cohort – a series of training measures for sixteen- to twenty-five-year-olds were introduced after 1983 at the initiative of the social partners (CEC 1995b): guidance contracts for unqualified young people, lasting three to six months, with specified college-based modules or on-the-job training, under agreement with the trainee; qualification contracts lasting between six months and two years, building on initial training, with the trainee paid a salary and guaranteed training for at least 25 per cent of the working week; and adaptation contracts alternance training for specific job-related skills. These contracts are financed by an additional 0.1 per cent payroll levy on companies, and have grown significantly in importance since their inception. Whereas in 1985 3,031 qualification contracts were signed, in 1990 101,706 young people were registered on such contracts. However, doubts have been expressed about the content of the training in such contracts, and there are fears about simple substitution of low-paid trainees for stable jobs.

In July 1994, responsibility for provision of training to young people was transferred to the regional authorities. The idea behind this move was to make training provision more responsive to local business needs, but it is not yet clear what effects the reform will have on training and the labour-market integration of young people.

To summarise, the schemes initiated in 1983 introduced a significant change into the French training system by creating second-chance training for those leaving college without qualifications. The introduction and expansion of work-experience placements into existing initial vocational training courses also strengthened the link between business and training and moved France away from its traditional institutional approach. However, although the German dual system is much admired in France, it has not been emulated wholesale. Instead, the French system may be considered something of a hybrid, since it has sought to retain the central elements of its institutional model whilst incorporating elements along the lines of the German system. This is undoubtedly for cultural reasons. For example, French trade unions are much weaker than their German counterparts and this is often cited as a reason why German methods would not work in France. Employers have learned to live with the levy system and the state-sponsored youth employment schemes, although their effect on unemployment is limited. Youth unemployment is particularly high in France: one in four French citizens between the ages of sixteen and twenty-five is unemployed, and only one in four is now working without the aid of a government grant or financial system of some kind.

As a result, there have recently been some calls for a radical overhaul of the training system. A 1996 report recommended that the entire system be scrapped and training provision be left to businesses to organise according to their own needs. Such a radical deregulatory solution is unlikely to be implemented and would take a good deal of political courage. It is interesting, however, to note that the publication of a report recommending a voluntaristic, neo-liberal approach to training represents a chink in the prevailing consensus on training, which has tended to promote the German model.

From these brief overviews, evidence of direct EC influence over national policy choices appears scarce. Rather, we see that national training systems are culturally specific, but open to change as a result of pressures created by rising unemployment, economic globalisation, demographic pressures and so on. In this context, the European Union can provide a forum for the exchange of information and ideas, and some financial backing for necessary changes. Through the PETRA programme, too, member states have used the opportunity to build a Community dimension into major national initiatives such as the vocational baccalaureate in France, the reform of the *istituti professionali* in Italy, and the introduction of a new type of vocational school (*escolas profissionais*) in Portugal (CEC 1993a). The European Social Fund, too, has helped to finance the development of training schemes, particularly for the unemployed. In Italy and in Spain, ESF funding complements employer levies used for continuing training and employment training; in Portugal, ESF funding has helped to finance a radical overhaul of the vocational training system; and in Greece, individual projects have benefited, rather than the system as a whole, which remains somewhat piecemeal. Ireland too has benefited.

Of the three countries briefly surveyed above, Germany is closest to the model of a high-skills economy advocated by exponents of European integration. However, recent trends do not appear to be converging towards the German model. Indeed, the UK neo-liberal model seems to hold some interest for would-be reformers in France and Germany. Moreover, the UK's approach to accreditation and individualisation of training has much in common with EC training policy in the 1980s. (We have already noted the similarity between the EC's five training levels and the organisation of NVQs.)

This apparent contradiction could suggest that in the l990s the EU has come round to the British way of thinking on social matters and adopted a deregulatory approach to training, as British politicians often claim. More probably, the search for a 'lowest common denominator' likely to win approval from all member states leads the EU to a minimalist approach which resembles British 'voluntarism'. Effectively, this limits the EU to the 'neo-voluntarism' advocated by Streeck (1995) as the only realistic policy approach.

Divergent policy styles and the impact of EC policy

As already indicated, training policy reform reflects what we might term policy 'styles', following Esping-Andersen 1990, as well as strategic social and economic choices. British 'voluntarism', for example, blocks trade unions and other social actors from access to decision making. This helps to explain why the UK government is so keen to safeguard its autonomy and insistent on EU respect for the principle of subsidiarity. However, the style of EU policy making opens up a more 'open-textured, multi-level perspective' (Marks 1992: 192) in which the central role of national governments can be contested by regional and social actors. The increasingly frag-mented and technical nature of the EU offers greater opportunity for the formation of policy networks than at the national level (Mitchell 1993: 15). Subsidiarity not only allows national governments to challenge EU competence, but potentially gives greater power to sub-national levels of decision making. Moreover, as Spicker (1991) argues, subsidiarity can be interpreted in a horizontal as well as vertical sense: that is, policy making can be opened up to include non-governmental actors such as employers, consumers' organisations or trade unions. It is widely recognised that training particularly lends itself to corporatist modes of policy making because of the fundamental issue of trust which any training system seeks to address.

During the time of the Task Force, the Commission cultivated its own policy style which in many ways emulated German or Swedish-style neo-corporatism. The reason was partly ideological – a commitment to a 'high-skills equilibrium' – but also practical. In the absence of real legitimacy among member state govern-ments, the EC sought to create a wide policy network to legitimise its initiatives. Within the Task Force itself, the tripartite Advisory Committee on Vocational Training 'has, since [its establishment in] 1963, been the principal forum where the social partners have discussed, reflected on, and adopted positions on Community guidelines and actions' (CEC 1992). It was closely involved at an early stage in the preparation of texts which the Commission adopts or submits to the Council of Ministers. In this respect, the input of the ACVT was exceptionally high among the advisory committees (Milner 1993). However, after training poli-cies were streamlined in the wake of TEU ratification, the Commission appeared to have had less recourse to the Advisory Committee. The 1993 Commission proposals for future action (CEC 1993b) did not even mention the ACVT.

The ACVT constitutes a direct channel into national policy making networks, on a traditional tripartite basis. In this way, the Commission has sought to influence modes of policy formation in the member states, by inviting national governments to consult with employers' organisations and trade unions, and in some cases with training providers, before compiling national reports in response to specific policy objectives. This approach characterised the 1991 'Memorandum on Vocational Training' and, more recently, the 1995 White Paper on education and training. However, the result has sometimes simply been the submission of separate reports, for example, by the British government and the Trades Union Congress. Attempts in 1992–3 to set up tripartite discussion forums in each member state also failed to involve member states which were hostile to increased involvement of social partners. This suggests that national policy styles remain firmly resistant to EU influence. In addition, training policy was explicitly driven by the Summit-level social dialogue. Thus, for example, the 1993 Council Recommendation on Access to Vocational Training refer in its preamble to the November 1991 Joint Opinion signed by the social partners (the European Trade Union Confederation, the Euro-level employers' federation, UNICE, and the European Centre for Public Enterprises CEEP). Moreover, the Recommendation ended with an invitation to member states to provide a follow-up report within three years. This extra requirement, which was hotly contested by some countries but finally included, may thus be interpreted as a means of providing legislative back-up, via concrete commitments by member states, to the Joint Opinions reached by the social partners. However, the 1995 White Paper on education and training contains no such reference to the social partners in its preamble. In this respect, too, the link between the social partners, the EU and national policy making appears to have been weakened since 1991.

EU training policy undermines national autonomy in another key respect. The Structural Funds operate on the basis of a network of policy makers and providers, and, in some cases, users. EC training programmes – the 'European dimension' to training, essentially Leonardo and associated activities – follow this model. The avowed objective is to create dense multilateral links between local authorities, local associations and private bodies – companies, teaching and learning institutions, and trade unions – which, through the contact supported financially by EU schemes, gradually by-pass national governments. COMETT and FORCE were seen as exemplary in this respect, because of the representation of employer and worker interests on their advisory committees and the wide range of organisations participating in the programme networks, especially with respect to FORCE. Marks (1992) argues that such networks will increasingly contest the decision-making power of national government.

In the long term, transnational networks may help to break down differences between national policy styles by widening the menu of choices. In other words, this limited 'bottom-up' approach stands a greater chance of influencing national policy and practice than a 'top-down' attempt at harmonisation. However, for the moment at least, the scope for effective co-ordination of sub-national actors is often over-stated. Member states retain a large amount of control in the selection of projects (Allen 1996). Cross-national networks of sub-national actors can provide what Leibfried and Pierson (1995) term 'policy innovation and emulation' but they are less politically effective than national governments. Moreover, the territorialisation of policy in the Structural Funds and EU training programmes means that there is little or no spillover into mainstream EC social policy (Anderson 1995). But from the viewpoint of national government, the EU and sub-national actors, this situation might be helpful in providing a more open environment for policy innovation.

Conclusion

We have seen that national training systems are highly societally specific. There is considerable pressure for change from the global economic environment, rising unemployment and structural changes within national labour markets. However, although these pressures tend to push training systems towards a limited convergence, such trends are common to all industrialised countries rather than suggesting the existence of a 'European model'. Given the climate of change, the European Community has been able to create a role for itself in policy making as a forum for the compilation and exchange of information. It has, however, been reluctant to move beyond this role to advocate specific policies. This may be partly explained by the member states' strong opposition to any limits to their autonomy in policy making on training: training policy has financial implications, but it also reflects fundamental economic and social strategies and ideological choices. But the limited role given to the European Community under the principle of subsidiarity also legitimises EC action within its priority fields, and saves it from an ideological dilemma it is probably not equipped to face.

Notes

1 Council Decision, 63/266/EEC, 2 April 1963.
2 Note that in the UK separate arrangements exist for education and training in Scotland and Northern Ireland. The training system discussed here is that of England and Wales, but for the sake of brevity the term 'UK' is retained.

References

Allen, D. (1996) 'Cohesion and structural adjustment', in H. Wallace and W. Wallace (eds) *Policy-Making in the European Union*, Oxford: Oxford University Press, 209–234

Anderson, J. (1995) 'Structural funds and EU policy', in S. Leibfried and P. Pierson (eds) *European Social Policy*, Washington DC: The Brookings Institution

Balfour, C. (1972) *Industrial Relations in the Common Market*, London: Routledge & Kegan Paul

Bispinck, Reinhard (1990) 'Qualifikationsrisiken, berufliche Weiterbildung und gewerkschaftliche Tarifpolitik', *WSI-Arbeitsmaterialen*, Dusseldorf

Blancke, S. and Widmaier, U. (forthcoming) 'The politics of radical unemployment policies

SUSAN MILNER

in Germany', in H. Compston (ed.) *The New Politics of Unemployment in Western Europe*, London: Routledge

Caillods, F. (1994) 'Converging trends amidst diversity in vocational training systems', *International Labour Review*, 133/2

CBI (Confederation of British Industry) (1990) *Employment and Training*, London: Mercury Books

(CEC) Commission of the European Communities (1992) *Second Report to the Council, the European Parliament and the Economic and Social Committee on the application of the Community Charter of Fundamental Social Rights of Workers* (December)

—— (1993a) *EC Education and Training Programmes 1986–1992. Results and Achievements: An Overview*, COM(93)151 final, 5 May 1993

—— (1993b) *Working Paper: Guidelines for Community Action in the Field of Education and Training*, COM(93)183 final, 5 May 1993

—— (1995a) *White Paper on Education and Training, Teaching and Learning: Towards the Learning Society*

—— (1995b) *Education and initial training systems in the European Union*, Luxembourg: Official Publications of the European Communities

CEDEFOP (1995a) *Apprenticeships in the EU member states: a comparison*, Berlin: CEDEFOP

—— (1995b) *Financing Continuing Training: What are the Lessons from International Comparison?* Berlin: CEDEFOP

CEREQ (1993) *Formation Emploi*, no. 43 (special issue: Europe)

—— (1996a) 'Actualités: comparaison européenne des dispositifs d'insertion des jeunes', CEREO Bref, 120

—— (1996b) 'La formation continue dans les entreprises: la place de la France en Europe', CEREO Bref, 116

Coffield, F. (1992) 'Training and Enterprise Councils: the last throw of voluntarism?', *Policy Studies*, 13/4, 11–32

Cram, L. (1993) 'Calling the tune without paying the piper? Social policy regulation: the role of the Commission in European Union social policy', *Policy and Politics*, 21: 135–46

Crouch, C. (1993) *Industrial Relations and European State Traditions*, Oxford: Oxford University Press

—— (1995) 'Organized interests as resources or constraint: rival logics of vocational training policy', in C. Crouch and F. Traxler (eds) *Organized Industrial Relations in Europe: What Future?* Aldershot: Avebury, 287–308

DGB-Bundesvorstand (1992) 'Fortbildungsberufe starken – neue Weiterbildungsanforderungen umsetzen', Dusseldorf

Esping-Andersen, Gosta (1990) *The Three Worlds of Welfare Capitalism*, Cambridge: Polity Press

IES (Institute of Employment Studies) (1996) *In Brief*, 112

Lange. T. (1993) 'Training for economic transformation: the labour market in Germany', *British Review of Economic Issues*, 15/37, 145–68

Leibfried, S. and Pierson, P. (eds) (1995) *European Social Policy*, Washington DC: The Brookings Institution

Marks, G. (1992) 'Structural policy in the European Community', in A. M. Sbragia (ed.) *Europolitics. Institutions and Policy-making in the 'new' European Community*, Washington DC: The Brookings Institution, 191–224

Maurice, M. and Sellier, F. (1979) 'Societal analysis of industrial relations: a comparison between France and Germany', *British Journal of Industrial Relations*, 17:3, 322–36

Milner, Susan (1992) 'EC training policy', *European Business and Economic Development*, 1/1, 15–22

—— (1993) 'Understanding the impact of social actors on policy-making at EC level: the case of training policy', *Cross-National Research Papers*, Loughborough

Mitchell, Duncan (1993) 'Interest groups and the "democratic deficit"', *European Access*, no. 2, 14–17

Nielsen, Ruth and Szyszczak, Erika (1991) The social dimension of the EC, Copenhagen

Podevin, G. (1995) 'De la promotion sociale à la promotion de l'économique: le rôle du dispositif de formation continue depuis 1971', *Pour*, no.148, pp.65–79

Porter, Michael (1990) *The Competitive Advantage of Nations*, New York

Rainbird, H. (1993) 'Vocational and educational training', in M. Gold (ed.), *The social dimension. Employment Policy in the European Community*, Basingstoke: Macmillan, 184–202

Rose, R. and Page, E.C. (1990) 'Action in adversity: responses to unemployment in Britain and Germany', *West European Politics*, 13, 66–84

Sorge, A. (1995) 'Labour relations, organization and qualifications', in J. Van Ruysseveldt, R. Huiskamp and J. van Hoof (eds) *Comparative Industrial and Employment Relations*, London, Thousand Oaks and New Delhi: Sage, 243–66

Spicker, Paul (1991) 'The principle of subsidiarity and the social policy of the European Community', *Journal of European Social Policy*, 1/1, 3–14

Streeck, W. (1995) 'From market-making to market-building? Reflections on the political economy of European social policy', in Leibfried, S. and Pierson, P. (eds) *European social policy*, Washington DC: The Brookings Institution, 389–431

10

EC ACTION AND INITIATIVES IN ENVIRONMENTAL PROTECTION

David Freestone and Aaron McLoughlin

Introduction

This chapter argues that the expansion of EC competence in the field of the environment has been an exercise in 'Community opportunism'. The original Rome Treaty contained no authorising provision for an environmental policy, but it has nevertheless – through its range, degree of public support, and the legal instruments it has generated – become one of the more successful of EC policies.[1] Its development in both the domestic and international arena has inevitably come at the direct expense of state competence. The development of the EC agenda for environmental protection has for a number of member states[2] – particularly those, such as the UK, that are perceived as less 'green' – largely provided the national agenda for environmental policy.

The development of national and latterly regional and global agendas for environmental protection has been used skilfully by the Commission and the European Parliament to expand Community competence first internally, and then, by the doctrine of 'parallelism' (i.e. that Community competence in external relations expands in parallel with internal powers), externally, though this has in turn opened the EC to the charge that it has concentrated on the development of legal instruments at the expense of enforcement and that it has gone beyond its own infrastructure capabilities (MacRory 1992).[3] Post-Maastricht, this argument has been used as a justification for an attempt at 'roll back' of Community competence under the guise of the 'subsidiarity' doctrine.[4]

However, as in other areas of EC policy-making, even after 1992, the locus of power cannot be defined with precision. Relationships are still evolving, and the strength of particular actors varies according to political context and the constellation of alliances, including, most notably, those between the Commission and particular member states. External factors can also play an important role – most notably pressure from the United States, and threats of WTO adjudication.[5]

This chapter will address some of these complexities. In some instances the progress of EU environmental policy has been at the expense of the traditional competence of member states. This is not however a static relationship. Even in areas where member states perceive themselves as retaining 'sovereignty'[6] Community law may still impose restrictions on the exercise of their powers – as for example in the recent judgment of the English courts applying EC law in restricting the UK discretion unilaterally to define an 'estuary'.[7] The emergence of the doctrine of subsidiarity has also introduced another wild card, some arguing it should be used as justification for the increase in Community competence,[8] while others take the opposite view. It is certainly not axiomatic that subsidiarity involves a decrease in Community competence and a consequential increase in members states' powers in the environmental area. Environmental problems and their solutions are not restricted by national boundaries and article 3b of the EC Treaty (post Maastricht) provides for Community action 'only if and in so far as the objectives of that action cannot be sufficiently achieved by the Member States and can therefore by reason of scale or effects of the proposed action, be better achieved by the Community'.

EU institutions themselves are complex. Conflict is not unusual within the Commission, between and within Directorate-Generals, between Commissioners, and between the Commission, Parliament and Council.[9] The European Parliament, for example, is usually portrayed as a unitary actor, but its various committees often have very divergent views on environmental matters, although composite compromise amendments and resolutions do not always reveal these. Likewise, EP political groupings are often internally divided, often making national interest a stronger determinant of position than party group membership. It is thus simplistic to see institutions as monolithic and cohesive: policy outcomes are the result of a multitude of factors, both political and non-political.

This chapter seeks to illustrate these observations through a range of issues including enforcement, the role of the WTO in EU environmental policy, and the influence of lobbyists. It starts by outlining the development of EC environmental policy and the range of sectors it covers, the legal basis of the policy – which with the increase of majority voting has considerable political as well as legal significance – and looks briefly at the roles of the various EU institutions.

Origins

The true origins of the Community environmental policy lie in the 1972 Stockholm Conference.[10] Stockholm coincided with the formal end of the transitional period[11] and the negotiations for enlargement of the Community.[12] The end of the transitional period left a *lacuna* in policy. Not all the Treaty objectives had been met,[13] but most of what was then thought politically feasible was thought to have been achieved. The challenge of protecting the human environment raised forcefully by the Stockholm Conference provided a higher profile policy for the EC.

The famous 1972 Paris Summit of Heads of State or Government[14] officially acknowledged the direction of the Stockholm meeting, at which of course the EC

179

member states had participated. Despite the overwhelmingly economic objectives of the text of the Rome Treaty, the Preamble to the Paris Summit communiqué acknowledged that economic expansion was 'not an end in itself' but that economic growth should be linked to 'improvement in living and working conditions' of the citizens of the EC. This phrase was to form the tenuous basis for the development of a Community environmental policy,[15] the basic principles of which persist to the present.[16] The Summit called on the Commission to draw up a Community environmental policy and a year later the Council of Ministers approved an ambitious four-year Community Action Programme on the Environment.[17] This designated three areas of activity: reduction and prevention of pollution and nuisances; improvement of the environment and quality of life; and Community action, or common action by member states, in international organisations dealing with the environment.

The Environmental Action Programmes

The five Environmental Action Programmes (EAPs) established to date[18] demonstrate the extent to which EC policy-makers have both reflected, and contributed to, the evolution of the concept of sustainable development: the notion that development and environmental protection need not be in conflict. Reflecting Stockholm, the emphasis of the First Programme was on preventative action, but at the lowest cost to the Community. By the Third Programme (1983) the resources of the environment were coming to be thought of as the basis of – but also the limit to – further economic and social development.

The 1983 Programme also introduced the concept that environmental policy should be an integral part of other EC policies. This concept grew in importance until with the most recent programme 'the emphasis upon the integration of environmental considerations into the formulation and implementation of economic and sectoral policies was paramount alongside the concept of "sustainable development"'. This concept is defined in terms of securing 'continued economic and social development without detriment to the environment and the natural resources on the quality of which continued human activity and further development depend'. (COM(92)23, final 27 March 1992, 3).

The main priorities of the Fifth EAP are:

- improving the legal framework for environmental policy through more coherent and comprehensive approaches to specific sectors, through simpler legislative and administrative procedures, and by improving the enforceability of the measures adopted;
- enhancing the role and implementation of reporting requirements under Community environmental legislation;
- improving access to justice and facilitating public involvement in the implementation and enforcement of legislation;
- sanctions for non-compliance and enforcement of environment policies.

The means for achieving sustainable development are set out in article 4 of the Commission's proposed decision.[19] However, the agenda is hardly radical. In its recent review[20] of the Programme's progress the Commission itself stressed the need for improved integration of environmental concerns into other policies; for a broadening of the range of instruments, better means of implementation, as well as a reinforcement of the Community's international role. Significantly, in a change from the previous EAP the Commission has dropped from each heading of proposed action the phrase 'the Community will', thereby removing the potential threat of legal action if it were seen as having given a commitment to act and then failed to do so.

The European Parliament – whose role is important given that Action Programmes[21] go through the co-decision procedure, giving the EP in essence a right of veto – has been much blunter.[22] In its report at the first reading of the Commission's review of the Fifth EAP, the Parliament was highly critical of the Commission's position; its Rapporteur calling it a 'step backwards', claiming that the original obligations of the Fifth EAP had been 'completely watered down', and that there was no binding timetable as a statement of 'real political commitment'.[23]

Most recently, the Commission has proceeded with caution in the environmental area, reflecting both the modest political standing of DG XI[24] within the Commission and Jacques Santer's doctrine of undertaking 'less but better' legislation.[25] The 1997 Commission work programme contained only two new legislative proposals relating to the environment. The programme opted for realism, passing over proposals that had previously failed, or were being reviewed or updated. Thus for example, after the proposed directive on integrated pollution prevention control for small installations was dropped in April 1997, only one environmental legislative proposal remained – to regulate airport noise.[26] Even that proposal was withdrawn when it received support only from the Nordic countries and sustained opposition from industry and other member states.[27]

The legal bases for EC environmental policy

The Treaty of Rome

The Paris Summit found a mandate, albeit tenuously, for environmental protection in the commitment in the Preamble to the Treaty of Rome, to 'the constant improvement of the living and working conditions of their peoples'. This has been interpreted, somewhat expansively, to mean improvement in the 'quality of life' and thus the environment. There was also an argument, derived from market-building principles, that discrepancies in national environmental protection laws could result in distortions or obstructions to trade in that differing national standards could be used to discriminate against goods from other member states.[28] There were thus two separate Treaty bases for environmental legislation: articles 100 and 235.

Article 100 authorises directives approved unanimously 'for the approximation of such provisions laid down by law, regulation or administrative action in the Member States as directly affect the establishment or functioning of the common market'. The wording clearly signifies a link with economic policies and while it has provided a satisfactory basis for legislation in a number of spheres, such as water quality[29] or noise emission,[30] where different national standards could confer unfair trading advantage on certain enterprises, in other spheres it has proved too difficult to demonstrate that such discrepancies have affected the 'establishment or functioning of the common market'. Then recourse has had to be made to article 235 under which legislation not envisaged elsewhere is authorised if it is 'necessary to attain in the course of the operation of the common market, one of the objectives of the Community'. Here the Preamble was invoked to justify the argument that protection of the environment was one of the objectives of the Community,[31] leading, it should be said, to some strange results, such as the claim that the conservation of species of wild birds is necessary for 'the harmonious development of economic activities throughout the Community and a continuous and balanced expansion'.[32]

The Single European Act

The 1987 Single European Act[33] (new article 130, paragraphs R, S, and T) obviated the need for this juristic artifice. The SEA gave formal recognition to the Community environmental policy and provided for the first time a clear and unambiguous legal basis for EC environmental law. Article 130R defined the objectives of EC environmental policy: to preserve, protect and improve the quality of the environment; to contribute towards protecting human health; to ensure a prudent and rational utilisation of national resources. Article 130R(2) then set out the principles on which Community action to achieve these objectives should be based, namely that preventive action should be taken, that environmental damage should, as a priority, be rectified at source, and that the polluter should pay. It also required that environmental protection considerations be a component of the Community's other policies.[34]

Title II of the Single European Act envisaged that environmental legislation would be based on one of two main legal grounds. Article 130S, by providing specifically for the enactment of environmental legislation, freed it from the requirement noted above that it should serve economic ends,[35] but such legislation be adopted by unanimous agreement of the Council of Ministers, unless (by unanimity) it chose to define those matters as ones on which decisions shall be taken by a qualified majority.[36] Action taken under article 130 was subject to an early version of the principle of subsidiarity,[37] namely that: 'The Community shall take action relating to the environment to the extent to which the objectives [of EC policy] can be attained better at the Community level than at the level of the individual Member States.' It was also subject to the general safeguard provision in article 130T that: 'The protective measures adopted in common pursuant to article 130S shall not prevent any Member State from maintaining or introducing more stringent protective measures compatible with this Treaty.'

An alternative basis for environmental legislation was provided under article 100A. This article provides for action by majority vote in the Council (though member states are specifically permitted to adopt stricter measures of domestic environmental protection if they so wish).[38] To ensure that Single Market measures do not always take precedence over environmental considerations, the Commission is obliged when presenting proposals for environmental action under this article to 'take as its basis a high level of protection' (article 100A (3)).

The Treaty on European Union

The 1992 Maastricht text furthered the new constitutional recognition of environmental policy accorded by the SEA. Article 2 defined as a Community goal: 'the promotion throughout the Community, of a harmonious and balanced development of economic activities, sustainable and non inflationary growth respecting the environment . . . ' Article 3(k) included 'A policy in the sphere of the environment' as a means of reaching these objectives. The SEA commitment that environmental protection requirements were integral to other Community policies was reinforced by a further declaration that the Commission and the member states should 'take full account of their environmental impact and of the principle of lasting growth'. Alongside the principle of preventive action, article 130R(2) also introduced the so-called 'Precautionary Principle'[39] to join the existing principles that environmental damage should as a priority be rectified at source and that the polluter should pay.

The new Treaty also increased qualified majority voting on environmental issues – article 130R making it now the norm, except that 'by way of derogation' unanimity would, in the first instance, still be required for some classes of EC environmental legislation (fiscal provision, town and country planning, some sections of land use, and some measures affecting national energy policy).[40]

The Draft Treaty of Amsterdam

The Amsterdam Treaty made more modest changes, though at the time of writing full details had not been fully clarified, and the Treaty remains unratified.[41] The text reaffirms 'sustainable development'[42] as a cornerstone of EU policy and 'a high level of protection and improvement of the quality of the environment' as the norm.[43] Integration of environmental policies into all sectoral policies is strengthened with explicit Treaty references.[44]

The European Parliament is to be granted greater powers and the legislative process simplified to three procedures (assent, co-decision, co-operation). Most environmental legislation will be subject to qualified majority voting by the Council of Ministers. Unanimity will be preserved for those matters under article 130S(2) which touch on the politically sensitive matters of national policy.[45]

A controversial aspect of the draft Treaty, however, concerns an agreed derogation permitting member states to take more rigorous environmental protection
measures 'on grounds of a problem specific to the Member State'.[46] This conces-
sion, inserted at the demand of the Nordic states, is explicitly to protect those states
with high environmental standards, and in a certain sense is a repatriation of a
degree of environmental competence to member states. The Commission will
have six months to judge whether any national measures so introduced are justifi-
able on environmental grounds and 'do not constitute an obstacle to the
functioning of the internal market'.[47] This issue will arise again when the derogations in the accession Treaties of the most recent EU entrants (Austria, Finland
and Sweden) come up for review. The Commission – as well as many in the
business community – see these derogations as a potential threat to the integrity of
the internal market.

The forms of Community environmental legislation

Article 189 EEC authorises two main methods of Community legislation: the
regulation and the directive. The former has general application throughout the
member states and is directly applicable, becoming automatically part of the law
of the member states without implementation.[48] A directive, on the other hand,
specifically requires implementation into domestic law.[49]

The necessity of relying heavily on article 100 as a legal base in the early
development of environmental legislation dictated the use of the directive, for
that article, concerned as it is with harmonisation, only authorises action by
directive. Although article 235 does not impose a similar restriction it has been
suggested that the Commission, anxious not to be challenged as going beyond its
legal power, has been very cautious in its use of article 235 and other forms of
legal instrument.[50]

However, the way in which the directive has been used in environmental policy
areas is not strictly in accord with this distinction, and contains within it the implication of greater restriction on member states' margins of discretion or their
freedom to implement directives in particular ways which they would prefer. The
obligations imposed on member states by environment policy directives fall into
three broad categories often with different categories of obligation within the same
directive.[51] The first category contains the 'typical' directive – imposing a clear
result obligation, but genuinely leaving the means to the member states.[52] In practice such obligations are often procedural, as in the enforcement of obligations
imposed elsewhere in the instrument. The second category is of the 'regulation
type' imposing detailed substantive obligations, (prohibitions, standards and tolerances, etc.) often contained in annexes with simplified amendment procedures,
which give no effective leeway or discretion to member states.[53] The third is the
framework directive, such as the classic aquatic environment[54] directive which
simply provides a framework for future supplementation by more detailed 'regula-
tion-type' directives, where there is often no need for the framework directive itself

to be incorporated into national law. Rehbinder and Stewart conclude that 'with respect to substantive law the distinction between regulation and directive has been blurred, although it has retained most of its validity in the field of proce-dure'.[55] The Court of Justice has implicitly approved this elision of legislative forms.[56]

Largely as a result of the regulatory way that directives are often phrased, the ECJ has on occasions found that certain provisions of directives fulfil the require-ments of the doctrine of direct effectiveness – they are 'complete and legally perfect'.[57] This means that an individual (whether natural or legal) could rely on such provisions in the national courts in proceedings against the government,[58] in suits alleging failure to implement or faulty implementation. This doctrine, a judi-cial development by the European Court of Justice, has made a significant impact in other sectors of Community law, though as yet not significantly in the environ-mental area. It is noticeable however that although there was a trend for environmental directives and proposals to be drafted in unequivocal terms which might be found to fulfil the requirements of direct effectiveness,[59] the incorpora-tion of subsidiarity into the legislative programme has tended to reverse this trend.[60]

It should be added that the regulatory approach which manifests itself in the specificity of the obligations imposed by directives in this sector is in fact a hall-mark of the nature of EC environmental instruments as well as their form. Taking its lead perhaps from the majority of domestic policies of the member states, it is notable that the overall approach of Community environmental law has been regulatory: harmonised standards, such as environmental quality standards, and product and process (for example, emission) standards, are imposed on member states which have the responsibility to implement and enforce them under the supervision of the Community.[61] Very little use has been made to date of other types of powers; indeed the EC has seldom taken anything other than a passive regulatory approach, that is, amending existing laws to keep up with technological advances rather than seeking to force technological developments by setting progressive standards – an approach sometimes taken in the United States of America (where it is known as 'technology-forcing'). Again, it may in the past have been the use of the harmonisation devices of article 100 which inhibited such approaches.

Commentators have pointed out that a number of devices other than passive regulation are available for the development of environmental policies,[62] and in many member states public opinion may well have swung, or be in the process of swinging, towards support for environmentally progressive taxation such as the differentiation which now exists on lead-free petrol in the United Kingdom and other European states.[63]

The directive on waste oils does require member states to organise and subsidise the collection, regeneration and combustion of waste oils, and current proposals on waste encourage recycling and national self-sufficiency,[64] but the systematic use of subsidies always threatens to fall foul of the prohibition on state aids in article 92. In the Fourth Action Programme some priority was attached to the development of appropriate instruments for environmental protection, in particular the 'development of efficient instruments such as taxes, levies, state aid, authorisation of negotiable rebates with a view to implementing the principle that the polluter pays'.[65]

Environmental politics and the role of EC institutions

The Environmental Action Programmes described above have not emerged in a political vacuum. They have been generated in response to a wider European issue agenda in which environmental politics have increased in importance over the last decade, both at EC and national level.[66] However, that response has been shaped by a range of factors, including the variations in the salience and direction of environmental politics at national level, the tendency for EC policies to respond to crises and high-profile events, the complexities in inter- and intra-institutional relationships at EC level, and perhaps most importantly of all, the complex legal and administrative politics of implementation and enforcement.

Despite the undoubted achievements of the Action Programmes, critics of their shortcomings have been vigorous and persistent. First, there is, perhaps predictably, considerable dissatisfaction with the trade-offs which are made between environmental and commercial issues. Secondly, both the SEA and the Maastricht Treaty have been criticised: the former because article 130R(3), if rigidly adhered to, is seen as imposing virtually insurmountable obstacles to new legislation;[67] the latter in particular for its explicit incorporation of the principles of subsidiarity and proportionality, which are frequently seen as a reason for Commission inaction. Finally, with the choice of some ten different legislative processes available for Community environmental legislation, procedures are seen as having become far too complex and the process itself an arcane exercise masterable only by a tiny handful of experts. This lack of transparency and reliance on technocrats[68] is not unique to environmental issues, but is as acute within it as anywhere.

As in areas of social policy described in other chapters of this book, therefore, the extent to which EC institutions really lead the Community agenda, and the extent to which member-state autonomy is genuinely limited by Community action can only be understood by reference to the politics of environmental questions within the EC institutions, to which we now turn.

The Council of Ministers and the European Council

It is in the Council of Ministers that national differences of perspective, culture and approach inevitably come to the fore, with protracted and sometimes bitter disputes. The positions of the northern states – Denmark, The Netherlands, and Germany, the earliest converts to an environmental agenda – frequently contrast with the Mediterranean countries which are often accused of putting development (even non-sustainable development) before environmental concerns.[69] The northern position has been strengthened with the accession of Austria, Finland and Sweden. The UK position has also been distinctive in areas such as water quality standards[70] and automobile emission control.[71] Its claims for distinctive standards suiting local conditions[72] have been increasingly perceived as a defence of lower standards, and a defence of British industry's 'dirty' practices, rather than genuinely scientifically based policy alternatives.[73]

The dynamics of agreement or consensus formation within the Environment Council (the Council of Ministers of the Environment) meetings are complex, and illustrate the significance of intricate and highly interactive policy networks in operation. Von Moltke[74] sees the process in terms of a 'consensus cycle' under which national policy proposals provide the initial impulse for Community proposals;[75] these proposals although not adopted by the Council are often taken up by other member states which then introduce them domestically. The Community proposal, albeit often in modified form, then emerges as a consensus position. Dashwood's more cautious 'radiator effects' theory suggests that the substance of a novel Community proposal is often taken over as a national policy; this national adoption will often 'radiate' back to the Community process, thus making the Commission proposal more acceptable.[76]

As Rehbinder and Stewart suggest,[77] both approaches over-simplify, but environmental policy formation at national and Community levels certainly operates symbiotically. National policies in the sector are relatively young and undeveloped, particularly when compared with, for example, fiscal or economic policies. On occasions the early involvement of the EC appears to have facilitated an often surprising degree of consensus among member states.[78] Notwithstanding the resultant danger of 'lowest common denominator' policies, the evidence does not support the view that EC environmental policy always moves at the pace of the slowest. It may not always meet the aspirations of the 'greenest' but it has provided an important policy 'spur' to most national environmental policies. For example, the proposals to implement EU-wide legislation to label packaging waste is a move to curtail the possible effects of distortion of the internal market caused by the German DSD (Duales System Deutschland) system. EU measures on packaging waste and marking of packaging waste will bring to many states regulation were none existed before, albeit not as stringent as existing German regulation.[79]

The European Council naturally plays a more demonstrative but also more occasional role, frequently through 'disaster driven' responses to *causes célèbres*, as in the case of the specific sea pollution programme agreed shortly after the wreck of the Amoco Cadiz, or in 1980s when the acid rain effects on the Black Forest were first highlighted, and the 1983 Stuttgart European Council decided that environmental protection policy should be a priority within the Community, emphasising the need particularly to reinforce the fight against pollution and the dangers to European forest areas. The March 1985 Summit designated 1987 as the European Year of the Environment.[80] In its now famous Rhodes Declaration, the European Council pledged itself to 'play a leading role in the action needed to protect the world's environment' and to continue to strive for 'an effective international response . . . to such global problems as depletion of the ozone layer, the greenhouse effect and the ever growing threats to the natural environment.'[81] More recently the European Council meetings have been a forum for political deals on the implementation of subsidiarity in relation to environmental instruments.[82]

The European Parliament

Despite its still limited powers,[83] the EP is comprised of able and ambitious politicians who have taken advantage of the political capital to be made from a greater environmental awareness among electorates. An early success was the adoption by the Council in 1983 of a ban on the import into the Community of seal pup skins, after a series of Resolutions by the Parliament drawing attention to the culling issue.[84]

Since then major parliamentary initiatives have generally been the result of the work of the Environment, Public Health, and Consumer Protection Committee which has established itself as an important, high-profile influence. Through its work, Parliament has been able to provide sophisticated inputs into debates on legislative proposals on a variety of issues including environmental impact assessment and hazardous waste transport,[85] to establish its own inquiries into controversial issues such as the handling of waste,[86] and to flag up important issues not yet receiving attention, such as sea-level rise.[87] It has also conducted inquiries into the implementation of a number of key environmental directives: dangerous substances (76/464), drinking water (80/778) and bathing water (76/160).[88] Environmental policy has also benefited from general moves by Parliament to strengthen its own position within the Community decision-making process, including the strengthening of areas of non-obligatory expenditure[89] and its successful pressure on the Commission to present an annual report[90] to Parliament on the Commission's work in the monitoring of the application of Community law.[91]

However, the EP is split into numerous party groups,[92] national political groupings, committees, delegations and inter-groups,[93] the internal politics of which are complex and frequently divisive, as for example in relation to bio-technology or nuclear power. Thus in the bio-technology area the Research and the Environment Committees have taken markedly different lines, with the former being identifiably more sympathetic to industrial development.[94] Divisions on nuclear power were evident, for example in the Soulier report[95] on the Commission's communication on the future of nuclear power, with French interests in nuclear power sheltering under the claimed environmental benefits of limiting the output of carbon dioxide, in opposition to exponents of an increase in funding for renewable sources of energy, which exclude nuclear power.[96]

The Commission, implementation, enforcement

As initiator of legislation and guardian of the Treaties,[97] the Commission has the central role both in the development of the action programmes and in implementing legislative proposals. The factors which condition its role as policy initiator are complex and depend to a large degree on political conditions within the member states, and their willingness to allow the Commission a leadership role. As with other Directorate-Generals, such factors also include:

- the style of the Presidency (where Delors' permissiveness towards legislative initiatives contrasts with Santer's[98] chastened caution);
- relations between directorates general (DG XI's brief requires both a great deal of co-ordination with other DGs – some with diametrically opposed interests – and the capacity to persuade them to undertake environmental evaluations of their portfolios and programmes);
- the resources available to the lead DG itself;[99]
- the status of the Commissioner in charge (the recent vicissitudes of the colourful Ritt Bjerregaard and her misfortunes before the EP Environment Committee have been seen by some as highly prejudicial to DG XI's current influence.[100]

However, in the area of environmental policy, where the range of legal instruments adopted over the years is large, questions of enforcement and implementation are no less fundamental than those of policy initiation, and it is in this area that the real controversy has been focused in recent years.[101] As with enforcement in other sectors, such as competition policy and state aids, the Commission's decisions about the actions it takes to enforce rules in cases of apparent non-compliance are likely to involve delicate judgements and essentially political considerations, with member states often able to escape legal challenges because the Commission decides it is impolitic or impractical to be aggressive.[102] Certainly, the Environment Commissioner is the regular target of complaints about lack of action against member states' non-compliance.[103]

The Commission's efforts to ensure compliance were extensively documented in its 1995 *Communication on the Implementation of Community Environmental Law*,[104] which identifies several types of problem including those arising from the quality of legislation; lack of transparency; poor co-operation between member states and the EC; difficulties in monitoring and evaluation of the effects of legislation; limitations on knowledge of EC environmental law amongst practitioners; and lack of Community funding of the implementation of Community environmental legislation. The Commission proposed that in some cases new voluntary agreements would be more appropriate instruments than the traditional, top-down, regulatory methods. It also raises the possibility of expanding the role of the European Environmental Agency[105] to become an independent enforcement agency.[106] The latter, it was argued, could be given powers to investigate alleged failures to implement and apply European environmental laws, to make binding protective and final orders, and to levy fines, separating the enforcement function from the Commission's legislative role and from the political constraints imposed by the Commission's general relationship with the member states. It may be recalled that this was in fact the original role envisaged for the EEA.

The desire to de-politicise environmental enforcement, or make it more independent, is felt by many NGOs and legal practitioners.[107] Indeed, it has expressed been alleged that some member states have disliked the zeal with which officials in DG XI have acted and have sought to interfere in its internal administrative politics, and even in staffing policy.[108] However, since the EEA is primarily an information gatherer, and relies on the trust and support of national governments and agencies, endowing it with enforcement power would put that relationship under pressure.

Other enforcement problems arise from the fact that most environmental legislation is in the form of directives, which purport to give member states extensive discretion in implementation, and often making full and proper national transposition and implementation very slow. Other problems result from the delays and complexity involved in the cumbersome mechanisms provided by the Treaty under articles 169–171 under which states may be brought before the ECJ for violations of Community law.[109]

Special problems of implementation also arise in member states with highly devolved power structures, where regions or federal states have to transpose directives into their own law, as in the cases of Belgium and Germany. There are also often problems when EU legislation requires member states to amend existing national rules. Problems with applying EU environment law are most frequent in the areas of nature protection, environmental impact assessment, waste disposal and water pollution, frequently because of incorrect or incomplete transposal of directives or a lack of the technical infrastructure needed to meet EU requirements.

Enforcement: law and politics

Articles 169, 170 and 171[110] provide mechanisms by which, respectively, the Commission may take a member state before the ECJ for breach of Community law, member states may take another state before the Court for the same reason and by which the Commission can request the ECJ to impose fines on member states which, having been found by the Court to have been in breach of Community law, have not remedied that breach.[111] Article 169 has to date been the primary method for enforcement of Community environmental law.[112] Use of the inter-state action under article 170 is as yet extremely limited, and politically highly sensitive, [113] but there are signs that the new power to fine under article 171 introduced by the Maastricht Treaty may prove a significant weapon in the enforcement armoury of the future.

One example demonstrates the highly charged political atmosphere in which formal actions against member states take place. In 1996 Ireland started to investigate the possibility of taking the UK before the ECJ over plans to set up a nuclear waste treatment plant near Sellafield on the Irish Sea coast.[114] The Irish argument apparently was that Britain's nuclear waste agency had not disclosed the details of alternative sites, contrary to the environmental impact assessment directive,[115] and that the coast of the Irish Sea was an inappropriate location for such a facility. For political reasons the Irish government did not proceed with the formal action, but did support a private lawsuit to shut down the controversial British Nuclear Fuels reprocessing facility at Sellafield, brought by Irish citizens from Dundalk on the western coast of the Irish sea, who claimed that Sellafield was a serious health threat. The Irish government support was itself an attempt to deflect an action brought against it by the same citizens, who claimed that Ireland had been negligent in failing to check the expansion of Sellafield in the past, particularly during the planning and commissioning of the THORP plant, in use since 1995. The Irish government reportedly decided in principle to provide financial and other support to the Dundalk plaintiffs, including scientific investigation, research and legal work, on condition that the case against itself was dropped. In 1997, the Irish government also intervened for the first time in a UK planning inquiry by objecting to a preliminary scheme to store radioactive waste underground at Sellafield.[116]

Though article 170 has yet to be used in the environmental arena, applications to the ECJ under the new article 171(2) for financial penalties against member states which have not complied with previous court judgments have begun to be used.[117] In June 1996, the Commission adopted criteria[118] for assessing when to request penalties and their size. Its intention is to levy fines that have real deterrent effect, and reflect the seriousness of the infringement and its duration, taking into account economic prosperity and population size. The Commission exercised these new powers on 29 January 1997, making applications to the ECJ against Germany and Italy for failing to implement previous judgements of the Court for infringing European environmental law. It requested that financial penalties be levied on Germany for infringements in the areas of bird protection[119] of ECU 26,400 per day, groundwater[120] (ECU 26,400) and surface water[121] (ECU 158,400); and on Italy in the areas of waste disposal[122] (ECU 123,900) and radiation protection[123] (ECU 159,300).

Commissioner Ritt Bjerregaard said of the implementation of the power that 'we have decided the amount of penalties to propose to the ECJ concerning five court cases – all within the field of the environment. It is the first time that the Commission makes use of its powers according to article 171 in the Treaty. It is also high time. The public and the EP are waiting impatiently as they rightly see article 171 as needed to improve . . . implementation in general and in the environment and internal market in particular.'[124]

This statement perhaps inadvertently draws attention to the wide discretionary power which the Commission enjoys in relation to all powers to pursue enforcement proceedings. The Treaty itself gives the Commission considerable freedom of manoeuvre, which, it might be argued, is essential given the realities of environmental politics at EC level. If the Commission decides not to exercise its discretion to institute an action against a member state under article 169, for example, that failure to act, whatever the political realities, cannot be challenged. Nor does the Commission make public the documents related to the various steps it has to take in initiating proceedings.[125]

Given the limited rights of direct action against the Commission which the Treaty gives to the individual[126] and the very restrictive way in which even those limited rights have been interpreted by the European Court[127] the opportunities for individuals or groups of individuals to challenge the exercise of this discretion are negligible. MacRory has commented that 'a more mature legal system should begin to address these issues'[128]

Although the European Court of Justice has shown signs of taking a proactive stance on environmental issues[129] it has made no concessions in relation to the rights of *locus standi* (or legal standing) of individuals or NGOs before the Court. In the *Spanish Canaries* case,[130] which centred on a challenge by Greenpeace and local residents to the legality of a Commission grant of structural funds for the construction of power stations in the Canary Islands, the issue was whether the award of aid had been in conformity with environmental requirements contained in the relevant structural fund regulations, especially those concerning environmental impact assessment. The Court refused to consider the substance of the case, ruling that the applicant had no standing. It took a similar position in the *French Polynesian Nuclear Tests* case.[131] In the *Irish Tourist Board – WWF* case[132] the plaintiffs challenging the grant of aid to build a tourist centre in an area of outstanding natural beauty, the Court of First Instance again did not find the case admissible.

On some funding matters, however, the Commission has recently made a markedly pro-environmental policy switch. In April 1996, the European Commission proposed taking legal action against the Irish government over its decision to proceed with a controversial sewage plant at Galway Bay.[133] The Commission argued that the project would infringe the habitats directive[134] because the island plant would be built on a significant bird sanctuary. At the time of writing, the issue was still being argued between the Irish government and the Commission, which through its regional affairs Commissioner has made clear that no Commission funding will be forthcoming. This is the first time that the Commission has refused funding on environmental grounds.[135]

Inevitably political questions may be asked about the criteria which the Commission uses to determine whether or not to institute legal proceedings against member states. In March 1996 the Commission opened proceedings against Sweden for requiring vehicles already type-approved elsewhere in the EC to obtain a Swedish national exhaust-emissions certificate.[136] The Swedish system required, *inter alia*, that producers and importers recall cars if their emissions reduction equipment were found to degrade too quickly. The Commission claimed that the requirements discriminated against imports and went beyond pre-existing EC certification rules, pointing out that the scheme was being challenged before the ECJ by a car manufacturer. Significantly, however, the Commission has not yet taken any action against the German government which operates a similar scheme. The reason for the Commission decision not to treat the two member states in the same way appears difficult to justify, and many observers argue that although the EC is a union of equal states the political reality is that some are more powerful than others.[137]

Rather similar considerations apply in relation to the Commission's relations with European business interests.[138] Environmental policy touches the economic nerve of leading vested interests.[139] For example, Greenpeace claims that since 1990 nearly $15 billion of taxpayers' money has been used to support Western Europe's fossil fuel and nuclear industry, and that, between 1990 and 1995 the UK government gave an annual subsidy to the fossil fuel industry of $1217.9m, $2885.9m to nuclear energy, and $94.9m to renewable energy sources.[140]

Industry naturally has a legitimate right to protect its vested interests.[141] Indeed companies are usually obliged to do so by their duty to their shareholders under domestic company law. The main instrument for achieving this objective is lobbying. Lobbying is an inherent part of the democratic system and Brussels is fast becoming as much a city of lobbyists as technocrats. There are estimated to be over 20,000 lobbyists in the city. Major lobbying firms are credited with turning around public opinion on the issue of the use of furs and have helped promote the benefits of genetically modified food.[142] For example, during the passage through the European Parliament of the controversial biotechnology patents directive,[143] MEPs were subject to a constant barrage of faxes, information-packs, and letters from the biotechnology industry and environmental movement. It is widely thought that the massive lobbying effort by the biotechnology industry helped overturn the European Parliament's initial rejection of the directive. The debate over genetically modified soya and maize also saw the biotechnology industry orchestrate a major lobbying campaign, eventually helping to persuade the Commission to authorise the use of these products in the EC, despite the opposition of some member states. As a result, Austria, which implemented the ban after a national referendum,[144] now faces legal action for its ban on their use, as the Commission contends its unilateral action is contrary to the free trade provisions of the Treaty.[145]

The scope of community environmental policy

We turn now from actors and instruments to the policies themselves. Space does not permit an examination of every aspect of environmental policy,[146] but two areas in particular highlight the dynamics of the Community/member-state interaction, nature protection and water quality.

Nature protection

In this area, in addition to intervention in response to high profile campaigns (such as the imposition of restrictions on imports of seal skin and whale products)[147] there have been more generalised measures on species and habitat protection such as directive 79/409 on the conservation of wild birds,[148] which imposes strict obligations on member states to maintain populations of wild birds, to protect their habitat, to regulate hunting and trading and to prohibit certain methods of killing and capture, and establishes a centralised system of monitoring. Perhaps sensing a degree of strong public support on this issue, the Commission has adopted a relatively high profile, proactive role on enforcement policy, not only in relation to the prohibition of hunting for protected species in the southern countries but also in relation to the protection of important habitats. In response to NGO complaints to the Commission, the UK was persuaded to abandon proposals for expanding whisky production in the Isle of Islay on a designated bird site.[149] In 1989, in the first of three significant case before the European Court, Germany in the *Leybucht Dykes* case, faced violation proceedings under article 169 EEC for engineering work in an important wetland site.[150] Although the Court did not find that Germany was in violation of its obligations under the directive, the strict terms of its judgment considerably strengthened the impact of the directive. In the light of that case, and later cases against Spain[151] and the UK,[152] much of the discretion which member states had presumed that they possessed in relation to the designation and alteration of such sites appeared to have been removed, and the obligations appeared considerably more rigorous than they had previously thought. However, even as the Court was considering its judgment in the Spanish case, the habitats directive was being negotiated and, reportedly at the instigation of the UK, provisions were inserted purporting to reverse the effects of the Court's jurisprudence[153] so as to allow member states to impinge on protected areas for 'imperative reasons of overriding public interest, including those of a social or economic nature' (article 6(4). The habitat directive keys in with and expands the approach of the wild birds directive, and the network of sites established by both directives will form a European network of special protection areas by the year 2000.[154] It seems likely however that the restrictions on state discretion that the ECJ was developing in the birds directive cases have been rudely curtailed by the Council.[155]

At the same time, utilising the doctrine of parallelism, the Commission has also been able to develop the competence of the EC on the international scene, so that the Community has become a party to a number of important wildlife protection treaties, notably the 1979 Berne Convention on the conservation of European wildlife and natural habitats,[156] (implemented by the wild birds directive) the 1979 Bonn Convention on the conservation of migratory species of wild animals,[157] the 1973 Washington Convention on international trade in endangered species of wild flora and fauna[158] and the 1980 Convention on Antarctic marine living resources.[159]

Water

Water pollution policy was given priority status by the first action programme,[160] and more than twenty-five legal instruments have been adopted in this sector. From the beginning the policy had two main goals: to establish 'water quality objectives' which must, by a given time, be met for waters used for specified purposes, and to regulate the quality of contaminated emissions from fixed installations.[161] To ensure member states meet both, detailed and legally binding standards set maximum contamination levels and compulsory monitoring proce-dures.[162]

Water quality objectives have been established for surface water for drinking,[163] bathing water,[164] water for freshwater fish life[165] and shellfish waters.[166] Directives designate basic parameters (for example, for physical, chemical and microbiolog-ical characteristics), which waters must meet or aspire to meet. The competent authorities of member states are responsible for monitoring in accordance with the directive, but it is the member state itself which is responsible for designating the waters to which the directive applies (although of course the member state cannot in good faith use this discretion in order to defeat the objectives of the directive).[167] The only exception is the 1980 drinking water[168] directive which established mandatory standards for all water intended for human consumption. These standards have caused problems for the member states. A large number of article 169 actions have been taken to the European Court of Justice for non-compliance.[169]

A second group of directives seeks to control emission standards. This approach has been the subject of a long and much reported controversy between the United Kingdom and the rest of the Community which has been well analysed by Boehmer-Christiansen who suggests that the controversy 'was never primarily technical, but political'[170].The United Kingdom, which had a relatively estab-lished practice of regulating the pollution caused by emissions to ambient water quality,[171] objected to a system of EC standards for all emissions from fixed instal-lations. This dispute came to a head with the enactment in May 1976 of the framework directive 76/464 on the discharge of dangerous substances into the aquatic environment[172] and resulted in a mixed regime. Dangerous substances (based on toxicity, persistence and bioaccumulation), are placed on List I (the black list), while List II substances 'are characterised by the fact that their deleterious effects on the aquatic environment are confined to a given area and dependent on the characteristics and location of the waters into which they are discharged'.[173] Member states are obliged to eliminate pollution from List I substances by enforcing maximum limit values of these substances in discharges or in receiving waters (that is, either a 'uniform emission standards' (UES) or 'environmental quality objectives' (EQO) approach). List II substances are controlled by an EQO approach, enforced on the basis of the quality of the receiving waters. Implementation has not been without difficulty, however. Although 129 List I substances have been proposed only four directives establishing limit values were passed until 1986[174] when the framework directive was amended to expedite deci-sion making.[175]

Water legislation has been a major battleground in the subsidiarity debate.[176] In response to the demands of the 1992 Edinburgh European Council, the Commission's plans for adapting water legislation to the demands of subsidiarity were set out in its 1993 Report to Council.[177] Accepting that the previous emission control approach has not been entirely satisfactory the Commission proposed a more integrated, source-oriented approach to supplement the existing regime.

Important examples of this new approach are the directives on municipal waste water and pollution by nitrates from agricultural sources (both creatures of the International North Sea Conference – discussed below). These make a real attempt to attack the root of the problem by seeking to change waste-water treatment and farming practices. Crucially, and in line with the principle of subsidiarity, member states are themselves to designate the vulnerable zones to which these directives apply and the less vulnerable zones in which less stringent measures will be acceptable. It is not difficult to see the potential for conflict and even abuse of this approach. Already the UK government has been disciplined by its own courts for a breach of Community law in seeking to exclude important estuarine areas from its domestic application of the waste water directive.[178]

The 1996 directive on integrated pollution prevention and control (IPCC) is set to formalise this more integrated approach to water pollution control.[179] Similar insights into the nature of EC environmental law in the post-subsidiarity era are also provided by the proposed directive on the ecological quality of surface waters. It is no longer envisaged that this will become law in its present form, but very similar provisions are planned to form the basis of a new framework directive on water resources.[180] The draft text of the ecological quality directive[181] envisaged that the member states would set the operational targets for good ecological quality as defined by the directive and they would draw up integrated programmes to meet these targets. The obligations of the draft are not of result – as in previous water quality directives – but of procedure: member states must take the necessary procedural steps indicated in the directive, allowing the elaboration of solutions tailored to the needs of individual waters. In the Commission's communication on a European water policy of 21 February 1996[182] it articulates the need for a new framework directive on water resources, which reflects the new approach of the waste water and nitrates directives, and the proposal for a directive on the ecological quality of water. It seems therefore that in the water quality sector at least there has indeed been some conceptual 'roll back' of the role of the Community, conferring wider discretion on member states.

International aspects

In tandem with measures for the regulation of water pollution within the EC itself, the Commission has also sought to play an active role in the international regulation of water pollution. Under the doctrine of 'parallelism' developed by the Court of Justice in a line of cases starting with the classic ERTA case,[183] the external relations powers, or competences, of the Community mirror, or parallel, its internal competences. The development of internal Community environmental law from 1973 has resulted in the corresponding expansion of the external competences of the EC to represent the member states, most notably in the area of water. The EC is party to the 1974 Paris Convention on land-based pollution,[184] and thus participates, alongside its contracting member states in the Paris Commission (Parcom). It is party to the 1983 Bonn Agreement for co-operation in dealing with pollution of the North Sea by oil and other harmful substances.[185] It has also signed the 1982 Law of the Sea Convention[186] and participates in the International Maritime Organisation. It is a party to the International Rhine Convention,[187] the 1976 Rhine Chemical Convention[188] and participates in the Rhine Commission. The EC has observer status at the Oslo Commission as, for competence reasons, it has not ratified the Oslo Convention[189] and has also participated at the three international conferences on the protection of the North Sea.[190] The EC also participates in UNEP conventions and is a party to a number of relevant UNEP regional seas conventions.[191]

The EC has also played a significant role in the first three International North Sea Conferences (1985 Bremen; 1987 London, 1990 The Hague) not only as a negotiator but also as the body responsible for producing implementing legislation to meet the objectives agreed through that process. Notable legislative outcomes are the urban waste water directive and the nitrates directive. The EC has also been involved in the discussions on the possible establishment of Exclusive Economic Zones in the North Sea as well as a number of other resulting issues.[192]

Commentators are divided on the value of the EC's input into these fora.[193] Because of the parallelism concept Community external relations competence is continually developing and expanding. Hence it is difficult, if not impossible (and from the EC perspective certainly undesirable), for it to state categorically at any time the exact limits of its external relations competence. This causes difficulties: sometimes measures cannot be approved at international meetings because the EC currently lacks internal competence to put them into effect (that is, it acts as a brake) whereas in other situations the existence of Community competence, and the presence of EC member states with a united and progressive position, may well provide an important impetus to the success of international negotiations. Here too the process can be symbiotic. The international conferences for the protection of the North Sea have provided objectives for the participating states in an area in which the EC is probably the most important single actor. Agreements within Parcom[194] as well as EC legislation[195] stem directly from the declarations issued by these meetings. However, issues of Community competence have also been reported to be to blame for the five-year delay in the coming into force of the 1992 OSPAR Treaty.[196]

Policy implementation

International trade and the environment

Just as the EC limits the autonomy of its member states, so wider international economic regimes limit that of the EC – a limitation which in turn affects the member states themselves, though it should be noted that, from the perspective of certain such states, especially those opposed to higher environmental standards, the effect is by no means always negative. In practice, the existence of GATT rules and WTO arbitration procedures adds an additional tier of decision making to certain environmental issues, and means that the EC will be restrained in certain areas – eco-labelling, for example – from acting for fear of causing difficulties for itself at WTO level.[197]

The international trade and environment debate revolves around the lack of explicit environmental standards for trade in the GATT (General Agreement on Tariffs and Trade). EU law, however, has been explicit in permitting environmentally protective actions since 1974.[198] The trade rules of the World Trade Organisation WTO are based on the principle of non-discrimination, which in effect prevents trade prohibitions or quantitative restrictions on imports or exports other than duties or taxes; tariffs are the only acceptable trade barriers.[199]

Article XX of GATT allows some exemptions for trade barriers 'necessary to protect human, animal or plant life or health' or 'relating to the conservation of exhaustible natural resources if such measures are made in conjunction with restrictions or domestic production or consumption'. However, despite the development of some positive jurisprudence on the issue within the GATT dispute settlement panel, in practice this article has not allowed the EU to pursue the multilateral environment agreements sought by many proponents in the Commission, the Parliament,[200] and the more environmentally minded governments. The December 1996 WTO meeting in Singapore made little progress on this matter, and EU efforts to obtain a strengthening of article XX met the resolute opposition of a number of developing nations, who perceive attempts to introduce environmental conditions into international trade as environmental imperialism – a position also shared by the ASEAN states.

The case of the EC eco-labelling scheme illustrates some of the Commission's dilemmas in this area. Regulation 880/92[201] granted a European-wide quality label to those products which have better environmental characteristics than others, to date affecting products such washing machines and dishwashers, laundry detergents, soil improvers, toilet paper and kitchen rolls. Certain member states also possess their own national eco-labelling regimes, though one of the most well-known – the German 'green dot' scheme whereby the packaging can be left at designated places to be collected by the DSD (Duales System Deutschland) – has been the subject of complaints[202] to the Commission for anti-dumping violations, and anti-competitive behaviour contrary to article 85.[203]

Certainly, systems of eco-labelling raise complex trade-related issues, and in member states with high environmental standards can easily favour home-country products against imported, whether intentionally or inadvertently, since requirements which may be very meaningful in the importing country, for environmental reasons, may, however, be of little or no significance in the exporting country because of its environmental objectives. Problems – for example regarding transparency of conditions – are also posed by whether the scheme is an official government one, or, as in The Netherlands, a non-governmental scheme.[204]

However, when the Commission recently proposed a directive on the marking of packaging[205] to implement an EU-wide system of standard labelling for packaging, to resolve some of these difficulties, it ran into an immediate threat of inconsistency with ISO standards,[206] and of WTO litigation, and seems likely to be withdrawn.[207] The issue of eco-labelling came up alongside that of reform of article XX of GATT at the 1996 Singapore WTO meeting, but met the same difficulty. The Commission therefore faces a delicate balancing act, destined to last for some years, between on one side the demands of its more environmentally active member states, EC lobby-groups, and the European Parliament, and on the other its trade partners in the wider world. The European Parliament has criticised the Commission for its refusal to take a tough stance on the genetically modified maize labelling issue, an animal testing ban, and novel food labelling, because of potential conflicts with the GATT provisions.[208] The USA has been vocal in its threats to use the WTO to seek resolution of any potential discriminatory trade measure the EU may implement,[209] and currently the Commission's operational policy appears to be to avoid potential WTO referrals. Its willingness to take a tougher line depends ultimately on the political will of member states to force the issue by lodging a complaint at the WTO on the details of the case and the wider circumstances in which it arises.[210]

Conclusions

The rapid expansion of Community action on the environment into a programme illustrates the effectiveness of the tactical opportunism of the Commission, and its ability to occupy the moral high ground identified by Giandomenico Majone in chapter 2 of this book. In terms of the quantity and range of the legislation enacted under its auspices, and in terms of its increasing popular support, environmental policy has become one of the Community's more successful policies in the social domain. Initially concerned with preventing obstructions to trade, environment policy now has an independent existence and rationale derived largely from global arguments about the sustainable use of resources. Although the environmental policy field was not empty at the national level when the EC began its First Action Programme it has used the developing global and regional environmental awareness to develop it own competences. Having established a certain legitimacy as an appropriate arena for EC action, the next task is to establish a parity with other sectors in order that environmental considerations are given full weight in wider EC policy development. To date, the results of this are mixed: more progress has been made in the sphere of fisheries, for example, than that of agriculture.

Admittedly, problems of competence, of the impact of subsidiarity and of the often related difficulty of securing agreement on a uniform policy stance, mean that it can also sometimes act as a brake on regional and international developments, and from the point of view of substance, even the environmental policy's strongest proponents accept that there is a down side.[211] As its policies cut deeper there are increasing problems of enforcement, and the number of treaty violation procedures is increasing. Political compromises sometimes result in a incoherent legal documents.[212] Nevertheless, the achievements should not be underestimated.

There have been a number of major changes in environmental practices within the Community as a direct result of its environment policy, most notably in water quality control in member states. The wild birds directive also, while not offering a model at the level of compliance, has necessarily resulted in fundamental changes in habits in some member states, particularly in the Mediterranean. The policy has generated significant public law developments, such as the recent directive on freedom of access to information on the environment, and on wildlife habitat; proposals on the disposal of waste and carbon emissions are in the pipeline. Some member states – most notably Denmark – have not been reticent to voice the view that common standards will mean lower standards, but there can be little doubt that, delinquencies aside, the common policy does more to encourage the laggards than to hold back the leaders.

At the wider international level, although the ability of the European Union to act further may be curtailed by a WTO that has no explicit environmental agenda, the European Union is a powerful force in the international arena, with an influential environmental agenda capable of having a direct impact on neighbours and non-European states and companies. To return finally to the issue of erosion of sovereignty, it is interesting to note that the impact of the EU in this wider arena is often considerably greater than the sum of its parts.

Notes

The views expressed in this chapter are those of the authors and should not be attributed to their employers.

1 See generally S. P. Johnson and G. Corcelle, *The Environmental Policy of the European Communities*, Graham and Trotman, London, 1989; P. Birnie, 'The European Community's Environmental Policy' in E. D. Brown and R. R. Churchill (eds) *The UN Convention on the Law of the Sea: Impact and Implementation: Proceedings, Law of the Sea Institute Nineteenth Annual Conference*, Law of the Sea Institute, Hawaii, 1987, 527–556; E. Rehbinder and R. Stewart, *Environmental Protection Policy*, Vol. 2 of *Integration Through Law*, De Gruyter, Berlin,1985; N. Haigh, *EEC Environmental Policy and Britain*, Longman, Harlow, 2nd edn 1987. Also N. Haigh *et al.*, *European Community Environmental Policy in Practice*, 4 Vols, Graham and Trotman, London,1986 onwards. D. Freestone, 'European Community Environmental Policy and Law' in Churchill, Warren and Gibson (eds), *Law, Policy and the Environment*, 1991, 135–154. D Judge (ed.) *A Green Dimension for the European Community* Special Issue of *Environmental Politics*, Winter 1992; David Freestone and Diane Ryland, 'EC Environmental Law after Maastricht', *Northern Ireland Legal Quarterly*,1994, 45, 152–176.

2 Ludwig Kramer, *European Environmental Law Casebook*, Sweet and Maxwell, London, 1993, v.

3 Richard MacRory, 'The Enforcement of Community Environmental Laws: Some Critical Issues' *Common Market Law Review*, 1992, 29, 347–369.

4 See this argument analysed further in David Freestone and Han Somsen, 'The Impact of Subsidiarity' in Jane Holder (ed.) *The Impact of EC Environmental Law in the UK*,1997, 87–99.

5 'EU/US to Hold Talks on Eco-Labelling', *Environment Watch Western Europe (EWWE)* 5:20:6.

6 For a convincing critique of the traditional concept of sovereignty see: K. Ohmae, *The End of the Nation State: The Rise of Regional Economics*, 1996, 12.

7 *R v Secretary of State for the Environment ex parte Kingston-upon-Hull City Council* and *R v Secretary of State for the Environment ex parte Bristol City Council and Woodspring District Council*, The Times Law Report, 31.1.96. Judgment reprinted in the *Journal of Environmental Law*, 8, 2, 336–344.

8 Jan Brinkhorst, 'Subsidiarity and EC Environmental Policy: A Panacea or a Pandora's Box?', *European Environmental Law Review*,1993, 3, 8; See also House of Lords Select Committee on the European Communities, *Report on the Implementation and Enforcement of Environmental Legislation*, Session 1991–92, Ninth Report, HL Paper 53–1, para 87. And Freestone and Somsen, n. 4.

9 T. Burke, 'Sir Leon Sets a Trap', *New Statesman*, 8 August 1997, 20–21.

10 United Nations Conference on the Human Environment (UNCHE) held in Stockholm, 5–16 June 1972, UN Doc. A/CONF.48/14/Rev.l. Although some environmental legislation had been adopted before then, mainly to eliminate distortions in the common market, e.g. First environmental directive adopted 67/548/EC, on classification, packaging and labelling of dangerous substances.

11 Under 8 EEC. the transitional period was designed to run for twelve years, 1958–70; in fact it was accelerated.

12 The proposed accession of Denmark, Eire, Norway and the United Kingdom; Norway of course withdrew after a referendum voted against membership.

13 For example, the failure to develop a common transport policy, which was the subject of an article 175 EEC action (for 'failure to act in infringement of [the] Treaty' by the European Parliament, see *European Parliament v. Commission and Council* case 13/83[1985] I 138.

14 The predecessor of the European Council, and now formally recognised by article 2, Single European Act.

15 Note also that article 2 EEC designates 'an accelerated raising of the standard of living . . . as one of tasks of the Community'.

16 These are set out at length in the First Programme (OJ 20.12.73 C112), reproduced in Johnson and Corcelle, n. 1, pp 12–14 and summarised well in Birnie, n. 1, p. 354, and *The European Community and the Environment* European Documentation, 3/1987.

17 OJ 20.12.73 C 112. The five main objectives were as follows: to abolish the effects of pollution; to manage a balanced ecology; to improve working conditions and the quality of life; to combat the effects of urbanisation; to co-operate with states beyond the EC on environmental policy on environmental problems (p. 445). Of the eleven implementing principles 'prevention at source' and 'the polluter pays' have been the most significant.

18 For texts see: Second Programme (1977–81), adopted 17 May 1977, OJ 13.6.77 C139; Third (1982–86), adopted 17 February 1983, OJ 17.2.83 C46; Fourth (1987–92), adopted 19 October 1987, OJ 7.12.87 C328.

19 Proposal for a EP and Council Decision on the review of the European Community Programme of policy and action in relation to the environment and sustainable development 'Towards Sustainability' COM(95)647, final.

20 The review of the Fifth Environmental Action Programme, 'Towards Sustainability', Proposal for an EP and Council Decision'. (COM(96)648).

21 Article 130s(3) EC Treaty.

22 'Committee Tables Over 100 Changes to EC Action Programme', *Environment Watch* 5:19:15.

23 'Ritt Bjerregaard Comes Under MEPs' Scrutiny Over Fifth Programme', *European Report*, n. 2175 – 16 November 1996, 16.

24 'Doubts over Bjerregaard Dampen EU Policy Expectations for 1996', *Environment Watch* 5:1.
25 *The Commission's Programme for 1997*, Jacques Santer, Strasbourg, 22 October 1996.
26 An initiative by DG VII, Transport.
27 *Environment Watch*, 6:8:1–2.
28 These arguments are very fully discussed in Rehbinder and Stewart, n. 1, pp. 15–30.
29 See further below.
30 See Johnson and Corcelle, n. 1, pp. 220–236.
31 See n.1, also *Commission v Italy (Re Detergents directive)* [1981] I CMLR 331.
32 Directive 79/409, 10th preamble, note also that 'harmonious' and 'balanced' have been interpreted to imply respect for conservation and natural resources – see Johnson and Corcelle, n. 1, ch. 1.
33 UKTS 31 (1988), Cm. 372; EC12 (1986), Cmnd. 7958; 25 ILM 506. On the environment policy after the SEA, see J. S. Davidson, 'The Single European Act and the Environment', *International Journal of Estuarine and Coastal Law*, 1987, 2, 259, 63; P. Kromarek, 'The Single European Act and the Environment', *European Environment Law Review*, 1986, 1, 11.
34 Article 130R (3) also obliges the Community, when preparing its action relating to the environment to take account of: available scientific and technical data; environmental conditions in the various regions of the Community; the potential benefits and costs of action or lack of action; the economic and social development of the Community as a whole and the balanced development of its regions.
35 See further H. Somsen, 'EC Water Directives', *Water Law*, 1990, 1, 93.
36 Article 1 30S (second indent). The Commission had proposed that the procedure for adding new substances to the annex of directive 76/464 on dangerous substances be changed (by unanimous vote) to a majority approval procedure, see further below.
37 In fact the EC appears to have adopted such an approach in the past regarding environmental legislation: see *Progress Made in Connection with the Environmental Action Programme and Assessment of the Work Done to Implement it* (Communication from Commission to Council), COM(80)222, final, 7 May 1980, cited Birnie, n. 1, p. 551.
38 Subject, that is, to the procedure of article 100A(4): 'If, after the adoption of a harmonisation measure by the Council, acting by a qualified majority, a Member State deems it necessary to apply national provisions on grounds of major needs referred to in article 36, or *relating to protection of the environment* . . . , it shall notify the Commission of these provisions (emphasis added). The Commission shall confirm the provisions involved after having verified that they are not a means of arbitrary discrimination, or disguised restriction on trade between Member States.' Note also the Danish declaration attached to the SEA (quoted in Davidson, n. 33, p. 259) and A. Toth, 'The Legal Status of the Declarations Attached to the Single European Act', *Common Market Law Review*, 1986, 23, 802.
39 There is an extensive literature on this but see David Freestone, 'The Precautionary Principle.' in Robin Churchill and David Freestone (eds), *International Law and Global Climate Change*, 1991, pp. 21–40. More recently see David Freestone and Ellen Hey (eds), *The Precautionary Principle and International Law: the Challenge of Implementation* (1996).
40 For a more detailed discussion of this see Freestone and Ryland, op. cit.
41 Consolidated Draft Treaty Texts, 30 May 1997, to be examined on the 5–6 June with a view to presenting the draft Treaty for Amsterdam.
42 Amendment to 7th indent of the Preamble to the TEU, Amendment to article B of the TEU.
43 Amendment to article 2 of the TEU.
44 New article 3d in the TEC: 'Environmental protection requirement must be

integrated into the definition and implementation of Community policies and activities referred to in article 3, in particular with a view to promoting sustainable development'. This will lead to the deletion of article 130r(2). Declaration to the Final Act: 'The Conference notes that the Commission undertakes to prepare environmental impact assessment studies when making proposals which may have significant environmental implications.'.

45 'Reform of EC Treaty', *ENDS Report*, June 1997, 269, 44.
46 'Nordic Success Pleases "Green" Groups.' *European Voice*, 3, 25 (2 July 1997), 18.
47 Ibid.
48 Indeed such implementation is contrary to Community law: see, for example, *Commission v. Italy (Slaughtered Cow Case 11)*, Case 34/73 [1973] ECR 101.
49 Article 189(3) reads: 'A directive shall be binding, as to the result to be achieved upon each member State to which it is addressed, but shall leave to the national authorities the choice of form and methods'.
50 Rehbinder and Stewart, n. 1, pp. 245–252.
51 Ibid., pp. 33–36, 137ff.
52 For example, directive 90/313 on freedom of access to information on the environment, (OJ 23.6.90 L158/56).
53 For example, the early water quality directives, below.
54 Directive 76/464, below.
55 Rehbinder and Stewart, n. 1, p. 36.
56 Case 91/79, *Commission v. Italy* [1980] ECR 1099; Case 92/79, *Commission v. Italy* [1980] ECR 1115.
57 There is an enormous literature on this concept. Notably see J. A. Winter, 'Direct Applicability and Direct Effect: Two Distinct and Different Concepts in Community Law', *Common Market Law Review*, 1972, 9, 425 and A. Dashwood, 'The Principle of Direct Effect in European Community Law', *Journal of Common Market Studies*, 1978, 16, 229. See also T. C. Hartley, *The Foundations of European Community Law* (OUP, 2nd edn 1 988),183ff., and Freestone and Davidson, *The Institutional Framework of the European Communities*, Croom Helm, London, 1988, 27–44.
58 Which includes 'an emanation of the State' (per ECJ in *Marshall v Southampton and Southwest Area Health Authority*, Case 152/84 [1986] I CMLR 688. This means 'any body providing a service under the State's control' ECJ in *Foster v British Gas* [1990] 2 CMLR 833, (1990) 1 *Water Law*, 54.
59 For example, directive 90/313 on freedom of access to information on the environment, above; see also the Commission proposal for a directive on civil liability for waste, OJ 4.10.89 C251/.
60 See Freestone and Somsen, n. 4.
61 See: 'Report of the Group of Independent Experts on Legislative and Administrative Simplification.' COM(95)288. Molitor Report, 51–64, 86–80.
62 For example, Rehbinder and Stewart, n. 1., pp. 226–231.
63 'UK and Ireland move on Green Taxes', *EWWE* 5:23:5.
64 Directive 75/439 on the disposal of waste oils, OJ 25.7.75 L194/23 (as amended). Note also the recent proposals on waste, OJ 19.11.88 C295/3 and 8, which adopt similar approaches.
65 See Council resolution on the implementation of a European Community policy and action programme on the environment (1987–1992) of 19 October 1987, (87/C328/01) item(s).
66 *Eurobarometer 1992*, and *Eurobarometer Top Decision Makers Survey Summary Report* (1997). 5 per cent of top decision makers cited the environment amongst the most serious problems. This was in comparison to 85 per cent of the general public who in 1992 considered environmental protection as an 'immediate and urgent concern'.

67 Somsen, n. 35.
68 For a critical analysis of technocracy see Fischer, *Technocracy and the Politics of Expertise*, Sage, Newbury Park, 1990.
69 G. Pridham and M. Cini 'Enforcing Environmental Standards in the EU: Is there a Southern Problem' in *Environmental Standards in the EU in an Interdisciplinary Framework*, 1997.
70 Directive 76/464, see further below.
71 See Johnson and Corcelle, n. 1, pp. 126–136 for a detailed account of the negotiations and the final approval of the directives on 3 December 1987, for texts see OJ 9.2.88 L36/1.
72 The UK claimed that controls on sewage dumping at sea were not necessary due to the coastal tides. It was the last North Sea state to stop dumping sewage sludge. After considerable pressure from the other North Sea states it announced immediately prior to the 1990 Hague Conference that it would end sewage dumping by the end of 1998. See further D. Freestone, 'The Third International Conference for the Protection of the North Sea', *Water Law*, 1990, I, 17, 18.
73 The United Kingdom has insisted on adding the rider that 'best available technology' means 'not entailing excessive cost' (BATNEEC), see the footnote to this effect in The Hague Declaration, 1990 (reproduced D. Freestone and T. IJlstra (eds) *The North Sea. Basic Legal Documents on Regional Environmental Co-operation*, Graham and Trotman/Martinus Nijhoff, London and Dordrecht, 1991, 6) reported to have been included at the insistence of the United Kingdom.
74 K. von Moltke, *Institute for European Environmental Policy, Annual Report* 1981, 4ff, cited Rehbinder and Stewart, n. 1, p. 265.
75 There would be historical reasons for this in the 1973 Council 'Standstill' Agreement, OJ 15.3.73 C9/1, under which the member states agreed to inform the Commission as soon as possible of their intention to introduce national environmental measures, and then to suspend such national action for at least two months to allow the Commission to decide whether it should propose Community measures instead.
76 A. Dashwood, 'Hastening Slowly: The Community's Path Towards Harmonisation' in H. Wallace, W. Wallace and C. Webb (eds) *Policy Making in the European Communities*, 1973, 195–6. His theory is not restricted to environmental issues.
77 Ibid, p. 266.
78 See further, for example, S. Saetevik, *Environmental Co-operation between the North Sea States*, Belhaven, London, 1988.
79 See later section on International Trade.
80 Johnson and Corcelle, n. 1, p. 20.
81 EC Bull. 12 1988, point I. I. I l; reproduced in Freestone and IJlstra, n. 73, p. 232.
82 Report of the 1992 Edinburgh Council in *EC Bull.*, no 10, 12, 129–130; and *Commission Report to the European Council on the Adaptation of Community Legislation to the Subsidiarity Principle*, COM(93)545, final, 24 November 1993, at p. 3. Discussed in Freestone and Somsen, n. 4, p. 92.
83 For discussion of the EP's current powers, see Freestone and Ryland, n.2, and above at 183–4.
84 Initially by a resolution of 5 January 1983 OJ 18.1.83 C14, calling on Norway and Canada to examine the issue further, and subsequently by directive 83/129, OJ 9.4.83 L91/30. See *Johnson and Corcelle*, n. 1, p. 241. See directive 85/444, OJ 1.10.85 L259/70.
85 Rehbinder and Stewart, n. 1, p. 269.
86 EP Report 1 1376/83, Resolution OJ 14.5.84 C127/67.

87 EP Report Doc A 2–87/89 on the consequences of a rapid rise in the sea level along Europe's coasts, 19.4.89.

88 K. Collins and D. Earnshaw, 'The Implementation and Enforcement of European Community Environmental Law', *Environmental Politics*, 1, 1992, 213–249, 235.

89 In the 1991 Draft Budget the European Parliament at its first reading increased the environmental allocation from the initial Commission proposal of 74m ECU (reduced by the Council to 56m) to more than 190m ECU, of which it wished to see 36m go to a new 'Environment Fund'. The remainder would go to existing schemes: environment and regional development (ENVIREG), 125m; Mediterranean (MEDSPA), 13m; biotypes and nature improvement (ACNAT), 15m; and action by the Community on the environment (ACE), 5m, see *Water Law*, 1991, 2, 4. Also see: Joint Meeting on Integrating environmental protection requirements into Community budget and policy. Committee on the Environment, Public Health and Consumer Protection and Consumer Protection and Committee on Budgets. Strasbourg, 16 July 1996.

90 See *Seventh Annual Report, Luxembourg, Office of Official Publication.*, p. 34. In addition the European Parliament has passed a number of resolutions on the monitoring of the application of environmental law which the Commission is following up: for example, on water, OJ 11.4.88 C94/155; air, OJ 11.4.88 C94/151; habitats, OJ 14.11.88 C290/137.

91 See, more generally, *Report on the Enforcement of Community Environmental Law*, Rapporteur Ken Collins (A4 – 109/97). COM(96)0500, 21 March 1997.

92 Political groups of the European Parliament are PES (Socialists) [214], EPP (People's Party) [181], UFE (Union for Europe) [55], ELDR (Liberal) [41], EUL/NGL (Green/Left Parties) [33]; Greens [9]; ERA (Radical Alliance/Progressive Left) [20]; I-EN (Anti-Integrationists) [18]; Independent [NF, Lega Nord, Ian Paisley].

93 e.g. Intergroup on the Welfare and Conservation of Animals.

94 Report on the Review of Directive 90/200/EEC in the Context of the Commission's Communication on Biotechnology and the White Paper. COM(96)630.

95 [F-EPP] (A4–131/97).

96 'Parliament Calls for a Huge EU Boost to Renewables' *EWWE* 5:14:15.

97 See article 155 EEC, and Freestone and Davidson, n. 57, 57–66.

98 See 'EU Political Horse-Trading', *European Voice*, Legal Briefing, 9–14 May 1996, 20.

99 DG XI has sixteen lawyers who spend 60 per cent of their time on enforcement actions. DG XI is able only to undertake one to five investigatory visits to the member states per year. Ludwig Kramer, HL Select Committee, Evidence. p. 6.

100 'Doubts over Bjerregaard Dampen EU policy expectations for 1996', *Environment Watch* 5:1:1.

101 See the House of Lords Select Committee on the European Communities, 9th Report 1991–92, *Implementation and Enforcement of Environmental Legislation*. R. MacRory, 'The Enforcement of Community Environmental Law: Some Critical Issues', *Common Market Law Review*, 1992, 347–369.

102 See n. 98.

103 In 1995 there were 265 suspected infringements of EC environmental legislation. This is a marked decrease from 455 in 1991, but still constitutes the second largest area of complaints received by the Commission. DG XV, dealing with the internal market, had 512 suspected infringements out of a total of 1,252. see: *Thirteenth Annual Report on the Monitoring the Application of Community Law* (1995), COM(96)600, final.

104 *Communication from the Commission on the Implemention of Community Environmental Law* (COM(96)500. Also see the opinions: Rapporteur: Mr Ken Collins 'Working

Document on Implementation of Community Environmental Law' 9 October [PE 219.420], and 'Draft Council Resolution on the Drafting, Implementation and Enforcement of Community Environmental Law' [Adopted 19/20 June 1997].

105 Regulation 1210/90 OJ 1990, L 120/1. Despite pressure from the European Parliament to give the agency a more explicit inspection and enforcement function, the Regulation restricts its activities broadly to the gathering and assessment of environmental data. Article 20 however provides that after two years after entry into force of the Regulation, the Council, having consulted the Parliament and on the basis of a report from the Commission, must decide on further tasks for the Agency including 'associating in the monitoring of the implementation of Community environmental legislation, in co-operation with the Commission and existing competent bodies in the Member States'.

106 It is reported in the *European Voice*, 31 January 1996, 'Plans to strengthen environment laws' (p. 2) that 'Officials in DG XI . . . believe that the establishment of EU-wide inspectorate could be another effective means of cracking down on member states that fail to fulfil their legal obligations'.

107 Proposal for a Council Decision on a Community action programme promoting non-governmental organisations primarily active in the field of environmental protection. COM(95)573, final.

108 Action brought on 4 July 1996 by Ludwig Kramer against the Commission of the European Communities. Case T-104/96. OJ No C 247/20.

109 See L. Kramer, *EC Treaty and Environmental Law*, Sweet and Maxwell, London, 2nd edn, p. 153–155.

110 As amended by the Maastricht Treaty.

111 Article 171(2) TEU.

112 See some examples cited below; an increasingly important means is by preliminary reference from an action before the national courts, under article 177 EC, see e.g. Case C-44/95, *Sec of State for the Environment, ex parte Royal Society for the Protection of Birds*, judgment of 11 July 1996.

113 Article 170 has been used only once in Case 141/78, *France v United Kingdom* [1979] ECR 2923. This was a dispute involving the Common Fisheries Policy.

114 'Ireland Backs Private Lawsuit to Shut Down UK Nuclear Plant'. *EWWE* 5:22:8.

115 Council directive 85/337/EEC on the assessment of the effects of certain public and private projects on the environment. OJ L.175, 5 July 1985.

116 Also see 'UK Nuclear Fuel Company Taken to Court' *EWWE* 5:19:8.

117 Press Release, 'The Commission for the First Time Seeks Financial Penalties Against Non-Compliance with European Court Judgements', Commission IP/97/63. 29 January 1997.

118 IP/97/5 rev. Council of Ministers.

119 Council directive 79/409/EEC on the conservation of wild birds, OJ L 103, 25.04.1979.

120 Council directive 80/68/EEC on the protection of groundwater caused by certain dangerous substances, OJ L 20, 26.1.1980.

121 Directive 75/440/EEC on the quality of water intended as drinking water, OJ 194, 25.7.1975.

122 Council directive 75/442/EEC on waste, OJ L 194, 25.7.1975.

123 Council directive 84/466/Euratom OJ L265, 5.10.1984.

124 See above, note 117.

125 See further R. MacRory, 'Community Supervision in the Field of the Environment' in H. Somsen (ed.), *Protecting the European Environment: Enforcing EC Environmental Law*, Blackstone, London, 1996.

126 See e.g. articles 173, 175, 184, 215. Article 177 has been more productive.

127 See e.g. the earliest, classic case: Case 25/62, *Plaumann & Co v EEC Commission* [1963] ECR 95.

128 McRory, n. 125, at 21.

129 See the *Leybucht dikes* case and others below and P. Sands, 'The European Court of Justice: An Environmental Tribunal?' in Somsen, n. 125.

130 Case T-858/93, T-585/93 *Stichting Greenpeace Council (Greenpeace International) and Others v Commission* [1995] ECR II2205 Now the subject of a second action as C-321/95.

131 Case T-219/95, *Danielsson and others v Commission*, 22 December 1995.

132 Case T-461/93, *An Taisce a.o. v. Commission*, [1994] ECR at II-733.

133 'EU Commission Moves Against Controversial Irish Project' *Environment Watch* 5:7:10.

134 Directive 92/43 on the conservation of flora and fauna. OJ L206/7.

135 See n. 133.

136 'EU Executive to Start Legal Action Over Swedish Emissions Rules', *EWWE* 5:5:7.

137 'EU Commission to Tolerate German Car Tax Incentives', *EWWE* 5:22:6.

138 See K. Middlemas, *Orchestrating Europe: The Informal Politics of the European Union 1973–1995*, Fontana, London, 1995, chs. 10–12.

139 In 1996 it was reported that twelve of the world's largest oil and chemical companies had formed an exclusive lobbying group with the purpose of fighting environmental taxes in general and an EU-level carbon dioxide/energy tax in particular.(see e.g. Proposal for a framework model for a carbon dioxide/energy tax, COM(95) and proposal for a directive on taxation of energy products, COM(97)30).

Particular controversy arose over the claim that the work of the group would include efforts to influence the outcome of EC-funded research on the environment. This was fuelled by a subsequent decision by the Commissioner responsible for research funding to cut off funds to an individual – known to be hostile to the so-called 'double dividend', model set out in the Commission's 1993 white paper on growth, competitiveness and employment, according to which, environmental tax, shifting the focus of taxation from labour to natural resources, will create jobs and benefit the environment at the same time. A letter from the CBI member informing EU officials of these activities was subsequently published by the Danish newspaper *Borsen*. ('CBI Member Blows Whistle on Anti-Green Tax Lobby Group', *EWWE* 7 June 1996, p. 14.; For a more detailed analysis of the issue of regulatory capture see: S. Peltzman, 'George Stigler's Contribution to Economic Analysis of Regulation' *Journal of Political Economy*, 1993, 101, 5, 818–832.)

140 Greenpeace, 'Energy Subsidies in Europe: How Governments Use Taxpayers' Money to Promote Climate Change and Nuclear Risk' , Greenpeace, London, 1997.

141 See: M. G. Cowles, 'The EU Committee of AMCham: The Powerful Voice of American Firms in Brussels', *Journal of European Public Policy* 3, 3, September 1996, 339–58.

142 'The Acceptable Face of Disaster' *The Guardian*, 13 August 1997, G2, 2–3.

143 Proposal for a European Parliament and Council directive on the legal protection of biotechnological inventions. COM(95)661.

144 One-fifth of all Austria's voters (1.2m) voted against the release and patenting of GMOs 'Strong Vote Against GMOs in Austria', *EWWE* 6:811.

145 'Brussels Set to Order Austria to Lift Transgenic Maize ban', *EWWE* 6:10:11.

146 For a comprehensive coverage of EC Environmental Legislation see: Commission of the EC, Directorate-General for Environment, Consumer protection and Nuclear Safety, European Community Environmental Legislation, 1967–1991. Brussels, (1992). Seven Vols. and 1991–1994 (1996) Vols. 1–7. These two texts are known as the 'Green' and 'Grey' books respectively.

147 Council regulation 348/81 on common rules for import of whales and other cetacean products, OJ 12.2.81. L39/1.

148 OJ 10.2.82. L103/1.

149 S. Lyster, *International Wildlife Law*, Grotius, Cambridge, 1985, 67.

150 See David Freestone, 'The *Leybucht Dikes Case*: Some Wider Implications', *Water Law*, 1991, 4, 2, 152–156. An application for an interim order preventing further work – the first application of its kind – was also unsuccessful.

151 Case C-355/90, *Commission v Spain (Marismas de Santoña case)* [1993] ECR-I 4221.

152 Case C44/95, *Secretary of State for the Environment, ex parte the Royal Society for the Protection of Birds (Lappel Bank)* case (not yet reported).

153 See article 6, particularly 6(4), and 7 of the habitats directive, for a more detailed discussion of these cases see David Freestone, 'The Enforcement of the Wild Birds Directive: A Case Study' in Somsen, n. 125, pp. 229–250.

154 For text of original proposal see OJ 21.9.88 C247/3, and for text of proposed annexes see COM(90)59, final. For the final text with the amendments see directive 92/43 on the conservation of natural habitats and of wild flora and fauna, OJ 1992 No. L 206.

155 See Freestone, 1996, op. cit.

156 See directive 79/409 on the conservation of wild birds. It is noticeable that the directive makes no mention of the 1979 Berne Convention which it clearly implements – is this an example of contemporaneous parallelism – where internal and external powers are claimed virtually simultaneously?

157 Council decision 82/72, OJ 10.2.82 L38/1.

158 Council decision 82/461, OJ 19.7.82 L210/100.

159 Implemented originally by Council regulation 3626/82, OJ 31.12.82 L384/1 (now much amended).

160 See Johnson and Corcelle, n. 1, p. 25. By contrast, the first air pollution legislation was in 1980.

161 Although do note the more recent diffused source controls below.

162 These requirements are so strict they are in reality more like regulations, see further above.

163 Council directive 75/440 concerning the quality of surface water intended for the abstraction of drinking water, OJ 15.7.75 L 194, as amended by Council directive 79/869, OJ 29.10.79 L271 /44.

164 Council directive 76/160 concerning the quality of bathing water, OJ 5.2.76 L31/1.

165 Council directive 78/659 on the quality of fresh waters needing protection in order to support fish life, OJ 14.8.78 L222.

166 Council directive 79/923 on the quality of shellfish waters, OJ 10.11.79 L28 1/47.

167 See, for example, bathing water directive, above, article 1.

168 Council directive 80/778 relating to the quality of water intended for human consumption, OJ 30.8.80 L229/11.

169 Somsen, n. 35, p. 96.

170 S. Boehmer-Christiansen, 'Environmental Quality Objectives Versus Uniform Emission Standards' in D. Freestone and T. IJlstra, *The North Sea. Perspectives on Regional Environmental Co-operation*, Graham and Trotman/Martinus Nijhoff, London and Dordrecht, 1990, 139.

171 Somsen, n. 35, points out that the United Kingdom as an island state with short, relatively fast-flowing rivers derived some competitive advantage from such a system, and that the use of UESs conflicted with the British 'tradition of decentralised and pragmatic pollution control'; see further D. Vogel, *National styles of regulation: environmental policy in Britain and the United States,*1986.

172 Council directive 76/464 on pollution caused by certain dangerous substances discharged into the aquatic environment of the Community, OJ 18.5.76 L129/23.
173 Somsen, n. 35, p. 97.
174 For mercury: Council directives 82/176, OJ 27.3.82 L81/29 and 84/156, OJ 17.3.84 L74/49; cadmium: Council directive 83/513, OJ 24.10.83 L201/1; HCH: Council directive 84/491, OJ 17.10.84 L274/11. Note that the 129 substances were listed in Council resolution of 7 February 1983, OJ 17.2.83 C46, and that Council directive 80/68 on the protection of groundwater against pollution caused by dangerous substances, OJ 26.1.80 L20/43 was enacted pursuant to article 4 of directive 76/464 and follows the general approach of that directive.
175 By Council directive 86/280 on limit values and quality objectives for discharges of certain dangerous substances included in List 1 of the annex to directive 76/464, OJ 4.7.86 L181/16. Progress remains slow and the Commission seeks to change the basis on which substances are added from unanimity to QMV. See COM(90)9, final for original version of proposal and for comment, Somsen, n. 35. Of course, under the procedure of article 130R EEC, such a proposal must be approved unanimously by the Council.
176 For a more detailed discussion see Freestone and Somsen, n. 4, pp 92–97.
177 *Commission Report to the European Council on the Adaptation of Community Legislation to the Subsidiarity Principle*, COM(93)545, final, 24 November 1993.
178 *R v Secretary of State for the Environment ex parte Kingston-upon-Hull City Council and R v Secretary of State for the Environment ex parte Bristol City Council and Woodspring District Council*, Times Law Report, 31.1.96. Judgment reprinted in the *Journal of Environmental Law*, 8, 2, 336–344. See also Philippe Sands and Caroline Blatch, 'Estuaries in European Community law: Defining Criteria', *International Journal of Marine and Coastal Law* 1998,13, 1–22.
179 Directive 96/61, OJ 1996 L275.
180 COM(93)680, final. See now COM(96)59, final.
181 COM(93)680, final.
182 COM(96)59, final.
183 *Commission v Council (Re European Road Traffic Agreement)*, Case 22/70 [1971] ECR 263. See also A. Nollkaemper, 'The EC and International Environmental Co-operation – Legal Aspects of external Community powers', *Legal Issues of European Integration*, 1987, 2, 55–91.
184 1974 Paris Convention for the prevention of pollution from land-based sources, UKTS 64 (1978; Cmnd. 7251); 13 ILM 352 (1974); and with amending Protocol, see Freestone and IJlstra, n. 73, 128ff.
185 1983 Bonn Agreement for co-operation in dealing with pollution of the North Sea by oil and other harmful substances; UKTS Misc 26 (1983; Cmnd. 9104); and with 1989 amending decision, see Freestone and IJlstra, n. 73, pp. 171ff.
186 For the text of the EC Declaration on signature of the Law of the Sea Convention on 7 December 1984, listing its legislation in the field, see Freestone and IJlstra, n. 73, pp. 228ff.
187 1963 Berne Agreement on the International Commission for the protection of the Rhine against pollution, 994 UNTS 14538 (1976), supplemented by 1976 Bonn Agreement; see further A. Nollkaemper, 'The Rhine Action Programme: A Turning-point in the Protection of the North Sea?' in Freestone and IJlstra, n. 170, p. 123.
188 1976 Bonn Convention on the protection of the Rhine against chemical pollution, 27 ILM 625 (1988), and see OJ 19.9.77 L240.
189 1972 Oslo Convention on the prevention of marine pollution by the dumping from ships and aircraft, UKTS 119 (1975); Cmnd. 6228; 11 ILM 262 (1972); for text with amending protocols, see Freestone and IJlstra, n. 73, pp. 91ff.

209

190 For the full texts of three Declarations, see Freestone and IJlstra, n. 73, Bremen, 1984, pp. 62–90; London, 1987, pp. 40 61; The Hague, 1990, pp. 3–39.
191 See generally, P. Sand, *Marine Environment Law*, Tycooly, Dublin, 1988; for example, 1976 Barcelona Convention for the protection of the Mediterranean Sea against pollution (and protocols) 15 ILM 290 (1976); also the 1983 Cartagena Convention for the protection and development of the marine environment of the wider Caribbean region (and first protocol) 22 ILM 221 (1983).
192 See generally Freestone, 'Some Institutional Aspects of the Establishment of Exclusive economic Zones by the EC Member States', *Ocean Development and International Law*, 23, 1992, 97–114. and Freestone, 'The Declaration on the co-ordinated Extension of Jurisdiction in the North Sea', *The International Journal of Marine and Coastal Law*, 8, 1993, 171–175.
193 See for example, Saetevik, n. 78, and J.-L. Prat, 'The Role and Activities of the European Communities in the Protection and Preservation of the Marine Environment of the North Sea' in Freestone and IJlstra, n. 170, p. 101.
194 See, for example, Parcom recommendations 89/1 on the precautionary principle, and 89/2 on best available technology, reproduced in Freestone and IJlstra, n. 73, pp. 152 and 153 respectively.
195 For example the current EC Commission proposal for a directive concerning the protection of fresh, coastal, and marine waters against pollution caused by nitrates from diffuse sources. Original text at COM(88)708, final, as amended in light of EP proposals COM(89)544, final, and see *Water Law*, 1990, I 6.
196 See Hey, IJlstra and Nollkaemper, 'The 1992 Paris Convention for the Protection of the Marine Environment of the North East Atlantic: a Critical Analysis', *International Journal of Marine and Coastal Law*, 1993, 8, 1–50. The full text of the new Convention is annexed at pp. 50–76.
197 See: D. A. Reid, 'Trade and the Environment: Finding a balance. The EU approach'. *European Environmental Law Review*, May 1996.
198 *Procureur du Roi v Dassonville*, Case 8/74 [1974] ECR 837 at p. 852.
199 Report on the Communication from the Commission to the Council and the European Parliament on trade and the environment. Rapporteur: Mr W.Kreissl-Dorfler (A4-0319/96).
200 Report on the Communication from the Commission to the Council and the European Parliament on trade and the environment. (A4-0319/96). Rapporteur Mr W. Kreissl -Dorfler.
201 Council Regulation 880/92/EEC on a EU award scheme for an ecolabel. OJ L99, 5.11.1992.
202 See L.Gyselen, 'The Emerging Interface Between Competition and Environmental Policy in the EEC', Ch 3 in J. Cameron *et al.* (eds) *Trade and the Environment: The Search for Balance*, Cameron and May, London, 1995.
203 Press Release IP(93) 820 of 30 September 1993.
204 WTO Trade and Environment Committee Discusses Market Access, TRIPS and Eco-labelling. WTO Press/TE 009.1 May 1996.
205 Proposal for a directive on the marking of packaging and the establishment of a conformity and assessment procedure for packaging. COM(96)191, final.
206 'ISO Group Agrees on Dual Meaning for Moebius Loop', *EWWE* 2 May 1997, p. 4.
207 'ISO Pressures EU Draft Packaging Marking', *EWWE* 5:18:1.
208 see Kreissl-Dorfler, n. 199.
209 'Trade Strains Possible as EU Gene-Tech Maize Decisions Delayed even further', *EWWE* 5:17:15.
210 See generally: J. Morris, *Green Goods? Consumers, Product Labels and the Environment*, London, Institute of Economic Affairs, 1997.

211 Johnson and Corcelle, n. 1, p. 9. A recent example is the delay in the EU ratification of the 1995 UN Agreement on Straddling Stocks, see further David Freestone and Zen Makuch, 'The New International Environmental Law of Fisheries', *Yearbook of International Environmental Law, 1996*, 7, 3–51.
212 Johnson and Corcelle, n. 1.

11

CONCLUSION

The European Union, member states and social policy

Hussein Kassim and David Hine

This book, with its three companion volumes, has examined the extent to which developments at the EU level have constrained or enhanced the autonomy of the member states. It has investigated how these developments have affected the substance of national policy, national policy processes and national actors. Claims that power has migrated from national capitals to Brussels cannot be properly assessed without careful examination of this dimension of the relationship. If we are to understand European integration fully, we need to examine not just institutional action and policy development in Brussels, but also what Moravcsik has called, 'substantive domestic policy adaptation' (Moravcsik 1993: 473). In the first section of this concluding chapter, the extent to which the European Union has affected the autonomy of the member states in the specific area of social policy will be examined, while in the second section we shall compare the findings of this volume with the conclusions reached in the companion volumes dealing with other sectors.

The European Union, national autonomy and social policy

The chapters of this book demonstrate that while there is clearly a difference between rhetoric and reality, and between the aspirations expressed and the development of policy, the contention that little has been achieved by the EU within the social realm (Lange 1992; De Swann 1992) cannot be sustained, nor can the corollary – that the integrity of territorial sovereignty of member states has been maintained. Even if policy development across the social dimension falls far short of an EU welfare state or a comprehensive social policy, the Union is active across a wide range of fronts. Member states remain the primary institution of European social policy, and have in general resisted EU action in this domain, but important inroads have been made nevertheless.

The picture that emerges from the case studies, in terms of the impact of EU action on national policy, is therefore complex and highly differentiated. In some areas, such as women's rights, the EU has been the primary force; in others, such as environmental policy, it has played the role of opportunist, taking advantage of the prevailing political climate to persuade member states to grant competence to the EU. In others still, such as workers' rights, it has made progress on a few issues, but not on many others. There is no single explanation for this variegated picture. It is the consequence of the interaction of a range of factors, some positive, some negative, of which the most important are:

- the treaty base itself, giving a very strong constitutionally protected position to member states in social policy, underpinned by their reluctance to cede authority upwards, and by the suspicion of several of them about the policy ambition of the Commission;
- the large differences in the detailed operation of the European welfare state across member states (even if in broader comparative perspective, there are common features of a 'European' model) most notably in the way in which welfare is delivered, and the emphasis which different states put on particular areas of provision (pensions, health care, income support, unemployment benefits);
- the absence of a *central* EU regulatory function, as exists for example in competition policy for industry and commerce, or through direct market intervention for agriculture;
- the capacities of the Commission, in the absence of this central 'hard-law' regulatory function, to exploit other 'soft-law' opportunities, and to establish a moral and didactic leadership in the social policy sector;
- the important but uneven impact of the Court of Justice, which, like all other constitutional courts, can only influence policy on issues that reach it through the legal system in a slow, almost haphazard manner;
- the prevailing policy climate as affected not just by national political developments, but by changing perceptions of the general economic and social values the Union should pursue, and indeed by broader global attitudes towards welfare, markets and social choice – perceptions which inevitably feed through to national opinion leaders at different rates.

How these factors combine to make for the uneven purchase of social policy across the Union can be best illustrated by considering the difficulties encountered in particular sectors. Here we look particularly at the areas of 'social dialogue' and collective bargaining. Article 4 of the protocol outlines two ways in which EU-level agreements can be implemented and enforced. The first is 'in accordance with the procedures and practices specific to management and labour and the member states'. The second – which is restricted under article 2 to certain areas like health and safety, information and consultation and equal opportunities – is through a Council *decision* on a proposal from the Commission, by request from the signatory parties. Parental leave and part-time work were the first two issues taken under the latter procedure. Part-time work was the subject of a draft agreement concluded in May 1997 by UNICE, CEEP and ETUC.

Now the Declaration on article 4(2) of the social protocol makes clear that member states are under 'no obligation . . . to apply the agreements directly or to work out rules for their transposition, nor any obligation to amend national legislation in force to facilitate their implementation'. Clearly, then, such an agreement – unlike a directive – cannot be relied on to *guarantee* minimum standards across the EC. Moreover, there is a wide divergence between member states in relation to the nature of collective bargaining structures and the means to make them generally binding across a given sector. In Belgium and The Netherlands, for example, national procedures exist for the negotiation of national, intersectoral collective agreements that may then be proclaimed generally binding by due process of law. By contrast, in France, Germany, Spain, Portugal and Greece such a centralised approach is not the practice. Agreements in those countries are generally concluded at sector level and extension procedures may be invoked through the Ministry of Labour to ensure their application to non-organised employers and employees throughout a given bargaining unit (the conditions for extension naturally also vary from country to country). In Italy there is also sector-level bargaining, but extension procedures are likely to be considered unconstitutional. And, unlike their Danish counterparts, Irish unions and employers have little influence over their members who fail to comply with agreements. This is the situation also in the UK, where provision for the extension of collective agreements under Schedule 11 of the 1975 Employment Protection Act was abolished by the 1980 Employment Act.

There is also wide diversity between the states over the subjects that can be negotiated and the criteria for establishing the representativeness of the domestic negotiating partners. Differences also exist between states over the legal regulation of strikes and lock-outs as well as implementation of the terms of agreements. These factors, amongst others, 'show clearly that there is no homogeneous legal pattern of collective bargaining and collective agreement throughout the Community' (Weiss 1991: 64).

Very similar problems in the degree to which policy can establish a purchase arise in relation to collective bargaining at the European level. 'European' collective bargaining can, of course, refer to two quite distinct processes. The first is the process through which the results of collective bargaining in other member states are brought to bear on domestic negotiations at intersectoral, sectoral or company level. The second is the process through which employers' organisations and unions actually conduct negotiations face to face at European level in an attempt to conclude binding agreements. These agreements may themselves be of two sorts: procedural and substantive. For a *procedural* agreement employers and unions negotiate 'an operational mechanism which details and regulates the manner in which a specified issue is to be handled' (Salamon 1987: 387). To this extent, a number of such agreements have already been concluded at European level. We have seen in chapter 7, for example, that the social chapter itself was the result of negotiations between ETUC, UNICE and CEEP in October 1991, a few weeks before the Maastricht Summit. At sectoral level, procedures relating to training and other issues have been agreed and some 250 multinational companies have already established European works councils in some form or other, mostly following detailed negotiations.

Substantive agreements, by contrast, refer 'to those terms of employment, such as wages, hours, holidays, etc. which can be converted into monetary terms' (Salamon 1987: 289–90). At intersectoral level, the framework agreement on parental leave and the agreement on part-time work are so far the only examples. There are very few substantive agreements at European sectoral level, though the case of Danone is significant at company level. In April 1996, this French multinational signed an agreement with the unions to form a Joint Information and Consultation Committee, covering all its subsidiaries across Europe. Provision is made for this Committee to 'negotiate joint statements and measures, including with respect to employment, training, information, safety and working conditions, as well as to the exercise of trade union rights'. Some see this as 'the closest European works councils have yet come to some form of collective bargaining at European level' and the agreement as 'the first to accord an explicit negotiating role to the European works council' (*European Works Councils Bulletin* 1996a: 1).

Procedural agreements already exist at EC level. Whether agreements on *substantive* issues will be developed will depend on the degree to which recognition rights are extended to unions and employee representatives to bargain collectively at EC intersectoral, sectoral or company level. This in turn assumes that the problems of representation, implementation and enforceability analysed above can be satisfactorily resolved and, indeed, that the unions themselves actually demand it (Marginson and Sisson 1992: 44–5). One secondary factor which may eventually help is the capacity of European Monetary Union to make pay levels across the member states more transparent, and thus act as a catalyst for the gradual evolution of EC-wide agreements covering pay and other conditions.

Developments at the EC level in relation to information disclosure, consultation and the negotiation of procedural agreements have also been patchy and opportunistic, but that is scarcely surprising. The spread of recognition of employee representatives for these purposes over the last hundred years or so, even within any national economy, has been patchy and opportunistic. Union recognition – the process by which management formally acknowledges the legitimacy of a union's right to determine jointly terms and conditions – is a key stage in the development of an organisation's industrial relations system, but recognition too may proceed in stages: first the right to representation, then the right to consultation, and finally the right to negotiation. The social dialogue has played some role in enabling unions to gain the initial stages of recognition at EC-level, but the right to representation is best thought of at EC level not through the right to represent employees in individual grievances, but through the right to information – in other words, the right of unions at EC level to receive relevant information about events likely to affect their members across the member states and to represent their views accordingly in the light of it.

Recognition is not static however; once recognition has been granted by employers for certain defined purposes, it may become relatively easier for its boundaries to be spread further. For this reason, the mere fact that social dialogue has taken place at all is an encouraging sign for those who believe that labour market regulation should proceed on a voluntary, flexible basis. The problems encountered so far, including employer resistance, inadequate structures, lack of resources and economic recession, are not different in kind from those encountered during the process of *national* recognition processes, but they do inevitably mean that there will be no uniform or homogeneous legal pattern of collective bargaining and collective agreement throughout the Community (Weiss 1991: 64).

The role of the Commission

A second consideration which emerges from the preceding chapters is that the Commission's capacities for action in the realm of social policy do not depend solely on the national governments which define its legal and regulatory power and policy reach. They also depend on its own independent capacity to act as a central focus for the activities of a range of interested potential allies among parties, unions, employers, social policy agencies and professionals . . . and some national governments. Moreover, it is a capacity in which the Commission can, within the limits of its resources, do much for itself in sensitising elite and expert opinion to the possibility of problem-solving action at EU level, and assembling a critical mass of favourable opinion, especially if it is able to occupy the moral high ground in an area of policy debate where attitudes and values vary considerably within as well as between the member states. Inevitably such a capacity is greatly influenced by major variations in national circumstances, and is liable to substantial changes over time. However, time is often on the Commission's side. It will still be there when a particular national government has gone, and if it can extract concessions from that government's more sympathetic successor, they can be built in to the *acquis* in ways that are difficult if not impossible to reverse, even if there is a reversal in the state in question.

An important part of this capacity, as we have seen, is the Commission's ability to create networks, observatories and agencies, to commission research, and to publicise findings etc. This process of bureaucratic expansion and mutual learning absorbs apparently rather modest resources but enables the Commission to frame issues, design packages and structure the sequence of proposals that eventually reach the visible policy agenda. The range of such bodies is formidable. It covers employment policy, equal opportunities, public health, health and safety at work, 'social protection' (i.e. pension regimes, unemployment insurance, health insurance, and other forms of social assistance), and social partnership and social rights. Many of the programmes established under these headings are co-financed by the European Social Fund. Some of the most significant are EURES – the European labour market network; NOW (New Opportunities for Women); the main public-health networks covering AIDS, cancer, and drug abuse; the various working parties of the study group on the modernisation of social protection, covering disability, family policy, ageing policy, and social exclusion; and the range of framework agreements on part-time work, labour law, migration policy and action on racism.

Hand in hand with this semi-concealed role is a parallel declaratory one which may be said to have reached its most developed form at the 1996/7 intergovernmental conference on institutional reform. The latter, though originally convened to deal mainly with problems of decisional effectiveness in advance of enlargement of the Union to central and eastern Europe, was, conveniently for the Commission's agenda, to a large degree overtaken by the abrupt change in policy climate provoked by the election of a left-wing government in France, and by mounting EU-wide concern about the political consequences of rising unemployment. The result was the inclusion in the draft Amsterdam Treaty (at the time of writing in 1997 still, of course, unratified) apparently at a late stage in discussions, not only of the social protocol hitherto excluded from the formal Treaty by the British opt-out (renounced by the incoming 1997 Labour government) but also of a separate employment chapter, another on public health, and another on consumer protection. The contents of the employment chapter are, to say the least, pregnant with ambiguity, and the extent, if at all, to which it can, for the time being, *constrain* national governments, or be justiciable by the ECJ, remains doubtful. What it does do, however, is create new forums for policy discussion in these sectors, and in the case of employment this involves annual resolutions by the European Council, on the basis of a joint annual report from the Commission and Council of Ministers. These reports may, by qualified majority (and in consultation with the Economic and Social Committee, the Committee of the Regions, and the Parliament) be used to draw up guidelines which member states are required to take into account in their own national employment policies. Member states are also required to provide Council and Commission with an annual report on their policies in this connection, and, again by QMV, the Council can make specific recommendations to member states about employment policy.

Certainly, in view of the 'recommendatory' rather than mandatory framing of such procedures, a sceptic is likely to remain unconvinced that the chapter contains any real and immediate constraints. What is clear, however, is the long-term thinking in the chapter: the aim is to influence the context and the debate on employment, and to foster the creation of employment policy networks at the EU level. This is especially evident in article 5, which allows the Council to

> adopt incentive measures designed to encourage cooperation between Member States and to support their action in the field of employment through initiatives aimed at developing exchanges of information and best practices, providing comparative analysis and advice as well as promoting innovative approaches and evaluating experiences, in particular by recourse to pilot projects.

The EU has frequently been said to have proceeded in areas like social policy by the creation of 'soft' or indicative law and in the new draft Treaty the employment section is clearly towards the 'soft' end of EU constitutional law too. But once employment has been placed on the agenda, the Commission has greater administrative opportunities and considerably more legitimacy to build more solid foundations, gradually drawing into its orbit a range of sympathetic actors from the national level – including, most importantly, national administrations.

Social policy in comparative perspective

Since the relaunching of the European project in 1985 in the form of the 1992 programme, the scope and intensity of EU action have increased considerably. The Single European Act extended Community responsibilities along the social dimension to include social cohesion and the environment. It also made policy development easier in certain areas of social policy by changing the decision rule in the Council of Ministers from unanimity to QMV. By establishing a Community treaty base for European political co-operation, the member states signalled their intention of making the EC a more influential actor on the international stage, while a future commitment to economic and monetary union in order to underpin the single market and to strengthen European currencies was also undertaken. The Treaty of European Union further expanded the social policy competences of the Community and extended QMV. It brought justice and home affairs within the scope of the Union, transformed EPC into the CSFP, and set out a detailed schedule for realising EMU. The Amsterdam Treaty, as noted above, has continued this expansion.

Although the EU has expanded its activities both within existing competences and into new fields and new domains, its impact on the autonomy of the member states has not been uniform either between or within policy domains. This volume has found that even though action at the Union level has had significant consequences for national social policy, the impact has been greater in some areas than others and it has differed from member state to member state. In the areas of health and safety, women's rights, environmental policy, training and some aspects of industrial relations, EU-level action has been a major stimulus to policy change and development at the national level, while in employment, consumer affairs and with respect to some aspects of health policy, the EU has exercised a more limited degree of influence. By contrast, in the traditional areas of social policy, namely, social security, health service provision, welfare, and unemployment benefits, member states have been relatively unaffected by Brussels. In these latter areas, national governments have not been prepared to cede control, and although falling within the ambit of permissible action on the part of the Union, unanimity ensures that member states are able to prevent policy development in these areas.

The differential impact that EU action has had on member states results from the differences in social policy that they have historically pursued, reflecting the differing legacies of past social conflicts and social coalitions, as well as the influence of differing political cultures, state traditions and balance of political forces. Governments in western Europe have developed different types of welfare regime: the Scandinavian, the Germanic, the Anglo-Saxon and the southern European. National social policies reflect different conceptions of social citizenship and of the family (see chapter 8 in this volume). Moreover, certain countries, such as Germany and the Nordic states, have instituted relatively high levels of environmental protection, while other member states have shown rather less willingness to take action in this domain (see chapter 10 in this volume). Beginning from different starting points, it is not, therefore, surprising that the impact of EU action has produced different outcomes in different member states.

Differential impact along sectoral and national lines is not, however, unique to social policy. The impact of EU action in the industrial domain also betrays a similar pattern (see Menon and Hayward 1996). In some sectors, such as air transport, telecommunications and energy, policy development in Brussels had a very considerable effect on national policy, not only forcing changes in the substance of the policies pursued by governments, but also depriving states of the use of policy instruments that they had traditionally deployed (see Kassim 1996, Thatcher 1996 and McGowan 1996). In other sectors, such as aerospace and research and development policy, EU action at the Union level has had a far less significant effect on the member states (see Jones 1996 and Peterson 1996).

The contrasting experiences of these industrial sectors could not be explained in terms of reference to a single key factor, but were rather the outcome of the interaction of a number of factors influencing the likelihood and direction of EU policy development, as well as the impact of Union action on national policy. These include the following: the extent of EU competence under the treaties; the institutional arrangements governing the division of responsibilities and powers between EU institutions, and the decision rule operative in the Council of Ministers; the preferences of the member states; the orientation and calibre of the relevant Directorates-General within the European Commission; interest group mobilisation, organisation and strategy; intervention by the European Court of Justice; the nature of the international and regional regimes governing the sector, and its domestic organisation; the role of technology in the sector and the consequences of technological advance; the political salience of the sector; and the strategic importance of the sector. It was not possible to establish any authoritative hierarchical ordering of these factors, since the relative importance of each changed over time and there was constant interaction between them.

As we have seen, some of these factors are also at work in social policy and may help to account for the differential impact of EU action in the various areas of the social policy domain. Constitutional and institutional differences, for example, have made it easier for policy to be developed at the Union level in health and safety, where QMV has been the decision rule in the Council since 1987, than in areas where unanimity is required. Also, entrepreneurship on the part of the Commission has played an important part in the development of environmental policy. However, there are also differences in the importance that certain of these variables have had in the social policy field. For example, technological change is much less relevant to social policy. There is no case comparable to energy or the audiovisual sector where technological change has undermined the traditional rationale for organisation into national markets, operated by state-owned monopolies and regulated by national authorities, and opened the possibility to European-level regulation.

The same point applies equally to national differentiation. Factors such as the differences between state traditions, political culture and the balance of political forces can help to explain the differential impact of EU action between member states in all policy domains in general. However, additional country-specific features are also relevant. Thus, whilst conceptions of social citizenship, the nature of the welfare state and official concern for the environment must be invoked in order to explain patterns of national differentiation in social policy, the differential impact of EU action in industrial policy from member state to member state can only be explained with reference to natural resource endowment, the history of trading relations, the organisation of policy networks, and industrial strength and competitiveness. In macroeconomic policy, by contrast, the differences in national experience result from differences in the openness of the economy, in economic structure and in economic performance (Menon and Forder 1998), while in defence they relate to geography, the strength of Atlanticism and military tradition (Freedman and Menon 1997).

The experience of social policy bears close comparison with industrial policy in terms of two other important aspects concerning the effects of EU action on state autonomy: the first is the magnitude and nature of the impact of the EU, and the second is the relative importance of the impact of the EU. With respect to the first, the consequences of Union-level action have undoubtedly been considerable in the social policy domain, sectoral and national differentiation notwithstanding. This has also been the case in industrial policy, where member states have been compelled to adapt their existing policies in a significant number of sectors. The same is not true, however, in the areas of macroeconomic and defence policy. Despite appearances to the contrary, in macroeconomic policy, national autonomy has not been significantly affected as a result of EU action (see Menon and Forder 1998 from which the following extensively draws). Firstly, although there is an apparent convergence between economic policies within the Union, this tendency should not be attributed to action on the part of Brussels. It is not the ERM that has convinced states to believe in the centrality of lowering inflation as a means of achieving economic success. Rather ERM and EMU are the outcome of this consensus. Moreover, even when states have joined the ERM, it is not necessarily their participation that is responsible for the fall in inflation that they may experience. Secondly, although the ERM does impose limits within which exchange rates can be set by governments, membership is not compulsory and participating states can decide to exit. In addition, the tools by which EMS obligations are met remain exclusively in national hands. Moreover, the ERM does not legally bind member states in the same way that the social chapter compels governments to recognise certain rights and to meet certain obligations. If the autonomy of the member states is circumscribed by membership of the ERM, the constraints are not legal, technical or practical, nor are they imposed by Brussels, rather they are of a political nature and self-imposed by national governments seeking the benefit of credibility for their economic policies. Finally, it is important not to be misled by the rhetoric of governments who may either refer to EU requirements in order to legitimate policy choices or use Brussels as a scapegoat when taking unpopular decisions. This applies generally and not just to macroeconomic policy.

Likewise in defence, action by the EU has not directly led to shifts in national policy, nor has the Union placed major constraints on state autonomy (see Freedman and Menon 1997). This runs counter to expectations that the end of the Cold War would bring an end to the dependence of West European governments on the US, which was institutionalised through NATO. However, US detachment from Europe has failed to bring about an increased role for the EU. Firstly, governments have shown a consistent preference for co-operative, intergovernmental arrangements which do not threaten national decision-making competence, rather than EU-style integration. Secondly, despite the efforts of supporters of a European defence capability, NATO is, and appears likely to remain, the principal framework for multilateral action and co-operation in the field of defence. Thus, the prospects for the EU's development as a security community seem distinctly limited. At most, hitherto, the EU has exercised a modest influence through indirect means, such as the pressures placed on public finances by efforts to meet the Maastricht convergence criteria, the intrusion of industrial policies, increased links between states in non-military areas and broadening conceptions of security.

Although social policy is closest to industrial policy in terms of the magnitude of EU impact, there are both similarities and dissimilarities in the way in which the member states have been affected. In both domains, action at the Union level has exercised direct and indirect influences. Direct impact has taken the form of sectoral policy development by the EU which has necessitated policy adaptation at the national level (telecommunications, energy and air transport on the one hand, environmental policy, health and safety, and workers' rights on the other). The rulings of the European Court of Justice have also led directly to the abandonment, introduction or modification of existing national rules (air transport, women's rights and workers rights). EU action has also indirectly affected the member states. For example, industrial and social affairs ministries have presided over cuts in public expenditure that have been imposed by national governments attempting to reduce budget deficits in order that they can meet the criteria for convergence and proceed to the third stage of EMU.

Beyond these similarities, however, there are important differences. This may result from the fact that, while industrial and economic objectives have always been at the centre of the European project, social policy has generally been of secondary importance. This is reflected by the energies that have been respectively devoted to the two policy domains, the powers granted by national governments to the European Union and the decision-making procedures instituted, as well as the greater powers exercised in Brussels by the Commission directorates dealing with producer interests. Firstly, although there have been numerous action programmes in the social policy domain, none has galvanised the Community to a degree comparable to the extent to which the 1992 project mobilised governments and business actors towards the realisation of the single market, generating a momentum that spilled over into virtually all areas relating to trade in goods and services. Secondly, in social policy, there has been no equivalent to the competition rules, which in the domain of industrial policy have proved powerful tools in the hands of Commissioners eager to liberalise sectors historically characterised by protectionist and collusive policies (energy, telecommunications and air transport). In social policy, changes have come about largely as a result either of sectoral policy developments at the EU level or of rulings laid down by the European Court of Justice, and not as a consequence of the application of general rules. Thirdly, in social policy, the impact of the EU on the member states has otherwise been exercised less directly and through different means. For example, soft law in the absence of tougher regulatory instruments has played a much more important role in EU social policy. Also, the action of networks, observatories and research projects sponsored by the European Commission has been very significant. These activities enable domestic interests to exchange information, to articulate common concerns, and to facilitate the formation of coalitions, as well as permitting direct communication with interested officials from EU institutions. The ideas which are floated or developed as a result can shape policy agendas in the member states, confronting governments with unpalatable policy options, modifying 'policy frames' (see chapter 9 in this volume) and subjecting them to unwelcome pressures. The autonomy of national government may thereby be restricted in ways that are more subtle than the implementation of EU regulations or interventions by the European Court of Justice. In these circumstances, the national government loses control of the policy agenda, it confronts transnational coalitions and it no longer acts as a gatekeeper for domestic constituencies that want to ensure that their interests are represented. Finally, in some industrial sectors, certain countries have sought to export their domestic policies to other member states through the adoption of EU rules. In the social policy domain, there is less evidence that member governments have attempted to impose their national models on their European partners in this way. A more pressing concern has been to avoid competitive disadvantage (see chapter 3 in this volume).

Not only does social policy bear comparison with industrial policy in terms of the magnitude of EU impact, but there are also similarities in terms of the relative importance of the Union as an influence on national policy and policy change. In industrial policy, Menon and Hayward (1996) have cautioned against exaggerating the role of the EU (see also Kassim and Menon 1996). Although EU action did exercise a considerable influence on policy in the member states, other factors, both internal and external, were significant too. Within the state, changes of government as well as government action remained key determinants of policy. Financial pressures constitute an additional domestic policy influence, preventing, for example, the state from offering high levels of financial support freely to its national champions. Also, the action of domestic lobbies can maintain or lead to the alteration of state preferences. Externally, governments find themselves subject to constraints imposed by economic interdependence, as the French Socialist government discovered in 1983. Technological change can also affect policy, rendering traditional policies obsolete or infeasible. Thus, for example, the revolution in telecommunications has forced governments to revise policies concerning the movement of capital, while the advent of satellite television has made it increasingly difficult for countries to maintain control over broadcasting.

If the continued influence of these internal and external factors on shaping national policy warns against overestimating the importance of the EU, the limits on what EU action can achieve should also be borne in mind, as Menon and Hayward (1996) note. Surveying a range of industrial policies, they observe that even in the area of competition policy where the European Commission disposes of extremely powerful instruments and enjoys considerable autonomy, its rulings on state aid have not prevented governments from directing funds to publicly owned companies. Also, in some key instances, the source of policy change can ultimately be traced to responses of governments to the pressures of internationalisation and the attempts to ensure that their economies are competitive rather than to initiatives launched by Brussels. Indeed, even where EU action antedates domestic policy adaptation, the stimulus may lie elsewhere. Finally, in some sectors, aerospace, for example, tightly organised domestic policy networks have been able to resist attempts to develop policy or policy capabilities at the European level.

Similar conclusions can be drawn from social policy. While the effects of EU action have been pronounced, the limitations are also worthy of note. Firstly, the traditional areas of social policy have remained largely untouched by Brussels and have been safely insulated by the member states. Governments have largely retained their sovereignty over health, welfare, social security and the treatment of the unemployed. Secondly, domestic constituencies and national governments have continued to exercise an important influence on the direction of policy (see chapter 3 in this volume). Thirdly, although it has played a significant role, the European Court of Justice, like other similar courts, is not capable of developing comprehensive policies. Its interventions may be decisive, but they are also episodic.

References

Cram, L. (1993) 'Calling the Tune without Paying the Piper? Social Policy Regulation: The Role of the Commission in European Community Social Policy', *Policy and Politics*, 21, April 1993, 136

—— (1997) *Policy Making in the EU: Conceptual Lenses and the Integration Process*, London: Routledge

Esping-Andersen, G. (1990) *The Three Worlds of Welfare Capitalism*, Cambridge: Polity Press

De Swann, Abram (1992) 'Perspectives for Transnational Social Policy', *Government and Opposition*, 27, Winter 1992, 33–52

Fraser, M.W. (1996) 'Television', in H. Kassim and A. Menon (eds) *The European Union and National Industrial Policy*, London: Routledge, 204–25

Freedman, L. and Menon, A. (1997) 'Conclusion: Defence, States and Integration in Europe' in J. Howorth and A. Menon (eds) *The European Union and National Defence Policy*, London: Routledge

Jones, C. (1996) 'Aerospace', in H. Kassim and A. Menon (eds) *The European Union and National Industrial Policy*, London: Routledge,88–105

Kassim, H. (1996) 'Air Transport', in H. Kassim and A. Menon (eds) *The European Union and National Industrial Policy*, London: Routledge,106–31

Kassim, H. and Menon, A. (1996) 'The European Union and state autonomy', in H. Kassim and A. Menon (eds) *The European Union and National Industrial Policy*, London: Routledge, 1–10

Lange, Peter (1992) 'The Politics of the Social Dimension', in Alberto M. Sbragia (ed.) *Euro-Politics: Institutions and Policy-Making in the 'New' European Community*, Washington DC: The Brookings Institution, 1992, 225–56

Marginson, P. and Sisson, K. (1992) 'The Structure of Transnational Capital in Europe: The Emerging Eurocompany and its Implications for Industrial Relations', in R. Hyman and A. Ferner (eds) *Industrial Relations in the New Europe*, Oxford: Blackwell, pp. 15–51

McGowan, F. (1996) 'Energy Policy', in H. Kassim and A. Menon (eds) *The European Union and National Industrial Policy*, London: Routledge,132–152

Menon, A. and Hayward, J. (1996) 'States, Industrial Policies and the European Union', in H. Kassim and A. Menon (eds) *The European Union and National Industrial Policy*, London: Routledge, 267–290

Menon, A. and Forder, J. (1998) 'Conclusion: State, the European Union and Macroeconomic Policy', in A. Menon and J. Forder (eds) *The European Union and Macroeconomic Policy*, London: Routledge

Moravscik, Andrew (1993) 'Preferences and Power in the European Community: A Liberal Intergovernmentalist Approach', *Journal of Common Market Studies*, 31, 473–524

Peterson, J.(1996) 'Research and development policy', in H. Kassim and A. Menon (eds) *The European Union and National Industrial Policy*, London: Routledge, 226–46

Pierson, P. and S. Leibfried (1995), 'The Dynamics of Social Policy Integration', in S. Leibfried and P. Pierson (eds) *European Social Policy: Between Fragmentation and Integration*, Washington DC: The Brookings Institution, pp. 432–65

Salamon, M. (1987) *Industrial Relations: Theory and Practice*, Hemel Hempstead: Prentice Hall

Thatcher, M. (1996) 'High Technology', in H. Kassim and A. Menon (eds) *The European Union and National Industrial Policy*, London: Routledge, 178–203

Weiss, M. (1991) 'Social Dialogue and Collective Bargaining in the Framework of a Social Europe', in G. Spyropoulos and G. Fragniére (eds) *Work and Social Policies in the New Europe*, Brussels: European Interuniversity Press

INDEX

Printed in the United States
by Baker & Taylor Publisher Services